THE MEN AND THE MOMENT

THE MEN AND THE MOMENT

THE ELECTION OF 1968 AND THE RISE OF PARTISAN POLITICS IN AMERICA

Aram Goudsouzian

The University of North Carolina Press | Chapel Hill

Designed by April Leidig
Set in Kepler by Copperline Book Services, Inc.
Manufactured in the United States of America

The University of North Carolina Press has been a
member of the Green Press Initiative since 2003.

Cover photos: Lyndon Johnson (courtesy Lyndon Baines Johnson Presidential
Library); Robert F. Kennedy (courtesy John F. Kennedy Presidential Library
and Museum); George Wallace (courtesy Alabama Department of
Archives and History); Richard Nixon and Hubert Humphrey
(courtesy Richard Nixon Presidential Library and Museum)

Library of Congress Cataloging-in-Publication Data
Names: Goudsouzian, Aram, author.
Title: The men and the moment : the election of 1968 and the rise
of partisan politics in America / by Aram Goudsouzian.
Description: Chapel Hill : University of North Carolina Press, [2019] |
Includes bibliographical references and index.
Identifiers: LCCN 2018045751| ISBN 9781469651095 (cloth : alk. paper) |
ISBN 9781469651101 (ebook)
Subjects: LCSH: Presidents—United States—Election—1968. | United States—
Politics and government—1963-1969. | Political parties—United States—History—
20th century. | Political culture—United States—History—20th century. |
Television and politics—United States—History—20th century.
Classification: LCC E851 .G68 2019 | DDC 324.973/09046—dc23
LC record available at https://lccn.loc.gov/2018045751

For mentors:
Randy Roberts, Janann Sherman

CONTENTS

ILLUSTRATIONS

AUTHOR'S NOTE

Throughout the presidential election of 1968, the backdrop was chaos. In February of that year, communist forces launched the Tet Offensive, intensifying questions about the U.S. role in the Vietnam War. In April, Martin Luther King was assassinated, triggering fury and angst among African Americans as well as terrible riots in inner cities. Later that month, the nation's cultural divide sharpened when radical students occupied buildings at Columbia University and the police brutally removed them. That summer, the Cold War hardened with the Soviet Union's ruthless invasion of Czechoslovakia. On the streets outside the Democratic National Convention, the Chicago police attacked peace activists, and the nation appeared to descend into political pandemonium. By Election Day that November, many Americans were questioning the basic stability of their core institutions.

That anxiety helps explain voters' choices. The 1968 election shaped the identities of our two major political parties. It signaled the end of a long liberal era in American politics that began with the New Deal of the 1930s. The Democratic coalition—which included the urban working class, African Americans, intellectuals, and white southerners—met its demise. The party has since struggled to advocate progressive policies while capturing the political center. Just as important, the election mobilized the conservative forces that dominated the era to come. The Republican Party resonated with the comfortable-yet-nervous middle class, spreading into the growing suburbs and the emerging South, while learning to absorb an emerging populist conservatism.

The presidential campaign of 1968 was a last hurrah for the "Old Politics," in which political machines and party leaders determined the major nominees. It also highlighted a "New Politics," in which candidates took their cases right to the people, through party primaries and modern technology. On both the Left and Right, candidates seized hot-button issues to alter the larger political dynamic. And more than any previous campaign, it showcased the transformative power of television to "package" candidates.

The candidates were extraordinary personalities. The Democrats
battled for the soul of their party. Like a cunning, tortured king out of
Shakespeare, Lyndon Johnson presided over the action, even after his
shocking decision not to seek reelection. Eugene McCarthy was the rallying figure for a remarkable grassroots campaign rooted in opposition
to the Vietnam War, even as he sabotaged his prospects through his dif-
fidence. Bobby Kennedy, both adored and despised, was evolving from
his brother's prickly lieutenant into a charismatic hero of common folk,
only to die at the hands of an assassin. Hubert Humphrey, bullied into
servility as Johnson's vice president, needed an independent strategy on
the Vietnam War to finally become his "own man."

On the Republican side, the magnetic figures of Nelson Rockefeller
and Ronald Reagan pulled on the left and right wings, respectively, of
the party. Meanwhile, the fiery George Wallace almost toppled the two-
party system with his aggressive politics of reactionary resentment. But
it was Richard Nixon who found the language of the Republican resur-
gence: "law and order" to contain urban violence, patriotic vagueness on
Vietnam, and appeals to "forgotten Americans" who resented the Great
Society's devotion of resources to the poor, oppressed, and black. By winning the presidency, Nixon completed the greatest comeback in modern
American political history. Only Nixon committed to running throughout the election cycle. Only Nixon calculated an approach of pragmatism over principle. Only Nixon exploited all the tools available to him—
from slick television ads to diplomatic deception. His narrow victory,
accomplished by dubious means, laid the foundation for the crisis that
ultimately befell him.

As you might imagine, many books describe the presidential election
of 1968. In its immediate aftermath, journalists from the United States
and Great Britain wrote long, detailed, insightful accounts. Popular writers have described the election alongside trends in American culture
and developments around the globe. Excellent biographies, enhanced
by archival research and personal interviews, depict all the major candidates. Political scientists have analyzed electoral strategies and party
processes. Academic historians have contextualized the election through
studies of grassroots politics.

This book seeks to pull together these strands into a short, engaging
narrative. It relies on the research and insights of many authors, along
with the profuse output of political journalists during that hectic year.

Each of the first eight chapters centers upon a single candidate, and the chapters toggle back and forth between Democrats and Republicans (until the chapter on George Wallace, who ran under the banner of the American Independent Party). Though the book moves forward through 1968, the chapters often cover overlapping developments. A timeline of major events, found in the appendix, can help keep the story straight.

The echoes of 1968 reverberate in our contemporary politics. We again have flamboyant demagogues who conjure fears of elite conspiracies, righteous progressives who seek to reclaim the ideals of the Democratic Party, liberal centrists who fail to summon a unifying message, and accusations of foreign interference in our democratic process. My hope is that readers can draw those parallels, yet understand the election of 1968 within its special context—particularly through the personal experiences of each candidate. These were all elite, influential white men in late adulthood. At times, they were put to the test. As the book and chapter titles illustrate, their notions of manhood shaped their political identities— sometimes in overt ways and at other times more subtly. But gender roles and expectations, on their own, cannot explain the presidential election of 1968. Each candidate was responding to the swirling forces of that tumultuous year, acting in a specific historical moment. Their critical decisions, which altered the nation's destiny, were shaped by their personal backstories, their public images, and their political odysseys.

"The whole secret to politics," confessed Republican strategist Kevin Phillips during the 1968 election, "is knowing who hates who." The same might be said about low-level academic administration, my other main professional endeavor during the time spent writing this book. But as my term of service closes, I better appreciate the lessons I have learned. For that, I am grateful for the models set by two great historians. Randy Roberts, my mentor since graduate school, reminds me why I ever decided to be a history professor. He keeps telling good stories. Janann Sherman, my predecessor as chair of the Department of History of the University of Memphis, inspires me with her example. She sees the best in everyone.

Randy and Janann both read this book manuscript and offered constructive feedback, as did a host of scholars of twentieth-century American history and politics. I am indebted to my friends and colleagues Jefferson Cowie, Robert Fleegler, Michael Nelson, Sarah Potter, Edward

Schmitt, Johnny Smith, and David Welky. The book is enriched by their ideas and their care. My further thanks to Brandon Proia and the University of North Carolina Press.

I am anchored by my family, including my parents, Nishan and Mary, and my brothers Steve and Haig. As usual, I owe my greatest thanks to my wife, Chrystal. She read this manuscript and had smart suggestions, as she tends to do. More vitally, she illuminates what is important, keeps me laughing, and plays "good cop" or "bad cop" as necessary with our boys, Leo and Ozzie. She remains my all-time favorite historian.

THE MEN AND THE MOMENT

—1—

HOUND BITCH IN HEAT

LYNDON B. JOHNSON no longer won many cheers. But as he strode into the chamber of the House of Representatives on January 17, 1968, to deliver the State of the Union address, the assembled senators, representatives, Supreme Court justices, cabinet members, and other dignitaries gave him a warm ovation. It was a sign of respect, perhaps, for a tormented leader in a time of trouble. Johnson took the podium. He recalled a remark from his mentor Sam Rayburn, the late Speaker of the House: "The Congress always extends a warm welcome to the President—as he comes in."[1]

Everyone laughed, but it was the evening's last real sign of affection. Johnson's tone was subdued. His words were straight. In previous State of the Unions, he had put forth expansive visions for a "Great Society," brimming with optimism about the federal government's power to transform American lives. This time, there was no mention of a Great Society. Peace in Vietnam, he asserted, would come only after a continued military commitment. He urged Congress to curb inflation by passing his proposed tax hike, and he called for some modest programs in job training, housing, child health, and consumer safeguards. Throughout the speech, the clapping was polite and perfunctory, and mostly from loyal Democrats. When he talked about new civil rights legislation, the chamber was quiet. He got the loudest applause when he said, "The American people have had enough of rising crime and lawlessness in this country."[2]

Reporters described a "new" or "real" Johnson, who was "shedding the never-too-convincing guise of folksy preacher and avuncular counselor." He wore a trimmer suit and new, rimless glasses. He grew his hair longer, without slicking it back, so it was grayer and puffier. His State of the Union speech matched this image. Liberals called it unimaginative, and

OVERLEAF: President Lyndon Johnson (D-TX) (courtesy Lyndon Baines Johnson Presidential Library)

conservatives decried it as big-government overreach. But his austere, responsible style matched the nation's mood. He was trying to project responsibility and experience in a time of crisis, both at home and abroad.[3]

"Tonight our nation is accomplishing more for its people than has ever been accomplished before. Americans are prosperous as men have never been in recorded history," proclaimed Johnson. "Yet there is in the land a certain restlessness—a questioning." The United States of America had great power, great wealth, and great expectations, but both radicals and conservatives aired sharp dissent. The broad swath in the middle had an eroding sense of confidence. Was Johnson the right leader for this moment? As he spoke, he reached into his pocket, fishing for a piece of paper— a surprise ending. The paper was not there. It was sitting in his White House bedroom, by his telephone. On some level, he knew this, but he reached into his pocket anyway.[4]

For now, he remained the leading candidate in the presidential election of 1968.

Johnson's life was politics, and he loved power. He had no real hobbies and few real friends. He worked long days with exceptional gusto. To his aides, he could be extraordinarily cruel: berating them, exhausting them with demands for work, carrying on discussions while plopped on the toilet. Yet he showered the same people with flattery and gifts, winning their loyalty. He was a man that knew how to use people. He studied their needs, their wants, their flaws. He was famous for the "Johnson Treatment," a combination of cajoling, earthy analogies, veiled threats, and physical force, all in the name of getting his way. He wallowed in a sense of inferiority, but he delighted in Texan showmanship—cracking crass jokes, bragging about his power, donning cowboy boots embossed with the presidential seal.[5]

His political hero was Franklin Roosevelt. The New Deal shaped his faith in the good power of government. After winning and then losing election to Congress, he grabbed a Senate seat in 1948. By the mid-1950s he was majority leader, a role for which he was born. With relentless drive, he mastered parliamentary procedures, employing his titanic skills of personal persuasion and patient horse-trading to wrangle legislation through the Senate. He was one of the most powerful figures in Washington, D.C. But he yearned for the White House, and he needed a national profile, so in 1960 he surprisingly accepted the vice president slot on John F. Kennedy's ticket. For the next three years, he chafed for action and power, burning at every perceived humiliation by the young and dynamic Kennedy team.[6]

When Kennedy was assassinated in 1963, Johnson jumped through his political window. Presenting himself as president of all the people, he won a landslide election against conservative Republican Barry Goldwater in 1964. Congress had liberal majorities, and grassroots protestors in the civil rights movement were demanding change. Johnson promised a Great Society, an expansion of the scale and responsibility of the federal government. In his first few years in office, he released a kaleidoscopic burst of legislation: the Civil Rights Act and the Voting Rights Act, War on Poverty funding, federal aid for education, Medicare and Medicaid, and dozens of other initiatives.

No president had done more for the downtrodden since Franklin Roosevelt. No president had done more for black people since Abraham Lincoln. For many more Americans, he had increased their level of security. The Great Society expanded the scale and responsibility of the federal government. It was the peak of Cold War liberalism, rooted in the belief that the citizenry embraced a common agenda of enacting reforms, expanding the economy, and fighting communism. Johnson's wide arms had grabbed a majority of Americans and pulled them into his liberal consensus.[7]

Yet the Great Society also garnered disillusion. "I'm fearful we are overpromised, overextended, and overenthusiastic," Johnson lamented in November 1967. The War on Poverty raised liberals' expectations, but his administration had devoted more energy to passing laws than to implementing them. Civil rights legislation dismantled Jim Crow but also heightened discontent among African Americans about their continuing second-class status. In the mid-1960s, hundreds of race-related outbreaks occurred in American cities, including massive riots in Newark and Detroit during the summer of 1967. On the Left, idealists demanded ever-more-ambitious antipoverty legislation. On the Right, conservatives griped about bloated government programs that focused on the poor and minorities. The LBJ brand of pragmatic, centrist liberalism was fading.[8]

While magnifying the responsibilities of the federal government, Johnson increased the burdens on the presidency. Even in realms where he exercised little direct power, he became the target of criticism. Yet he craved affection and respect. Through marathon days, he surrounded himself with a tornado of hard-driving advisers, television screens, and briefings.

In his mind, enemies lurked around every corner, including all those eastern, Ivy League types associated with the Kennedys. He sank into moods of prolonged gloom. Some White House insiders whispered that he was unbalanced, paranoid.[9]

He failed, moreover, to communicate effectively with the American people. In person, Johnson could be raw and compelling—a product of a fading era, perhaps, when politicians chewed the fat, traded favors, and bullied one another in back rooms. But in public, he wore a thin plastic coat of humility. At the same time, he skirted honest discussions about his agenda, and he alienated reporters by lying about mundane or petty items. His complex personality was an asset in manipulating people and passing laws. It was also his tragic flaw. After studying his television appearances, he made such adjustments as the "new Johnson" of the 1968 State of the Union. But many Americans wanted something less tangible, something more inspiring, someone authentic.[10]

At the center of the "credibility gap" between Johnson and the American people lay the Vietnam War. When he assumed the presidency in November 1963, Johnson inherited a mess: about 16,000 American troops were in Vietnam, Ho Chi Minh's communist regime in North Vietnam was winning the war, and a coup had deposed South Vietnamese president Ngo Dinh Diem.

Temperamentally, Johnson was much better suited to push legislation through Congress than to implement foreign policy. With more self-assurance in international affairs, he might have realized the pitfalls of large-scale military intervention. But he was a child of the Texas hill country, a graduate of Southwest Texas State Teachers College, operating among East Coast bluebloods and decorated generals. In his typical style, he demanded consensus among these esteemed advisers and then made careful decisions weighed by political concerns. But every choice was piecemeal, somewhat devoid of a big-picture analysis of the historical forces in both Vietnam and the United States. Moreover, Johnson excluded most of the dissenting voices from his inner circle. The effect was to concentrate the president's power, escalate the military's commitment, and heighten America's divisions.

In 1964, after reported attacks on a U.S. destroyer, Congress approved the Gulf of Tonkin Resolution, which sanctioned the commander in chief to combat communist forces in Vietnam. Johnson used this short-term measure as a blanket authority for waging war. In early 1965, after a raid on an air force station in Pleiku, Johnson started intense bombing raids in North Vietnam. That summer, U.S. ground forces started pouring into Southeast Asia. Out of some combination of Cold War principles and political calculation, he declared, "I am not going to lose Vietnam." By the end of 1966, 450,000 American personnel were there. Johnson sought military solutions, but he faced an essentially political problem: the communist Viet Cong controlled much of the South Vietnamese countryside, and the corrupt government in Saigon was losing legitimacy.[11]

Johnson never introduced a genuine Vietnam debate to Congress. Nor did he level with the American people. He failed to explain how the war served the national purpose, and he avoided any call for sacrifice. Why were half a million troops in South Vietnam by 1968? What did their military victories actually accomplish? The press started depicting Johnson as out of touch, surrounded by yes-men, a devious warmonger. For all his political talents, he won little loyalty or affection from average Americans. He polled as low as 23 percent about his handling of the war and his general performance. When *Time* declared him 1967's "Man of the Year," the cover caricatured him as King Lear—doomed by foolish pride, a tragic embodiment of a dwindling national spirit.[12]

By then, dissident liberals were leading a Dump Johnson movement, seeking a new Democratic nominee for the 1968 election. Some prominent politicians questioned the rationale behind the war. Intellectuals, clergy, and newspaper editors griped that the war abused American power and siphoned resources from the Great Society. College students and radical groups engaged in dramatic public protests. During a White House luncheon in January 1968, the entertainer Eartha Kitt scolded Johnson's wife, Lady Bird, blaming the war for the nation's larger disaffection. "You send the best of this country off to be shot and maimed," seethed Kitt.[13]

More and more, Johnson isolated himself in the Oval Office. Envisioning himself as an embattled wartime president in the mold of Abraham Lincoln, he stayed the course. He believed that Ho Chi Minh would exploit any bombing pause for military advantage, and he refused to compromise the security of American troops. A genuine peace also needed the consent of South Vietnam's president Nguyen Van Thieu, who refused to recognize the National Liberation Front, the communist political body within South Vietnam. At the end of 1967, Johnson emphasized Thieu's important role during a round-the-world diplomatic tour; he had transformed a visit to Australia (for the funeral of Prime Minister Harold Holt) into a minor Asian summit followed by surprise stops in Thailand, Vietnam, and Pakistan. The trip was classic Johnson, a whirlwind of secrecy and ostentation. The last stop was Rome, where he gave Pope Paul VI a bust of himself.[14]

Ultimately, for Lyndon Johnson, politics was a test of manhood. He had big, macho appetites. He drank whiskey, told dirty jokes, and enjoyed watching cows fornicate. He treated most women as simple creatures who served his base needs. This worldview shaped his leadership. He famously reflected that the Great Society was "the woman I really loved" and Vietnam was "that bitch of a war." The war, in his mind, demanded strong male traits such as toughness and sacrifice. If Vietnam fell to communism, then people would label him "a coward. An unmanly man. A man without a spine."[15]

Once, reporters kept pressing him: *Why are we in Vietnam?* He lost his temper. He unzipped his pants and yanked out his penis. "This is why!" he declared.[16]

Perhaps Johnson could imitate Harry Truman. Twenty years earlier, Truman had suffered defections on both flanks of the Democratic Party, yet he rallied his base to win reelection as president. But Truman had personal warmth, a common touch. Johnson did not. LBJ was a big, meaty target for those who saw a rickety national scaffolding, undermined by inner-city race riots and an inconclusive war. He was losing loyalty among his party's traditional supporters, including Jewish, black, and young voters.[17]

Meanwhile, the larger Democratic coalition was eroding. Since the New Deal, the Democrats had pulled together a diverse lot, including white southerners, liberal intellectuals, big-city party bosses, labor unions, farmers, and racial and ethnic minorities. But the Great Society's civil rights legislation disenchanted white southerners. Journalists, professors, clergy, and other liberal agenda-setters hated the Vietnam War. The influence of urban bosses had declined. Labor union leaders still supported Johnson, but the rank and file no longer professed automatic loyalty to the Democrats.[18]

At its foundation, the Democratic Party was built on what Franklin Roosevelt had called "the forgotten man at the bottom of the economic pyramid." The booming postwar economy, combined with a vigorous federal welfare state, propelled much of that population into the middle

class. By 1968, the "average voter" in the United States was the most prosperous citizen in world history. Statistically, this person was white and
middle-aged, had a mortgage on a relatively new suburban house, owned
at least one car, and despite higher taxes, had seen a 20 percent rise in income since 1960. Fewer Americans considered themselves poor. Instead,
they shared anxieties about the future. Would their homes maintain
value? Could their children get college educations? Were their sons going
to die in Vietnam?[19]

Yet through the winter of 1968, the Democrats' nomination of Lyndon
Johnson seemed inevitable. Party members started endorsing him, and
a majority of delegates for that summer's Democratic National Convention supported him. His only open challenger was Minnesota senator
Eugene McCarthy, a lazy politician with a slapdash campaign. New York
senator Robert Kennedy, a more serious threat, kept waffling on a presidential run. Johnson eschewed campaigning in the primary elections in
New Hampshire and Wisconsin. Instead, he sought to project authority
from the White House. After the State of the Union, he kept delivering
speeches that touted domestic achievements and maintained commitments to Vietnam.[20]

But Johnson endured only more troubles. The international gold market
was in crisis, and the United States faced huge trade deficits. The Vietnam
War cost $20 billion a year. Inflation threatened the economy. Confidence
in the American dollar declined. In the House of Representatives, Wilbur
Mills, the influential chairman of the Ways and Means Committee, refused to endorse the president's request for a 10 percent tax surcharge. In
the Senate, conservatives blocked Johnson's civil rights initiatives, including a bill to ban racial discrimination in the sale or rental of housing.[21]

That winter, the presidentially appointed National Advisory Commission on Civil Disorders issued a widely read analysis of the urban crisis.
The Kerner Report, as it was known, called for more government spending to help poor blacks in American cities, warning that the nation was
"moving toward two societies, one black, one white—separate and un-
equal." Johnson considered the Kerner Report a personal attack. Even
though he agreed with its recommendations, he fumed that the commission failed to acknowledge his accomplishments. Anyway, he lacked the
political leverage to enact its recommendations. So he ignored it.[22]

Humiliations piled on top of frustrations. On January 23, 1968, North
Korea seized the *Pueblo*, a small naval vessel collecting electronic intel-

ligence. Eighty-three American sailors were held hostage. The communist regime of Kim Il Sung demanded that the United States apologize and promise to avoid similar missions, even though the *Pueblo* had been beyond North Korean waters. While battering American prestige, the hijacking stoked fears of a wider Asian war; about 50,000 American troops were already stationed in South Korea, patrolling the Demilitarized Zone.[23]

Johnson cautiously avoided any intensification of the dispute, even as North Korea imprisoned American sailors. The Vietnam War was straining American resources. Anticipating a major North Vietnamese offensive during the winter of 1968, U.S. military forces amassed at Khe Sanh, in the northwest corner of South Vietnam. They expected a big, decisive battle.[24]

Instead, a massive invasion hit about 100 targets throughout South Vietnam, including the capital city of Saigon. It started on January 30, the Lunar New Year, a holiday known as Tet. The "Tet Offensive" devastated airfields, military bases, and most of the provincial capitals. Thousands of South Vietnamese civilians died; hundreds of thousands more were uprooted. It was more than a military surprise; for the American people, it was a psychological smack in the face. North Vietnam and the Viet Cong had proven their ability to keep striking.[25]

The press painted the Tet Offensive as a disaster. "President Johnson's strategy for Vietnam has run into a dead end," stated *Newsweek*. "As a consequence, the United States is seized by a crisis of confidence." An iconic photograph showed a South Vietnam general executing a Viet Cong official with a point-blank shot to the head. Television broadcast the carnage into living rooms. Walter Cronkite, the renowned and respected anchor for CBS news, finished a report on location with an editorial: "To say we are mired in stalemate seems the only realistic, yet unsatisfactory, conclusion."[26]

Tet made clear that a genuine victory, fought along the current lines, was impossible. The president could apply more military power, but that would cost a high political price, including the calling of reserve troops and more government spending. He could gradually withdraw, but that would abandon a commitment to South Vietnam, and he would be branded a loser. Instead, Johnson uttered the same language about waging war and seeking peace. He pored over details of military strategy. He shook hands with American troops. His own two sons-in-law were soon shipping to Vietnam. He looked so tired. "I don't know how to do anything better than we are doing it," he said. "If I did, I would do it. I would take the better way. We have considered everything."[27]

General William Westmoreland, commander of U.S. forces in Vietnam, had long chafed that the president was waging a limited, gradual war. He saw the Tet Offensive as an opening: it failed to spark a grassroots uprising in the South Vietnamese countryside, and it exposed the North Vietnamese army. To exploit the military opportunity, Westmoreland requested troops beyond the current ceiling of 525,000. But a massive troop surge would signal a total Americanization of the war.[28]

Meanwhile, the Senate Foreign Relations Committee grilled Secretary of State Dean Rusk throughout a long, live televised hearing. Chairman William Fulbright blasted the administration for making military decisions without consulting Congress. Stuart Symington, once a proponent of escalation, now confessed "increasing doubts," asking, "What do we win if we win?" Throughout this period of confusion, Johnson stayed in the White House, consulting with a revolving cast of advisers, his mindset a mystery.[29]

At the end of February, Robert McNamara left his position as secretary of defense. A brilliant, driven man who had introduced corporate management techniques to the Pentagon, McNamara was a key architect of the calculated military escalation in Vietnam. In time, though, he brooded that their efforts had failed. At his farewell luncheon, McNamara's eyes welled with tears: the United States had dropped more bombs in Vietnam than in Europe during World War II, and it was a terrible waste.[30]

Johnson replaced him with Clark Clifford, a wealthy attorney who had dispensed trusted advice to Democratic presidents since the Truman administration. The urbane, precise Clifford generated great respect. He had connections throughout Washington. The media assumed that he supported the current policy, though when asked if he was a hawk or a dove, he replied that he was "not conscious of falling under any of those ornithological divisions."[31]

Clifford led a task force that considered deploying more troops to Vietnam. But the more he learned, the more he doubted the war itself. Unlike other cabinet members, Clifford did not owe his career to Johnson. Nor did he bear responsibility for escalating the conflict. So he asked fresh questions. How many troops would it take to win? Did bombing North Vietnam have any effect? The Joint Chiefs of Staff had no good answers. In his smooth and sensible style, Clifford steered discussions away from

troop escalation and toward an eventual withdrawal. Johnson felt betrayed. The president thought that he had appointed a loyal supporter.
Instead, for the first time since 1965, his advisers engaged in a genuine
debate about the nature of the Vietnam War.[32]

In late March, at Clifford's suggestion, Johnson gathered fourteen distinguished figures known as the "Wise Men." They included former secretary of state Dean Acheson, Generals Omar Bradley and Maxwell Taylor,
Supreme Court Justice Abe Fortas, and diplomats and advisers such as
McGeorge Bundy, Henry Cabot Lodge, and Averell Harriman. These were
venerable, pragmatic Cold Warriors who were committed to American
credibility—the type of educated, elite, establishment figures that Johnson both resented and admired. When the Wise Men had convened in
November 1967, they had counseled Johnson to maintain the course in
Vietnam. A few kept giving that advice. But after Tet, the majority had
grown pessimistic about military progress. Even Acheson, the aristo-
cratic author of American policy in the aftermath of World War II, urged
diplomatic solutions.[33]

Johnson was cranky and oozing self-pity. His eyes were sunken, with
red sties bulging off his eyelids. Deep creases of skin hung off his fleshy
cheeks. He needed more troops, more taxes, more budget cuts. But the political climate was thick with despair. And it was an election year. What
about his commitments to South Vietnam? What about his great domestic programs? "I don't give a damn about the election," he moaned. "I will
be happy just to keep doing what is right and lose the election."[34]

A televised presidential address on Vietnam was scheduled for Sunday,
March 31. The original drafts of the speech began as a defense of the war.
Johnson remained skeptical of a bombing halt; when he tried it in 1965,
it failed to start negotiations. Since then, he had insisted that to stop the
bombardment of North Vietnam, the regime in Hanoi first had to agree
to peace talks. But by late March, as Johnson absorbed the conflicting
advice, his speech evolved. The first sentence now read, "Tonight I want
to speak to you of the prospects for peace in Vietnam." It promised a temporary stop to the bombing, with the hopes of starting negotiations. Even
Dean Rusk, the stoic secretary of state with a hard line on Vietnam, offered no objections.[35]

In one final meeting in the Cabinet Room, Johnson and his advisers pored over the language. As it wrapped up, presidential aide Harry
McPherson promised to write a short conclusion. "Go ahead, but don't

worry about the length of it," replied Johnson, while heading out the door. He had a little smile on his lips. "I may have a little ending of my own."[36]

Sometimes, when frustrated by Congress or Vietnam, or after too little sleep and too much whiskey, Johnson delivered woe-is-me rants. "I'm not going to take any more of this," he would say. "A man doesn't have to take this kind of thing." By late 1967, he was saying it more often. The intellectuals sniffed their noses at him. The college kids hated him. The press treated him like "a hound bitch in heat." His relationship with Congress was like that "of an old man and woman who've lived together for a hundred years. We know each other's faults and what little good there is in us." For all his talents in forging consensus, his country was divided. And for all his larger-than-life qualities, his ego was brittle.[37]

But Lyndon Johnson leaving office of his own will? It seemed impossible. Behind the scenes, Lady Bird worried about his health and happiness. His friend John Connally, the governor of Texas, urged him not to run. General Westmoreland confirmed that such a decision would not damage the morale of Vietnam troops. His aides Horace Busby and George Christian had helped draft a surprise ending for the State of the Union in January 1968. Despite Johnson's claim that he had forgotten the ending on his bedside table, he had not been ready to leave. He never forgot anything of political importance.[38]

Then came Tet. Amidst the renewed debate over Vietnam, Johnson suffered two more blows, both from within his own party. First, on March 12, Eugene McCarthy received 42 percent of the vote in the New Hampshire Democratic primary. Johnson did not campaign there and still won with 49 percent, but it was a shocking repudiation of a sitting president. Second, on March 16, Robert F. Kennedy announced his intention to run for president.

Bobby Kennedy! The literal embodiment of his personal insecurities, that "little shit-ass" who fought to keep Johnson off the 1960 presidential ticket, that "snot-nosed little son-of-a-bitch" who helped escalate the Vietnam War and now criticized it, the dashing heir to the martyred JFK, who could charm reporters and women and students and blacks and professors and everyone else who hated Lyndon B. Johnson. It was "the final straw," recalled Johnson. "The thing I feared from the first day of my Presidency was actually coming true. Robert Kennedy had openly announced his intention to reclaim the throne in the memory of his brother. And the American people, swayed by the magic of the name, were dancing in the streets."[39]

But Johnson rooted his identity—his manhood—in his political courage. Was he running from a fight? He ordered all his swirling emotions by reflecting on historical legacy. By abdicating the Oval Office, he could place himself above politics. In his final year as president, he could serve as a statesman, unifying the nation and crafting peace in Vietnam.[40]

Until his address on March 31, he kept his options open. He showed the ending of the speech to family members, Vice President Hubert Humphrey, and a few cabinet members and White House aides, with no promise to deliver it. On the day of his address, party officials briefed him about his weak campaign infrastructure. The next primary was in Wisconsin, where he would probably lose to McCarthy. Johnson said nothing about his plans. In fact, that same weekend, various friends reported that he seemed ready to battle for the Democratic nomination.[41]

One hour before the speech, Johnson added the surprise ending to the teleprompter. Even then, he was not sure. He began speaking at 9:01 P.M. With quiet seriousness, he announced the immediate cessation of bombing in most of North Vietnam. He called for Ho Chi Minh to respond to his gesture. He said that South Vietnam should absorb more military responsibility. He revealed a small injection of 13,500 additional troops. He called for the support of Congress, and he acknowledged the ruptures in American society. Finally, the ending rolled onto the screen. He glanced at Lady Bird. He started wiping some sweat from his brow, then caught himself, put his hand down, and said the fateful words: "I have concluded that I should not permit the Presidency to become involved in the partisan divisions that are developing in this political year. . . . Accordingly, I shall not seek, and I will not accept, the nomination of my party for another term as your President."[42]

It was jaw-dropping news. The tragic king was renouncing his throne! Though his harshest detractors refused to believe him, most of the press celebrated his personal sacrifice for international peace, and they applauded his effort to unite the American people. "By acting counter to every political instinct that has been credited to him," praised *Life*, "Lyndon Johnson has retrieved the chance to end his tenure on the highest note."[43]

For the moment, the president relaxed. He had pulled the bull's-eye off his chest, and he achieved clarity of mind and purpose. Hanoi soon responded to his overture, and in May, formal talks opened between the United States and Vietnam. But Johnson still held to a Vietnam policy on which he had staked personal and national honor, while governing a nation that was fraying at the seams. Moreover, his political rivals were usurping center stage. His pride was so great, his ambition so deep, his personality so forceful that he inevitably loomed over the coming election.[44]

—2—

THE LOSER

R ICHARD NIXON looked serene and confident, smothering his darker impulses. On the last day of February 1968, he was delivering his stump speech at a Knights of Columbus hall in Milford, New Hampshire. He always had a resonant voice and a command of the facts. But over time, he had learned to mellow his style, to force himself to appear relaxed. He even tossed in some self-deprecating jokes about his past failures, such as a line about being "a dropout from the Electoral College." Above all, he portrayed himself as a statesman, a man of experience, the voice of unity.[1]

He mostly ignored Michigan governor George Romney, his rival in the state's Republican primary, and took aim at Lyndon Johnson. His typical speech ended, "When the strongest nation in the world can be tied down for four years in the war in Vietnam, with no end in sight; when the richest nation in the world is plagued by rampant lawlessness, when the nation that has been a symbol of human liberty is torn apart by racial strife; when the President of the United States cannot travel at home or abroad without fear of a hostile demonstration—then it's time America had new leadership."[2]

On this afternoon, as Nixon stepped off the dais, two campaign aides hustled him straight to a bathroom and shut the door. "Romney's pulling out of the race!" they revealed. Nixon was surprised, but he composed himself. While Romney had bumbled his way through New Hampshire, Nixon led in the polls, won key endorsements, and ran a smooth campaign with select appearances before large crowds. But Romney's withdrawal could free challenges from more potent candidates, such as Nelson Rockefeller and Ronald Reagan. For now, Nixon needed to think. He had to show self-control. When he left the bathroom, Mike Wallace of

OVERLEAF: Richard Nixon (R-CA) (courtesy Richard Nixon Presidential Library and Museum)

CBS told him the news. He feigned shock. He refused to comment on "rumors," and until Romney gave his formal announcement later that afternoon, he proceeded with two more scheduled talks, delivered with the same professional comportment.[3]

Even among his staff, Nixon tried to exhibit this discipline. Back at his hotel, he declared that he would not watch Romney's press conference; he wanted to avoid an emotional response to a development that demanded rational calculation. So he asked his aides to report the details. After the press conference ended, campaign staffer John Sears walked down the hall, knocked on Nixon's door, and entered the room. He saw Nixon scuttling away from the television set. Obviously, Nixon had watched the news. But as Sears talked and Nixon listened, each man pretended that the candidate had resisted the temptation to watch his opponent's surrender.[4]

The media was calling him the New Nixon, but the Old Nixon lurked just beneath the surface—simmering with the resentments accumulated over a long political career and fueling this last determined quest for his ultimate ambition.

He was a loser.

In the presidential election of 1960, Nixon, doomed by his stubbornness and his image, lost to John F. Kennedy. He insisted on serving as his own campaign manager and visiting all fifty states, which sapped his energy. Unlike his charming competitor, he failed to court the press, and he bombed their first television debate, looking grumpy and haggard. By the end, his speeches seemed harsh and gloomy. Still, Kennedy edged him by the thinnest of margins. Two years later, Nixon ran for governor of California. He lost again. On November 7, 1962, in the aftermath of that humiliation, he blustered to reporters, careening from magnanimity to bitterness to self-pity, highlighted by a line that burned into the public consciousness: "You won't have Nixon to kick around anymore, because, gentlemen, this is my last press conference."[5]

In that moment, Nixon cracked his shell of self-control, exposing his festering rancor. Life, for him, was a series of tests, battles, *crises*. He had little capacity for affection, no close friends, no deep emotional attachments. He was uncomfortable around women. His father was mean; his mother was so pious that she was distant. A tireless worker, he possessed a deep sense of personal mission, as if his accomplishments would finally win him love. Yet his herky-jerky body language betrayed that, on some level, he thought that people disliked him. He compensated with discipline and calculation. He threw himself into public life, despite that fundamental shyness, manufacturing a hearty, sentimental persona that appeared insincere.[6]

He never won the acceptance of the privileged, the cultured, the intellectuals. At Whittier College, in the distant suburbs of Los Angeles, he organized his own student society, the "Orthogonians," after rejection from the elite "Franklins." He finished third in his class at Duke Law School, but top New York City firms tossed his application. As a freshman congressman in the late 1940s, he vaulted into the national spotlight by investigating the procommunist espionage of the government official Alger Hiss, an embodiment of the East Coast, Ivy League establishment that dominated Washington, D.C. In 1952, while running for vice president, he faced revelations about a personal slush fund. He defended his integrity on national television while admitting, mawkishly, to keeping one campaign gift: Checkers, the family dog. The "Checkers speech" defused an outcry and saved his spot on the ticket, but it also cast him as a self-righteous manipulator.[7]

He burned at the slights. As vice president, Nixon served as the anticommunist attack dog, keeping Dwight Eisenhower above the fray. In return, Ike almost dropped him before his 1956 reelection bid. In his second term, Nixon won respect by surviving violent anti-American protests in Venezuela and debating Nikita Khrushchev in Moscow. But when Nixon ran for president in 1960, reporters asked Eisenhower about major ideas contributed by Nixon, and the president responded, "If you give me a week, I might think of one." When Nixon lost, he fumed that Kennedy stole the election by manipulating returns in Illinois and Texas. Two years later, during his gubernatorial bid, he groused that the press screwed him.[8]

After that "last press conference," *Time* declared that "barring a miracle, Nixon's public career has ended." But Nixon could no more abandon politics than stop breathing. Before the 1964 Republican National Convention, he proclaimed that he was not a presidential candidate, though he stayed available as a centrist alternative to conservative Barry Goldwater and liberal Nelson Rockefeller. He had common cause with both party wings, but neither faction totally trusted him. He engineered a write-in campaign for the Oregon primary and fished for a Draft Nixon movement among Republican governors. Nothing materialized. Again, he was a loser.[9]

Nixon nevertheless began the greatest comeback in the history of American politics. Perhaps his single greatest talent was assessing the big picture and developing a strategy. Now, he gauged the state of the Republican Party. The 1964 election looked like a disaster. Nominee Barry Goldwater, the darling of grassroots conservatives, scared away mainstream voters. Advocating a bare-bones federal government paired with strong national defense, Goldwater boomed during his convention speech that "extremism in defense of liberty is no vice!" Lyndon Johnson's television ads suggested that Goldwater would destroy Social Security and deploy nuclear weapons. Pundits declared that Goldwater was a fringe candidate, that the Republicans were weak and divided, that conservatism was dying.[10]

Where others saw disaster, Nixon saw opportunity. He spent thirty-three days traveling to thirty-six states, stumping for his party. He praised local candidates, tried to burnish Goldwater, and blasted Lyndon Johnson. On Election Day, Goldwater carried only six states, and he soon lost his status as unofficial party leader. Nixon stepped into the vacuum. By then he had moved to New York City, become a partner in a prestigious law firm, bought a lavish apartment on Fifth Avenue, and joined exclusive clubs. With wealth and status, he grew more confident among the elite class. But he still strived for electoral success. He knew every important party official, and absent any direct political responsibilities, he stayed on the lecture circuit, urging an identity as "Lincoln Republicans: liberal in their concern for people and conservative in their respect for law." If the party was split, he would straddle the breach.[11]

In 1966, Nixon returned to the election grind, campaigning for 105 GOP candidates in thirty-five states. Night after night, he sat through boring rubber-chicken dinners, posed for photographs, slapped the backs of local officials, and delivered his speech. But he did it with energy. He maintained his discipline. He even managed to seem spontaneous. He would arrive just a little late, stride to the podium, and slam the Great Society with proven applause-generating lines. He stumped for any Republican, whether archconservative or moderate. At the same time, he met with influential party leaders, representatives, and senators. By spurring publicity and contributions for candidates, he earned political favors for 1968. Republicans gained 47 seats in the House, 3 in the Senate, and 540 in state legislatures, along with 8 more governors. The myth of a liberal consensus was eroding, and within GOP circles, Nixon was acquiring an air of inevitability.[12]

. Nixon further positioned himself as Lyndon Johnson's nemesis. They were, to some extent, mirror images: fascinating jumbles of self-doubt, ambition, brilliance, and arrogance. Nixon knew just how to poke the bear. He suggested that, in 1968, Johnson might have to replace Vice President Hubert Humphrey with Bobby Kennedy. He also needled Johnson on Vietnam, constantly countering the president's policy. In the fall of 1966, after Johnson conferred with American allies in the Philippines, Nixon's criticisms of the president got front-page coverage in the *New York Times*. Johnson hit back with a long tirade, soaked in sarcasm, that attacked Nixon's competence and integrity. "I don't want to get into a debate on a foreign policy meeting in Manila with a chronic campaigner like Mr. Nixon," he said.[13]

It was a coup for Nixon. Johnson was treating him like the chief opposition leader! Nixon staked the moral high ground by acting magnanimous. He looked more presidential than the president. On national television, while asserting that he always defended American involvement in Vietnam, he proclaimed, "I never was one that could be arm-twisted by anyone and frightened even by the towering temper of Lyndon Johnson." His stance of personal courage, wounded innocence, and principled patriotism cemented his status in the Republican Party.

But Lyndon Johnson, like Richard Nixon, was a political creature. LBJ knew that his tantrum would boost his rival. Why did he do it? At that point, Johnson still planned to run in 1968. Perhaps he preferred to confront someone else with a checkered history, someone else who inspired distrust. A loser.[14]

Political reporters had a new staple: analyses of Richard Nixon's chances for the presidency, weighing all the pros and cons. In his favor, Nixon possessed long experience in Washington, D.C., and deep knowledge of foreign affairs. He also had great stamina and public-speaking skills. Like no other Republican, he pulled together the party's two wings, and he had earned the respect of the rank and file. He strove to be a New Nixon— a seasoned, composed straight-shooter.

But Nixon lacked a base of political strength, since he now lived in New York, where rival Nelson Rockefeller was governor. More important, he had spent a generation in the public eye. Everyone remembered the Old Nixon, with the reputation of a shrewd bulldog. To his enemies, he was "Tricky Dick," the grinning choirboy who stole from the collection plate. Personally, he had no lightness, no capacity for small talk. He seemed dour, "square," more interested in political calculations than in actual people. Even his face—with its flipped-up nose, thick eyebrows, and floppy jowls—was a liability. One writer likened it to "zucchini squash left too long on the vine."[15]

In early 1967, Nixon gathered seven influential Republicans at the Waldorf Towers in New York. They urged him to capitalize on the 1966 victories by openly running for president, with television appearances and national lectures. But Nixon had the correct instinct. The likely delegates at the next Republican National Convention already supported him, and he worried that people would tire of him by 1968. So instead, for much of the next six months, he traveled the world. He met with NATO leaders in Western Europe and visited the Soviet Union. He toured Japan, Thailand, Indonesia, and South Vietnam, and then Peru, Chile, Argentina, Brazil, and Mexico. He ended with trips to Africa and the Middle East. By visiting with leaders, he polished his reputation as a statesman. Back home, he gave speeches about international affairs, casting himself as a thoughtful president-in-waiting.[16]

A Nixon for President committee opened an office one block from the White House. Still, Nixon avoided a formal declaration of his candidacy. This strategy allowed him to raise funds, plan primary campaigns, and assemble his team. His low-key, levelheaded law partner John Mitchell served as campaign manager. Close associates served in important roles, including California lieutenant governor Bob Finch, longtime secretary Rose Mary Woods, and New York lawyer Leonard Garment. He had a young and talented speechwriting trio of Ray Price, Pat Buchanan, and William Safire. They helped craft an image that reinforced his stability and competence. Furthering his image as a world leader, Nixon analyzed Asian geopolitics in the prestigious journal *Foreign Affairs*, which was then condensed for *Reader's Digest*, where it reached a huge middlebrow audience. Another *Reader's Digest* piece, "What Has Happened to America?," aired conservative grievances with a permissive Supreme Court, rising crime rates, and race riots.[17]

By the end of 1967, Nixon was openly analyzing his strengths and weaknesses as a campaigner, speculating on his governing style, and assessing his chances for the Republican nomination. "I'm the unifying candidate," he said. "Some people might not have me in their hearts, but I could get in their heads if I win in the primaries." He talked politics with Johnny Carson on *The Tonight Show*. Journalists analyzed his election strategy, from the nitty-gritty courting of Republican power brokers to the casting of a trustworthy national image. Others chronicled his career, and whether they admired or disliked him, they marveled at the revival of his fortunes.[18]

And yet, on the night of December 22, 1967, Nixon retreated to his den, pulled out a yellow legal pad, and wrote, "I have decided personally against becoming a candidate." He listed the reasons, which boiled down to his fatigue with fundraising, the media, and the campaign trail. When he told his daughters about his doubts on Christmas Day, they urged him to run. A few days later, he took a restful vacation at a Florida villa; his friend the Reverend Billy Graham said that he was the best-prepared man for the job. Finally, on January 15, 1968, Nixon gathered his family, his secretary, and his two beloved servants, who were Cuban refugees. "I have decided to go," he said. "I have decided to run again." His wife, Pat, dreaded another campaign, with its intrusions and strains and inevitable disappointments. A life in politics had already damaged their marriage. But she promised her support.

Had he truly considered *not* running? Just about every decision since the humiliating "last press conference" had pointed toward the White House. But Nixon needed the anguish, the conflict, the *crisis*—even if it existed solely within his brain. Besides, he knew that the election would compel sacrifices from his family. Even the stoic, resilient Pat had to profess her loyalty in front of those who loved them. She would stand by him, wearing a smiling mask. Everything now lined up perfectly. The presidency was his destiny.[19]

On February 2, 1968, 150,000 citizens of New Hampshire opened their mailboxes and found a letter from Richard Nixon. It declared him a candidate for president, branding him a leader with experience and knowledge. "During the past eight years I have had a chance to reflect on the lessons of public office, to measure the nation's tasks and its problems from a fresh perspective," he wrote. "I have sought to apply those lessons to the needs of the present, and to the entire sweep of this final third of the 20th century. And I believe I have found some answers."[20]

Nixon also entered the upcoming elections in Wisconsin, Indiana, South Dakota, Nebraska, and Oregon. These primaries were essential to his overall strategy. In some other states, a "favorite son" such as the governor was running, so that person controlled the state's delegates at the

Republican National Convention. In still other states, the primaries were just "beauty contests" with no influence on the votes of that delegation. And many states had no primary at all, just a convention of party officials. Although he had been greasing the party machinery, Nixon knew that to be a viable national candidate, he had to shed his "loser" reputation. Via these few open primaries, he could take his case to the people. He could be a winner.[21]

New Hampshire was a good start. The mass mailing was an assured, understated way to kick off the campaign. Nixon planned to convey dignity. "No baby kissing, no back-slapping, no factory gates," he commanded. He avoided the mistakes of 1960, when he burned himself out. Over the next six weeks, he spent about twenty days in New Hampshire, but only for choice and well-planned events. His first rally, at St. Anselm's College in Manchester, drew 5,000 people. He acted like he was already the Republican nominee. The state party's leaders endorsed him. He led in the polls. He appeared comfortable and confident. He even hosted a reception for his old enemies in the press.[22]

Reporters were flummoxed, however, when Nixon secretly left his hotel early one morning to film television spots. His campaign team had handpicked about twenty locals to interview Nixon at the Community Hall in Hillsboro. The clandestine taping session broke from the tradition of media availability. Absent reporters, Nixon relaxed. The people's questions and the candidate's answers were chopped into five-minute segments that aired in New Hampshire and beyond. Because they were unscripted, the spots seemed authentic, and they showcased Nixon on his best terms, as quick thinking and intelligent. On screen, this format worked better than a stump speech, where Nixon might appear combative and sweaty. The strategy revealed a larger trend in modern American politics: "packaging" a candidate through television.[23]

Television not only enhanced Nixon's campaign. To some degree, it transformed his entire operation. Nixon bore the scars of his disastrous first debate with John F. Kennedy. He had to show party leaders that he could thrive on television and thus win a national election. His new communications group started from the assumption that personal contact with voters mattered less than in previous elections: thirty seconds on the news, reported with soothing authority by Walter Cronkite, was worth more than months of face-to-face campaigning. Television allowed Nixon's team to take its narrative right to the public, on its own terms, bypassing the conventional press. The effect bounced back onto Nixon himself. With each successful rally or advertisement, he felt more like a winner.[24]

George Romney's withdrawal on February 29 guaranteed a Nixon landslide in New Hampshire. On March 12, there was a large Republican turnout, and Nixon won an impressive 78 percent of the vote. His campaign churned along. No competitors meant more big victories in the upcoming primaries. But that lack of opposition also slowed the candidate's momentum. If there was no real opponent, was he a winner? How could he display the New Nixon? If the campaign bogged down, would it rekindle skepticism about his character? He practically goaded Nelson Rockefeller to enter the primaries, but through the early spring, the New York governor kept his distance.[25]

Nixon's other challenge was Vietnam. For years, he had taken a traditional Cold War position by demanding an independent South Vietnam and rejecting peace talks. But especially after the Tet Offensive, he needed a more nuanced approach. The war frustrated the American people, whatever their politics—almost half the nation regretted intervention in Vietnam. Still, a majority opposed withdrawal, which would be a national embarrassment.[26]

Nixon thus offered something to both hawks and doves: he condemned Lyndon Johnson for wasting military advantage through a "misguided policy of gradualism," while also calling for diplomacy with the Soviet Union, which could pressure Ho Chi Minh to negotiate a settlement. Vietnam was LBJ's cross to bear. While campaigning in early March, Nixon said that if the war was still raging by Election Day, then "the American people will be justified to elect new leadership. And I pledge to you the new leadership will end the war and win the peace in the Pacific."[27]

Nixon was intentionally vague. A specific program might expose him to criticism. He hinted that he possessed an actual peace plan, but when critics pressed for specifics, he claimed that he could not expose bargaining points before taking office. On the campaign trail, however, he did label Vietnam "a deeply troubling lesson in the limits of U.S. power," signaling a shift in the Cold War. The campaign scheduled a television address for March 31, when he would explain his worldview while subtly preparing the American public for the future. "I've come to the conclusion that there's no way to win the war," he told his aides. "But we can't say that, of course. In fact, we have to seem to say the opposite, just to keep some degree of bargaining leverage."[28]

But Lyndon Johnson scheduled his own television address for March 31, forcing Nixon off the air. And after Johnson announced the bombing halt and his withdrawal from the election, Nixon shifted course. He promised a personal "moratorium" on Vietnam, to avoid interference with peace negotiations. From this point on, he avoided substantive comments on the war. According to one disaffected adviser, his strategy was "a cynical default on the moral obligation of a would-be President to make his views known to the people." But that same adviser admitted that it was "a brilliantly executed political stroke." The Republican front-runner had sidestepped controversy on the nation's most explosive issue. The debates over Vietnam were confined within the boundaries of the Democratic Party.[29]

On April 3, in another sign of his impending nomination, Nixon won 80 percent of the vote in the Wisconsin primary. For a man who defined himself by crises, things were going almost *too* smoothly. His campaign resolved to slow down, to cultivate party allies, to hone a general critique of Democrats. Meanwhile, the nation spiraled into chaos.[30]

On April 4, Martin Luther King was assassinated. The transcendent civil rights leader died in Memphis while supporting a strike of poor black sanitation workers. He had been planning a mass protest on the National Mall called the Poor People's Campaign. With King's death, the brief national optimism after Lyndon Johnson's withdrawal puffed into smoke. "America the Violent," cried an essay in *Time*, "a vast, driving, brutal land that napalms Vietnamese peasants and murders its visionaries along with its Presidents." Devastation and rage shook Black America. Riots plagued 130 cities, killed 43 people, caused $45 million in damages, and prompted 20,000 arrests. While many whites expressed genuine guilt and sorrow, many others muttered that King had invited his own death, arguing that his civil disobedience fomented violence and hatred. For them, the riots were not protests of racial inequality but symptoms of moral sickness.[31]

Nixon's camp debated whether he should attend King's funeral in Atlanta. This dark discussion illustrated a new Republican dilemma. He was courting southern party leaders, who had seen King as a dangerous rabble-rouser. But a legitimate national leader had to pay tribute to a slain Nobel Peace Prize winner. Ultimately, with some grumbles, he did go to the funeral. Black attendees griped that he was "politicking." When he leaned over a pew to greet Jacqueline Kennedy, the revered widow of another American martyr, she responded with an ice-cold glare.[32]

After the funeral, Nixon stepped off the campaign trail for a few weeks. He assessed the new circumstances. With Vietnam off the table, no Lyndon Johnson to vilify, and no Republican opposition, how would he remain a central voice of authority? The riots gave him an easy target. They heightened the sense of crisis. In Washington, D.C., troops with bayonets guarded the White House. *Newsweek* likened the city to "the besieged capital of a banana republic." Headlines in the conservative *U.S. News & World Report* painted a vision of Armageddon: "A Threat of Anarchy in Nation's Capital" . . . "Tragedy of Nation's Capital: A Story of Crime and Fear" . . . "Mobs Run Wild in Nation's Capital" . . . "More Violence and Race War?" The articles tended to ignore the causes of black discontent. Instead, they chronicled the greed of looters, the barbarity of violent destruction, and the inflammatory rhetoric of black radicals.[33]

When Nixon returned to campaigning, he tapped into conservative whites' racial worries. Earlier in the campaign, he had criticized the Kerner Report for blaming white racists rather than black rioters, and he had condemned government programs for fostering cycles of black dependency. Now he decried the "lawless society" fostered by liberals. His printed statement, titled "Toward Freedom from Fear," claimed a "staggering" 88 percent rise in crime since 1961. He castigated Lyndon Johnson, Attorney General Ramsey Clark, and the Supreme Court for their softness on criminals. The Great Society had tried to defuse urban riots by fighting poverty. "Poverty cannot begin to explain the explosion of crime in America," countered Nixon.[34]

Nixon did not mention black people. He did not have to. Crime and race were linked in the white imagination. By the 1960s, poor blacks were increasingly isolated in ghettoes, thanks to the surge of black migrants from farm to city, the decline in industrial jobs, and white opposition to integrated neighborhoods. At the same time, street crime was surging, and African Americans were arrested at exponentially higher rates than whites. White fears of murder, robbery, and rape mixed with unease about black riots and militant groups such as the Black Panthers. Conservative politicians made hay with this dread. In 1964, Barry Goldwater had decried Democrats for allowing "the license of the mob and of the jungle." In 1966, Republicans swept into office by charging the Great Society with coddling criminals. That message resonated with many working-class whites, who resented the decline in real wages due to inflation and higher taxes, as well as black encroachment on their neighborhoods and workplaces.[35]

Yet if Nixon's envisioned coalition included traditional conservative Republicans, white southerners, and disaffected white workers, it also sought to hold on to progressive Republicans, including middle-class blacks. To stake this position in the party's political center, he could not appear heartless to the plight of African Americans. He thus touted "black capitalism," with government promoting greater ownership in the free market, so poor blacks avoided welfare and public housing.[36]

Nixon even imagined black militants in his electoral coalition, since they wanted economic independence in black communities. But the Black Panthers were not voting Republican. Nixon's gesture actually targeted white swing voters, who could support Nixon without considering themselves racist. His simultaneous attack on lawlessness reassured the conservative base. He scorned the upcoming Poor People's Campaign, which planned to occupy the National Mall in Washington, D.C., since "the government must not be coerced into acting because the machinery of government has been disrupted and paralyzed by demonstrators."[37]

Nixon was equally harsh with radical student protestors. On April 23, students at Columbia University occupied five campus buildings. They objected to the university's plans for a new gymnasium that infringed on a black neighborhood, as well as Columbia's affiliation with a military think tank. While black students and Harlem activists occupied Hamilton Hall, white radicals took over Low Library, led by twenty-year-old Mark Rudd, a member of the Students for a Democratic Society who had visited Cuba and idolized Che Guevara. In the office of university president Grayson Kirk, they smoked cigars and urinated in his trash can. Radical icons such as Stokely Carmichael, H. Rap Brown, Tom Hayden, and Abbie Hoffman visited campus.

The administration toed a hard line, and one week later, 1,000 New York policemen removed the demonstrators with force. Over 700 were arrested, and 148 were injured. In this clash of generations and social classes, the idealistic and self-righteous activists were reimagining the priorities of American institutions, while the working-class cops loathed the attitudes and actions of these privileged youth.[38]

Nixon lashed at "the anarchic students at Columbia," calling the revolt "a national tragedy and a national disgrace." Even "more deplorable," he said, was "the conduct of those professors and teachers who have condoned or encouraged the lawlessness of their students." Like a strict father spanking his bratty children, he projected a firm, steady discipline. This stance had a new name: "law and order." The blanket term encompassed a conservative response to the forces of social chaos: poor blacks burning down the ghettoes, radicals plotting revolution, spoiled students undermining the Vietnam War, filthy hippies lacking basic values, thieves and rapists ruling the city streets.[39]

In 1968, wrote Garry Wills, there was "a quiet sour fear at the center of American life," spreading among the "vast middle range of the comfortable discontented." Nixon recognized these people. They did not hold picket signs or scream at politicians. "They just lock their doors. And they vote." So as Nixon developed this new defining issue, he groped for the right language. In a national radio address on May 16, he lauded "the millions of people in the middle of the American political spectrum who do not demonstrate, who do not picket or protest loudly." Pledging to represent this "silent center," he mined a larger cultural anxiety with protestors, criminals, and their liberal intellectual enablers.[40]

Richard Nixon wanted to be president. He knew it from the beginning. With calculation, he adapted to the political upheavals around him. Perhaps he was neither pure nor sincere, but for many Americans, that was okay. They, too, worked hard. They, too, were insecure about their place. They, too, wanted to be winners.[41]

—3—

ACT II MAN

EUGENE McCARTHY waited in the wings, fuming and grumbling and kicking a crushed paper cup. Two days earlier, the Minnesota senator had announced that he would enter four Democratic primaries in the upcoming presidential campaign. Now, on December 2, 1967, he was in Chicago to address the Conference of Concerned Democrats, an organization of Vietnam dissenters. McCarthy was set to give his first campaign speech. But he could not get on the podium. Allard Lowenstein, the whirling, rumpled orchestrator of this conference, was delivering a forty-minute oration that stirred the crowd's passions. It opened with a tooting brass band and it continued with fiery denunciations of a lying president. "Get this straight about Lyndon Johnson," he thundered. "If a man cheats you once, shame on him. But if he cheats you twice, shame on YOU!" McCarthy waited, his head down, his hands clasped, his mood irritated.[1]

Finally, Lowenstein finished. Beyond the 500 conference delegates, another 1,000 enthusiasts packed the auditorium. They roared, clapped, and waved signs that proclaimed, "We Want Gene." These were not radicals or hippies; they were mostly middle-aged, almost all white and educated, with semiprofessional experience in the Democratic Party. They were thrilled to have a big-time political figure representing their movement. They craved more inspiration, more fervor, more hoopla.[2]

Then McCarthy stepped to the rostrum. He read his speech in drab tones, smothering any potential high notes. Instead of blasting LBJ, he critiqued the nature of presidential power. After discussing the Vietnam War, he recalled the lessons of ancient Carthage and Rome. He never actually mentioned that he was running for president. The audience grew restless. A few people fell asleep.[3]

OVERLEAF: Senator Eugene McCarthy (D-MN) (courtesy Minnesota Historical Society)

From McCarthy's perspective, the speech was fine. The crowd needed less rousing and more knowledge of the basis for his challenge. Rather than lead a pep rally, he sought a serious discussion of American foreign policy. When he finished, some delegates surged forward to shake his hand, but McCarthy retreated to a back room. He also ignored a huge overflow crowd that watched his speech on closed-circuit television. "Please leave the auditorium now," announced the public address system. The event finished on an anticlimactic thud. "If he wants to be our leader," groused one attendee, "he damn well better start leading."[4]

Although the Conference of Concerned Democrats endorsed Eugene McCarthy, only about half the delegates voted, and the resolution's compromise proposal freed them to vote as individuals. Many complained about McCarthy's dull speech, lack of professional campaign staff, and absence of direction. But they went back home to work for him. An antiwar sentiment was building, and the crusade needed a legitimate presidential candidate. Eugene McCarthy was their only hope.[5]

There was Eugene McCarthy, the man. And there was the Eugene McCarthy movement. They were not the same thing. As the inauspicious debut in Chicago revealed, McCarthy and his supporters had different philosophies, goals, and tactics. And yet somehow, together, they scored remarkable victories, challenged the leadership of the Democratic Party, and compelled a growing number of Americans to question their nation's priorities.

––––––––––

Eugene McCarthy was subtle and witty, yet thin-skinned and haughty. His inspirations were long-ago giants of Catholic thought such as Thomas More and St. Augustine, yet he entered the cold-blooded, transactional world of politics. Though he stood for progressive principles, he was a languid legislator. This leader of an audacious struggle to topple the president was characterized by his restraint. His paradoxical appeal arose in the shadow of the shiny, cartoonish Lyndon Johnson. "If the Goliath in the White House were less flamboyant," wrote Shana Alexander, "McCarthy would not seem so attractively gray."[6]

He had once felt called to be a priest. Young McCarthy was the prize pupil of Benedictine monks at St. John's Preparatory Academy in Minnesota. Deep within him, he harbored a disquiet, a questioning, a disgust with American materialism and individualism. He valued historical precedents and established institutions. In 1942 he entered St. John's

Abbey to start training for the priesthood. After one year, he dropped out. He married his wife, Abigail, started a short-lived cooperative farm, taught economics and sociology at the College of St. Thomas, and then, in 1948, successfully ran for Congress as an anticommunist liberal in the mold of Harry Truman and Hubert Humphrey.[7]

Over five terms in the House of Representatives, the tall, handsome McCarthy won a minor national reputation, most notably for his courageous televised debate with Joseph McCarthy, at the height of the demagogic senator's influence. In 1958 he moved to the Senate. Although wry about the Senate's clannish, tradition-bound culture, he furthered his standing as a thoughtful liberal, projecting both morality and stability. "I do not suggest that there is need for a great structural change of our government," he wrote in 1960. "I believe that the Constitution and the traditions which have developed from it are flexible enough so that adjustments can be made within its framework."[8]

During the 1960 Democratic National Convention, McCarthy delivered an inspirational nominating speech for the darling of liberal intellectuals, former Illinois governor Adlai Stevenson. It garnered him acclaim, but John F. Kennedy won the nomination and the election. With another graceful, smart Catholic in the Oval Office, McCarthy felt frustrated and unappreciated. In the Senate, he developed an air of detached contempt. His political allies found him lazy and undependable. He had always possessed the gift for the artful wisecrack, but now those jokes got crueler. Lyndon Johnson considered him for vice president in 1964, and he wanted the job; but just before the convention, he realized that LBJ was stringing him along. The president had long planned on picking another Minnesotan, Hubert Humphrey. "What a sadistic son of a bitch," grumbled McCarthy.[9]

In 1965, McCarthy joined a small coterie of senators who challenged Johnson's handling of the Vietnam War. The president maintained that the South Vietnamese government was stable, that Vietnam was part of a worldwide battle over communism, and that the Gulf of Tonkin Resolution authorized him to wage the entire war. By contrast, McCarthy defended the right of Congress to determine foreign policy, and he questioned the premises behind the Cold War. In his 1967 book, *The Limits of Power*, he called for a retrenchment of American foreign policy obligations, to better match national constraints and an evolving global situation.[10]

For McCarthy, the escalation of the Vietnam War was a symptom of overconcentrated presidential power. He did not advocate peace at any cost, but he was "willing to pay a high price for it." Like many antiwar liberals, he urged a halt to the bombing of North Vietnam and a gradual military withdrawal. He also called for a negotiated settlement that included the communist National Liberation Front in the governance of South Vietnam. He considered Vietnam both an immediate moral problem and a long-term result of American hubris.[11]

That fall, McCarthy toured college campuses and other centers of Vietnam dissent, earning polite responses for his sober foreign policy assessments. He saw a young generation without political experience or historical perspective, but full of idealism. Its impulse for justice could enrich the nation's political conversation. McCarthy also saw it among his four children, ages thirteen to twenty. His daughter Mary, a sophomore at Radcliffe, had worked on an antipoverty program in Washington, D.C., volunteered to register black voters in the South, and marched on the Pentagon. She told her mother that he had to oppose Johnson. Abigail agreed that someone should run—but why Eugene McCarthy? "Mother!" exclaimed Mary. "That's the most immoral thing you have ever said!"[12]

McCarthy had toyed with a presidential run since March 1967, though he kept waiting for a prominent Democrat to enter the race. Discontent with LBJ intensified over the course of 1967. Still, challenging the powerful incumbent could undermine a politician's career. Other antiwar senators, such as Idaho's Frank Church and South Dakota's George McGovern, refused to imperil their reelection bids in 1968. Robert Kennedy could launch the most effective challenge, but he was dithering. So on November 30, in the Caucus Room of the Old Senate Building, McCarthy formally announced his entrance in four primaries. He hoped to not only challenge the Johnson administration's position on the war, but also start a conversation about America's global role.

His limited effort was a moral choice. It was not a strategic move. "I don't know if it will be political suicide," he cracked. "It'll be more like an execution."[13]

———

By the time McCarthy entered the Democratic primaries, the peace movement had grown bigger and stronger, but also more diffuse and chaotic. The first demonstrations and teach-ins took place in the spring of 1965. Driven by ideals of social justice and "participatory democracy," Students for a Democratic Society (SDS) lent much of the early, radical energy. But dissent came from many sources, including the Committee

for a Sane Nuclear Policy, Women Strike for Peace, and Clergy and Lay-
men Concerned About Vietnam (CALCAV). In February 1967, after 2,400
clergymen organized by CALCAV held a vigil in Washington, McCarthy
made his first statement against the war.[14]

The antiwar movement swelled in 1967. That April, Martin Luther King
formally denounced the Vietnam War. In Central Park, 300,000 people
demonstrated. Thousands of volunteers organized summer peace proj-
ects around the country. In October, over 100,000 marched from the Lincoln Memorial to the Pentagon—a protest that mixed the young with
middle-class professionals, liberals with militants, the peaceful with
the provocative. The demonstration revealed the growth of the antiwar
movement, though its image remained the domain of radical hippies,
drawn from a pool of indulgent youth.[15]

This Baby Boom generation had been raised amidst economic abun-
dance and sculpted by childrearing philosophies that nurtured individual expression. The Cold War dictated that they celebrate American
greatness, but they entered adulthood with political disillusion—John F.
Kennedy had been assassinated, the civil rights movement exposed the
nation's racism, and Vietnam showcased a brutal imperialism. As the college population doubled during the 1960s, a cadre of students saw huge
public universities, or "multiversities," as impersonal, alienating, and
serving corporate and military interests. These college activists made
little distinction between Cold War conservatives and establishment liberals such as Lyndon Johnson—they were all part of a power elite. Both
cynical and idealistic, activists demanded a more humanistic university,
a more humane national culture, a genuine bottom-up democracy.[16]

In 1968, the spirit of rebellion spread across the globe; students in
France, Mexico, Japan, Czechoslovakia, and elsewhere carried out mass
demonstrations. Though national circumstances shaped each protest,
television was fostering a global culture of leftist resistance. In the
United States, demonstrations rocked hundreds of college campuses.
Students agitated for an end to racism and imperialistic wars. Some protests descended into violence. Many vowed to resist the draft, especially
after the February 1968 government ruling to abolish most draft defer-
ments for graduate students. As more young people embraced a revolutionary spirit, they injected a radical energy into the antiwar movement,
expressing both passion and bitterness. But groups such as SDS were
rife with infighting, possessed different connections to communism, and

exhibited paranoia about government surveillance and co-optation by "the system."[17]

McCarthy's campaign stood at a distance from this radical action. Rather than disrupt the system, it brought the antiwar movement into the system. It built on the groundwork of reformers, not revolutionaries. Through much of 1967, Allard Lowenstein and Curtis Gans had organized a Dump Johnson movement within the Democratic Party. They traveled the country, recruiting allies from a wide network of antiwar groups typically populated by middle-aged, liberal, well-educated whites with mixed levels of political experience. By the fall, as LBJ's popularity waned, the bold idea gained some traction. All it needed was a legitimate candidate.[18]

When McCarthy stood before the Conference of Concerned Democrats, it was the culmination of a crusade. But the coming campaign faced enormous challenges. Even leading antiwar senators like William Fulbright and Wayne Morse failed to support him. Americans for Democratic Action—an influential coalition of liberal intellectuals, labor leaders, and civil rights advocates—did endorse him. But the vote was close, and seven members then resigned in protest. Democratic leaders accused him of dividing the party. Pundits complained that he presented no concrete solutions for Vietnam. Antiwar activists were ambivalent about him. No one thought he could oust a sitting president from his own party.[19]

McCarthy originally planned to avoid the New Hampshire primary. A handful of local Democrats had started a committee for him, but after visiting the state in mid-December of 1967, he leaned away from the race. New Hampshire was a Republican state without large centers of antiwar sentiment. Its most influential voice was William Loeb, the archconservative publisher of the *Manchester Union Leader*. And yet, New Hampshire was the first primary. A good showing could boost momentum for the cause. Moreover, New Hampshire residents took pride in their independence from the political establishment. Upon the New Year, hoping to sprout a grassroots campaign in this rocky, snow-covered ground, McCarthy announced a run in New Hampshire.[20]

The campaign tanked. By the end of January 1968, he trailed Johnson 4–1 in a national poll. McCarthy was accustomed to campaigning on his own terms, under his own authority, according to his own schedule. Instead of employing publicists or advance schedulers, he wanted to "live off the land," presenting his case to the people. He paid little attention to his big-money donors. Thousands of letters poured into his Senate office offering money and volunteer work; for weeks, they sat unanswered. He ignored local political officials. He kept speaking in a flat style that frustrated his fervent antiwar base. On his first day campaigning in New Hampshire, he missed the shift change at a Manchester textile mill, losing the chance to shake hands with voters. "Things couldn't be worse," assessed one staffer. "He had more support the day he announced than he does now."[21]

His saviors were college students. They arrived from the Ivy Leagues and the Seven Sisters; but they also came from small and obscure schools, and they traveled from as far away as Duke and Michigan. On weekends, they came by the hundreds, lugging their typewriters and sleeping bags. They were led by Sam Brown, a baby-faced graduate student at Harvard Divinity School, and Ann Hart, the tiny, twenty-year-old daughter of Michigan senator Philip Hart. A Cornell graduate student of theoretical physics organized the door-to-door canvassing effort. A Columbia grad-uate student in Chinese politics created a specialized system of maps. Ph.D. candidates in French literature from Yale campaigned in French Canadian neighborhoods.[22]

The McCarthy campaign gave these students a legitimate outlet for their antiwar convictions. Fearing any association between the candi-date and rebellious youth, local campaign leaders adopted the slogan, "Neat and Clean for Gene." No hippie style! The long hair was cut. The beards were shaved. Miniskirts and jeans were discarded in favor of plaids, corduroys, and Oxfords with rolled-up sleeves. Anyway, these kids were student leader types, not SDS radicals. They channeled their hatred of the war into practical politics. Subsisting on peanut butter and Beatles albums, they typed memos, mailed letters, answered telephones, passed out flyers during early morning shift changes outside freezing factory gates, and knocked on door after door, trying to personally reach every single Democratic voter. Rather than lecture people about an immoral war, they emphasized Johnson's foibles and the Vietnam War's problems. These clean-cut college students impressed New Hampshire voters, at-tracted national media attention, and transformed a moribund cam-paign into a noble "Children's Crusade."[23]

McCarthy's cool dignity lent respectability to their movement. Unlike LBJ, McCarthy conceived of the presidency not as a cudgel to wield but as a vessel for liberating the American spirit. Whether at a Rotary Club luncheon or a college rally, he refused to court laughs or cheers. His attitude conveyed respect: *This is me. These are my ideas.* That resonated with the students, who came to New Hampshire for a cause, not a personality. "He has liberated the idealism that was hidden by their beards and sneers," wrote Mary McGrory. If the candidate was wry and distant and vague, he nevertheless belonged to them—a dreamy, decent father figure who trusted his smart, creative, self-motivated children.[24]

The momentum built. The legendary Richard Goodwin—a Kennedy loyalist and former speechwriter for Lyndon Johnson—drove up from Boston and immediately started generating press coverage. Hollywood star Paul Newman left women voters agog as he pinned McCarthy buttons on their lapels. In the last stretch, the campaign staged a media blitz, and McCarthy thrived in television advertisements by speaking calmly, straight into the camera, transmitting a basic authenticity.[25]

His style further contrasted him with Johnson. The president's name was not on the ballot, but the state's leading Democratic officials engineered a write-in campaign. They declared that LBJ would prevail in a landslide. But they blundered by sending all registered Democrats a pro-Johnson pledge card. It had three parts: one for the voter, one for state party headquarters, and one for the White House. McCarthy derided this tactic as another heavy-handed power grab: "a brand on people . . . something they do in Texas." Many New Hampshire residents saw it as contrary to their independent tradition. Meanwhile, Governor John King harangued that McCarthy aided "the forces of appeasement" and "noisy and unruly" extremists—an old-fashioned Red-baiting attack that made McCarthy seem the calm and rational choice, especially as continuing news of the Tet Offensive spread doubts about Johnson's handling of the war.[26]

On the final weekends before the vote, about 1,000 students poured into New Hampshire (including an overqualified envelope-stuffer from Wellesley College named Hillary Rodham). The McCarthy campaign was developing nationwide legitimacy. His final campaign appearance in New Hampshire was at a shopping center in Salem. As he left, an old woman approached. "My grandson is fighting in Vietnam," she said. Staffers held their breath, fearing an attack on McCarthy's patriotism. They exhaled when she continued: "I don't know why he's there and I want him home as soon as possible. Senator McCarthy I'm going to vote for you and get the rest of my family to do the same."[27]

It was a good omen. On March 12, McCarthy got 42 percent of the Democratic vote, surpassing all but the most optimistic predictions. Johnson
won, but with only 49 percent. Factoring in Republicans who wrote in
McCarthy's name, Johnson edged him by only a few hundred votes. On
a separate ballot, the better-organized McCarthy slate also captured
twenty of the state's twenty-four delegates for the national convention.
As later polls showed, his supporters were not necessarily "peace" voters.
Many backed the Vietnam War, but they objected to Johnson. Nationally,
the reaction was shock; in the words of one editorialist, it was "an unmer-
ciful psychological defeat" for the president.[28]

McCarthy and his movement won some admiration. By 1968, pundits
were buzzing about "the New Politics." The vague term had different
meanings, but it essentially meant taking politics right to the people.
In the context of the McCarthy campaign, the New Politics entailed a
bottom-up challenge to the city bosses, party bureaucrats, and labor
leaders that dominated the Democratic Party. McCarthy had the courage to stand against the establishment. He refused to follow the habits of
traditional seekers of the Oval Office. His reward was an extraordinary
exercise in democracy. "As a man and a candidate," marveled the *New
Republic*, "he is bringing out the best in his supporters, young and old,
and demanding the best of our electoral process."[29]

The next morning, McCarthy flew back to Washington, D.C., in a jubilant mood. Upon landing, though, his jaw tensed. An aide informed him
that New York senator Robert F. Kennedy was planning his own bid for
the nomination. A barrage of reporters asked only about Kennedy. "He
wouldn't even let me have my day of celebration, would he?" grumbled
McCarthy.[30]

McCarthy and Kennedy soon met for a twenty-minute conversation
dotted with stubborn silences. Kennedy explained that he had feared dividing the party, but New Hampshire showed that the party was already
divided. McCarthy counseled Kennedy to wait until 1972; if McCarthy
won, he would serve just one term, in line with his philosophy of a limited
presidency. The next day, he said that he wished Kennedy "would leave the
primaries to me." Demonstrating his resilience, he entered two more primaries, in Indiana and South Dakota. After New Hampshire, his quixotic
challenge had transformed into a genuine national campaign.[31]

But McCarthy also bore a personal bitterness. "You know why I don't
get along with the Kennedys?" he asked Richard Goodwin. "They never

appreciated me." The privileged Kennedy brothers had surpassed him in reputation and influence. While his Catholic faith shaped his guiding principles, the Kennedys exploited their Catholicism for political support. He and Bobby were temperamental opposites: McCarthy was cerebral and withdrawn; Kennedy was emotive and impulsive. The press stoked McCarthy's resentments by constantly speculating that he was Kennedy's "stalking horse," paving the path for a more legitimate antiwar candidate. Now, on the heels of McCarthy's great triumph, Kennedy was stealing his thunder.[32]

On March 15, Massachusetts senator Edward Kennedy flew to Green Bay, Wisconsin, to meet McCarthy. The next day, Robert Kennedy would announce his candidacy, and younger brother Ted was acting as a peacemaker. It was a comic disaster. Kennedy missed his original flight, and McCarthy defiantly went to bed. When Kennedy arrived (by taking the freight elevator to sneak past reporters), Abigail refused to wake her husband. Finally, they roused Eugene and met at 2:30 A.M. After some idle banter, Ted confirmed that Robert was running. He had brought a reconciliation statement for McCarthy's approval, but it never left his briefcase. Campaign aides had hatched an idea to split six primaries between the two candidates, after which they could run against each other in California. The McCarthys nixed the idea.[33]

By dawn, Ted was back in Washington, informing Bobby about the meeting. At 10:00 A.M., McCarthy watched Robert Kennedy's televised announcement with a cutting smile. Then he went on television himself. "I committed myself to a group of young people and, I thought, a rather idealistic group of adults in American society," he stated. "I said I would be their candidate, and I intend to run as I committed myself to run." His resentment was clear: only he had the courage to run in New Hampshire, and now he needed room to keep running. "I can win in Wisconsin and I can go on to win elsewhere," he insisted.[34]

To his admirers, McCarthy emerged from the Kennedy challenge as pure and true, a folk hero. He spurned Kennedy's offer to campaign on his behalf in Wisconsin; he would beat Johnson on his own terms, not in the shadow of a swashbuckling political celebrity. The press recognized Kennedy's charisma and resources but decried his ambition and ruthlessness. Meanwhile, McCarthy's volunteer army saw Kennedy as an opportunist, in contrast to McCarthy, who fostered a new type of movement, built on his integrity. "The true significance of Eugene McCarthy is not that he gambled on himself," wrote Murray Kempton, "but that he gambled on us."[35]

In Wisconsin, another impressive grassroots effort fueled the McCarthy campaign. The state had a long progressive tradition, a center of activism at the University of Wisconsin-Madison, and some early antiwar groups. Though McCarthy had a small staff, he drew on a deep reservoir of local volunteers, most of whom were educated and middle class. "The real center of our support has come from the housewives, women who come into our headquarters and contribute $5 or $10 out of their grocery money without telling their husbands," reported one local coordinator.[36]

Another surge of students supplemented the locals. About 7,000 arrived for the final weekend, including eleven busloads from the University of Michigan. Campaign workers packed the headquarters in Milwaukee's Sheraton Schroeder Hotel, where they printed pamphlets and posters, coordinated canvassers, pored over data, and crashed on cots or sleeping bags in hallways. Despite the chaos, a representative of Eugene McCarthy reached 1.3 million homes, almost every voter in a large, spread-out state.[37]

Lyndon Johnson was dispatching cabinet members and Vice President Hubert Humphrey to campaign on his behalf, but McCarthy was winning hearts, minds, and crowds. The Minnesota senator kept calling for a president who limited his powers and forged a noble national purpose. He defended the right to dissent on Vietnam. In his speeches, he often quoted poetry, such as this verse from Walt Whitman:

> Poets to come! orators, singers, musicians to come!
> Not to-day is to justify me, and answer what I am for;
> But you, a new brood, native, athletic, continental, greater than
>   before known.
> Arouse! Arouse—for you must justify me—you must answer.

McCarthy had started writing his own poems. It was an art form that connoted respect for learning and justice. But poetry was also full of ambiguity and density, much like McCarthy himself. He described himself as an "Act II man," stuck in the middle of the drama: "That's where I live—involution and complexity."[38]

These qualities made McCarthy interesting, but they also compromised his campaign. As in New Hampshire, he was often late for campaign appearances. Sometimes he canceled them outright. While giving a speech or meeting voters, he seemed to have his mind on something else. He abhorred confrontation, so he imposed no order on his staff. Campaign manager Blair Clark, McCarthy committee organizer Curtis Gans, and wife Abigail each had unclear administrative power. The campaign finances were a mess. Local volunteers feuded with the national staff. The staff often failed to accommodate the press with advance speeches or travel arrangements.[39]

Furthermore, many liberals perceived McCarthy as distant from the great challenge of race relations. He had long voted for civil rights legislation, but his aloof manner often failed to resonate with African Americans. Moreover, McCarthy had no aspirations of maintaining Lyndon Johnson's Democratic coalition. He disdained interest group politics of all sorts, ignoring traditional power bases such as party officials, labor unions, and black leaders. Rather, he wanted "a constituency of conscience," forged through direct appeals to voters via his volunteer army and television. McCarthy thus shunned a walking tour through Milwaukee's black wards, a traditional ritual of Democratic candidates.[40]

In a microcosm of the Democrats' dawning cultural crisis, the campaign staff held a large and contentious meeting on the issue. The more idealistic staffers urged an intense campaign in black neighborhoods, while the more hardheaded aides cautioned that working-class, white ethnic voters would resent this racial appeal. Illustrating both their liberal principles and the campaign's haphazard discipline, press aides Seymour Hersh and Mary Lou Oates resigned in protest and leaked the controversy to the *New York Times*. McCarthy did care about the nation's racial divisions, and after the assassination of Martin Luther King, he pivoted to a sharper critique, even echoing Black Power militants by likening the inner city to an exploited colony. But he resented these political shows. In Wisconsin, he finally consented to a "ghetto walk" but rushed his way through it. Even more than usual, he acted indifferent, indignant, ironic.[41]

In his own mind, McCarthy fulfilled his particular moral obligation once he entered the primaries. As he sought a more passive presidency, he was a passive campaigner. He never asked for support, which he justified as an expression of his principles. But he also revealed his fear of rejection. He refrained from recruiting top-notch political professionals, instead using staffers who failed to challenge his authority. The mercurial candidate thus composed his campaign's jagged rhythms. "Again and again," reflected speechwriter Jeremy Larner, "he insisted on his personality, which one had to swallow whole on faith, not just in its principles but in its whims and moods." Like a poet, he would express his ideas and his values. Unlike a politician, he would not adapt to circumstances. He seemed resistant to actually *winning*.

Some volunteers began harboring misgivings, which intensified as the campaign shifted to Indiana and beyond. In closed-door meetings, they disclosed their doubts, asking one another, Should this man be president?[42]

On March 31, McCarthy was giving a dull speech at Carroll College in Waukesha. From the back, he heard yelps, then murmurs, then screams. As reporters rushed down the aisles, confused staffers hopped onstage to protect their candidate. "What is it? What is it?" cried McCarthy. When he learned the news, his jaw dropped, but he composed himself. "Things have gotten rather complicated," he announced to the confused audience. Then someone shouted it out: "JOHNSON'S NOT RUNNING!" The auditorium erupted in cheers.[43]

McCarthy was typically understated. He did not gloat. When Abigail called the White House to pay respects, she was the first to speak with both Lyndon and Lady Bird. Later, at headquarters in Milwaukee, television reporters appealed for interviews, but McCarthy told them to wait. "This is a night for reading poetry—maybe a little Yeats." After making the rounds, rather than discuss the campaign's next steps, he rambled about geography and recited poems.[44]

Three days later, McCarthy won 57 percent of the vote in the Wisconsin primary, carried seventy-one of seventy-two counties, and picked up forty-nine convention delegates. His protest candidacy had transformed into a genuine reach for the presidency. He had flaws and quirks, but he offered calmness, intelligence, and humanity in a period of national distress. Robert Lowell, a frequent companion during the campaign, applauded the candidate's "negative qualities"—the lack of charisma, drive, and ambition that distinguished him from LBJ. "But I am with him most for what he possesses," insisted the acclaimed poet. Lowell lauded his "tolerant and courageous mind," his "lungs that breathe the air." McCarthy stood for what was right: "When the race against President Johnson was hopeless and intractable, he alone hoped, entered and won."[45]

—4—

THE PEOPLE'S BILLIONAIRE

N ELSON ROCKEFELLER barreled straight to the podium, forgoing his usual smiles, handshakes, and greetings of "Hiya fella." His face looked pale. He gazed out at the ballroom of the New York Hilton, which was packed with cameras and about 300 reporters. The date was March 21, 1968, one day before the filing deadline for the primary election in Oregon. The *New York Times* was reporting that Rockefeller would announce his candidacy for president, and full-page ads in the New York papers were begging, "Please, Rocky—Say It." By challenging Richard Nixon, the governor of New York would reclaim the voice of the Republican Party's progressive wing.[1]

This moment had been brewing for a month. In late February, Rockefeller had admitted that he would accept a nominating drive in his name, though he still supported George Romney. A few days later, Romney dropped out, and the Draft Rockefeller movement took off. At a closed-door session before the National Governors Conference in Washington, D.C., he told GOP leaders that he was "ready and willing to serve the American people if called." Back in New York, Rockefeller mulled strategy at his Manhattan brownstone office. Republican officials were offering endorsements and starting local committees. On March 10, he assembled about twenty party leaders, who urged him to run. "Rocky" was their best hope: a man with vision and resources, a pragmatic and humane leader, a proven winner.[2]

Yet Rockefeller moved slowly, gathering information and opinions. He saw high barriers. It was too late for an effective write-in campaign in New Hampshire. Thanks to a quirky rule, if he joined the primary in liberal Oregon, he was automatically enlisted in conservative Nebraska.

OVERLEAF: Governor Nelson Rockefeller (R-NY) (*center*) (courtesy Rockefeller Archive Center)

About twenty of the nation's twenty-six Republican governors favored him, but few openly endorsed him, since that might jeopardize their own party standing. Meanwhile, conservative Republicans, including his old rival Barry Goldwater, appraised him with distaste. Most important, Richard Nixon already controlled a huge chunk of delegates for that summer's Republican National Convention.[3]

Then there was the question of Rockefeller himself. For years, he had relished the fight. He had loved challenging the right-wing hard-liners, selling himself as a fearless problem-solver who battled for justice. But now he bore scars from those clashes, and he worried about his family. He also resisted splitting the party again. To clear a path to the presidency, he needed Republican power brokers to block Nixon from a first-ballot majority at the convention. Then delegates might flock to him, since he was the most likely victor in a general election. That was a long shot, though.[4]

So on March 21, instead of announcing his candidacy, Rockefeller shocked the media throng by declaring, "I have decided today that I am not a candidate campaigning, directly or indirectly, for the presidency of the United States." Most party leaders favored Nixon, and in this moment of "perilous national division," the Republicans should present a united front. He was withdrawing from the Oregon primary and asking backers to cease organizing for him. If a genuine movement for his nomination arose from within the party, he would respond, but "I expect no such call. And I shall do nothing in the future, by word or by deed, to encourage such a call." At the end, he smiled and answered questions, looking relieved, his elbow leaning on the podium.[5]

The announcement was the latest curveball in an election that had already seen Eugene McCarthy's emergence and Robert Kennedy's entrance. Pundits mourned Rockefeller's decision, as the Republicans needed his fresh ideas and can-do approach. The party's progressive leaders were vexed. Kentucky senator Thruston Morton, his would-be campaign manager, called it a "tragic mistake." New York senator Jacob Javits mourned that with Romney's withdrawal and Rockefeller's disavowal, the moderate Republicans were losing their national voice. Maryland governor Spiro Agnew, the most enthusiastic proponent of Rocky's candidacy, had invited reporters into his office to watch the announcement. He prepared to brag about his own importance to the nominating effort. When Rockefeller started talking, Agnew's mouth went agape, then slithered into a pained grin.[6]

At this point, it appeared that the Rockefeller saga was over. In fact, it was just beginning. Nelson Rockefeller was at his most compelling amidst a crisis. He was stubborn and independent, optimistic and driven, astoundingly ambitious and frustratingly self-destructive. As the convulsions of 1968 kept rippling across the nation, he could not resist the responsibility to tackle huge problems, from the soul of the Republican Party to the fate of the American people.

When Nelson was a young boy, Theodore Roosevelt attended a gathering at the Rockefeller family brownstone. Nelson asked the former president how, after returning from big-game adventures in Africa, he got his giraffes through American railroad tunnels. An enthused Roosevelt launched into an explanation of a clever pulley system, and Nelson was impressed. The president must be a man who solves problems, who dreams big. He wanted to be president, too. "After all," he reflected, "when you think of what I had, what else is there to aspire to?"[7]

By 1968, Rockefeller's personal fortune was estimated at $6 billion to $10 billion. The mind-boggling wealth was a birthright, along with its presumptions of power. He was the grandson of not only the oil magnate John D. Rockefeller Sr., but also Rhode Island senator Nelson Aldrich. Yet he and his five siblings were raised to be sober and caring, to be well-rounded, to improve mankind. Nelson suffered from dyslexia, but he compensated with a grinding work ethic. He dedicated himself to public service. During World War II, Franklin Roosevelt appointed him to head a federal office that stimulated development in Latin America. After the war, he advised Harry Truman on foreign policy. Under Dwight Eisenhower, he chaired a committee to reorganize the federal government, served as undersecretary of the Department of Health, Education, and Welfare, and was a special assistant on foreign affairs.[8]

But Rockefeller craved more. He always wanted more. He was a man of staggering privilege and enormous self-confidence. He pursued the finest things before him, whether they were brilliant advisers, gorgeous mistresses, or more world-class art than he could possibly display. And he wanted power, the real power that comes from electoral office. In 1958 he won the election for governor of New York. On the campaign trail, he flipped the blue-blood connotations of his name and fortune, displaying a common touch. He could draw throngs on Coney Island or chat at a rural upstate coffee shop. He shook hands and slapped backs, scarfed down blintzes and tacos, offered a flirty glint for the girls and a hearty "Hiya fella" for the guys.[9]

As governor, he proved an emblem of progressive Republicanism, blending socially conscious policies with principles of fiscal integrity and individual dignity. While raising taxes to keep his budgets balanced, he oversaw a New York version of the Great Society: a new medical aid plan, a huge buildup of the state university system, a housing law that promoted racial integration, and increases in the minimum wage and workmen's compensation benefits. He distinguished himself from Democrats by averring that state government, rather than the federal bureaucracy, more effectively served the people.[10]

Given his popularity among general voters, Rockefeller stirred up Republicans during presidential election cycles. His gregarious independence made him a foil to the calculating party man Nixon. Though he refrained from running in 1960, he presented Nixon with the "Compact of Fifth Avenue." This fourteen-point statement, meant to shape the convention platform, included liberal initiatives to fund education and promote civil rights. While Nixon endorsed it to achieve party unity, conservatives were outraged. Arizona senator Barry Goldwater called it the "Munich of the Republican Party." The Republican right hated Rockefeller, who personified the elite, East Coast establishment.[11]

More than politics, Rockefeller's personal life derailed his presidential ambitions. It was not that he indulged in extramarital affairs—the press generally ignored such dalliances. It was not even that he divorced his wife Tod in 1962—their marriage had been long loveless. But in 1963, he married a new woman, Happy Murphy, who was divorcing her own husband, a scientist for the Rockefeller Institute. Most scandalously, Happy gave official custody of their four children to her husband. It was an era before conservatives' political emphasis on social morality, but there were certainly double standards for male and female behavior. Many voters judged the couple as flouting decency. Once considered the inevitable nominee, Rockefeller tanked in the polls. Stewart Alsop wrote that conservatives were "dancing gleefully on his grave." In 1964, he lost the critical California primary to Goldwater—in part because Happy had just given birth to Nelson Rockefeller Jr.[12]

Rockefeller's signature moment arrived during the 1964 Republican National Convention, when he condemned the far-right extremists behind Goldwater. With relish, even delight, he taunted the "kooks" in the gallery with denunciations of their "smear and hate literature, strong-arm

tactics, bomb threats, and bombings. Infiltration and takeover of established political organizations by Communist and Nazi methods!" The
"kooks" fulfilled their role by responding with boos, jeers, and shrieks.
The scene cast Rockefeller as the principled fighter for moderate Republicanism—and a misfit within his party.[13]

In 1966, Rockefeller rallied to win a third term as governor. While satu-
rating the state with advertising that touted his many achievements, he
again glad-handed his way among the people, luring new voters to the Republican Party, from Jewish liberals to African Americans to blue-collar
workers. The result vindicated him. He claimed to no longer desire the
presidency. He knew that another candidacy would stress his wife, split
the party, and expose him to another bruising fight.[14]

Through 1967 and into early 1968, Rockefeller supported the candidacy
of George Romney. Meanwhile, his own reputation rebounded, thanks to
his dynamic governing record and appealing moderate views. He kept
insisting that he was not a presidential candidate—which, paradoxically,
made him more alluring. His friends tried pushing him back into the
ring. Who better to dethrone Lyndon Johnson? Who better to solve the
riddle of Vietnam, the urban crisis, the diminishing American spirit? As
Rockefeller once said, "There's no problem that there's no solution to."[15]

The Republican Party had long championed economic growth and individual freedom. Historically, it united professionals, business owners,
white Protestants in the North, and African Americans in the South. By
the 1950s, however, the Republicans suffered from a split. The conservative wing, associated with Ohio senator Robert Taft, sought to disman-
tle the New Deal welfare state and pursue an isolationist foreign policy.
The other side, represented by President Dwight Eisenhower, advocated
a "Middle Way" between liberal centrists and conservative hard-liners.
It sought fiscal responsibility, accepted government as an economic
engine and social safety net, and embraced American leadership in foreign affairs. The moderates typically chose the candidate in the presidential election, at least until the 1964 nomination of conservative Barry
Goldwater.[16]

Despite the right-wing surge in 1964, the progressive Republicans re-
mained a potent force. Their tradition was rooted in the conscience of
Abraham Lincoln and the pragmatic reforms of Theodore Roosevelt. These
Republicans believed that local and state governments could provide

responsive leadership for American citizens, including the poor and racial minorities. Strongest along the East Coast and in other urban areas, the moderates lacked the grassroots organization or ideological passion of the conservatives, but their commonsense approach had national, cross-party appeal.[17]

In the mid-1960s, a new generation of Republicans rose in national standing. Though it included conservatives such as Ronald Reagan, dynamic moderates composed most of this deep talent pool. Oregon's Mark Hatfield, a dove on Vietnam, was elected to the Senate. Edward Brooke of Massachusetts became the first black Senator since Reconstruction. Governors such as Raymond Shafer of Pennsylvania, John Chafee of Rhode Island, and Daniel Evans of Washington sought to reorganize state government and address problems of race, class, and cities. Charles Percy of Illinois, once the CEO of the media technology corporation Bell and Howell at age twenty-nine, won a Senate seat while advocating creative ideas that blurred party lines, such as a home ownership program for poor families and an Asian conference to seek solutions in Vietnam.[18]

The moderate Republicans shared principles of fiscal responsibility and social justice, but they were singular figures rather than an organized faction. Their egos and ambitions sometimes collided—most notoriously in the rivalry between Rockefeller and New York City mayor John Lindsay. The tall, handsome, media-savvy Lindsay had a reputation for idealism and honesty, but his tenure reflected the difficulties of managing the modern American city. He struggled to muffle class and racial tensions while sparring with transit workers, police bureaucracies, and school-teachers. In February 1968, 10,000 sanitation workers went on strike. An estimated 100,000 tons of garbage piled up on the streets. Lindsay wanted Rockefeller to call out the national guard. Instead, Rockefeller appointed a mediation panel and gave the workers a modest raise. It was a practical solution to a potential crisis, but Lindsay won the public relations battle by painting Rockefeller as caving to the union.[19]

During the garbage strike, Rockefeller was still submerging his presidential ambitions. He not only endorsed Michigan governor George Romney but also gave him research files, mailing lists, political organizers, and money. Through most of the previous year, Romney had represented the moderates' best hope. He had a jutting jaw, a robust energy, a sincere moral grounding, and a track record in the business world. In the 1950s, he had saved American Motors by promoting the compact, fuel-efficient Rambler against the Big Three carmakers' "gas guzzling dinosaurs." In

1962 he won election to governor, and he soon enacted an impressive slate of programs to help workers, children, and the poor. He won reelection in 1964 while shunning Goldwater for courting extremists and southern segregationists. By 1966, when Romney won his third term, he was out-polling Lyndon Johnson and getting ballyhooed as presidential timber.[20]

In 1967, while Richard Nixon embarked on his world tour as a states-man, Romney occupied center stage, touring West Coast states and speaking before Republican groups. Just as Nixon calculated, Romney was too exposed, too early. His membership in the Church of Latter Day Saints also attracted controversy. Romney's Mormon faith shaped his en-tire persona: his sense of moral righteousness, his patriotism, his work ethic, his physical vigor, his missionary impulse to help others. It helped explain his appeal. But the cynical press corps found him boring and holier-than-thou. Moreover, Romney touted his civil rights record, but his church prohibited blacks from serving as priests.[21]

Romney plowed into everything with earnest stubbornness, whether it was courting his wife, jogging before dawn, or running for office. He did things because they were *right*. Yet on the early campaign trail, he offered no sharp ideas. Instead he exposed his tendency for fuzzy, fumbling lan-guage. Once, a reporter asked why he declined to provide specifics on his Vietnam policy. "Well, because I choose not to," he responded.[22]

The campaign faltered before it officially started. In July 1967, Detroit exploded in a massive riot, fueled by the outrage of its poor black citi-zens. The violence claimed forty-three lives, burned swaths of the city, and cost a half-billion dollars in damages. When Romney asked for fed-eral troops to restore order, the White House delayed, demanding the request in writing. In this way Lyndon Johnson embarrassed a potential foe whose programs had sought to improve the inner city and build the black middle class. A few months later, Romney toured seventeen cities in twenty days, meeting radical activists and poor people, seeking a na-tional moral reorientation on race and poverty. But he lacked the political skills to bridge the chasm in viewpoints on the urban crisis.[23]

Romney suffered most from a self-inflicted wound. An initial sup-porter of the Vietnam War, he then developed an independent stance that urged both military pressure against North Vietnam and open elections in South Vietnam. He even called the war a "tragic" mistake. Then, in a television interview, he claimed that while on a July 1965 tour of Viet-nam, "I just had the greatest brainwashing anyone can get." He meant to describe biased briefings from American generals and diplomats, but "brainwashing" conjured associations of nefarious tactics by totalitarian regimes. Both Democratic and Republican politicians slammed him. "Either he's a naïve man or he lacks judgment," grunted Vermont governor Philip Hoff. Romney could have claimed a slip of the tongue, but characteristically, he never backtracked. While he was on a monthlong world tour, the "brainwashing" gaffe kept haunting him.[24]

When Romney launched his campaign in mid-November, he already needed a comeback. Upon his January 12 arrival in New Hampshire, he trailed Nixon 5–1 in private polls. Romney plugged away, working sixteen-hour days, touring fish factories and insurance offices and supermarkets and living rooms. He brandished a huge lobster. He crashed on skis. He spent two hours outside a factory gate in subzero temperatures, greeting workers with a smile, eye contact, a grasp of the elbow, and a handshake. "Hello, I'm George Romney and I'm running for president," he said to one old lady. She stared back. "I think you are telling lies," she said.[25]

The underdog status was liberating, in a sense. Running from behind, he attacked with fervor. After Nixon sidestepped his challenge to televised debates, Romney blasted a "Johnson-Nixon policy of more and more military escalation," lumping the front-runners together on Vietnam. To students at Keene State College, he outlined his own policy, which emphasized political rather than military solutions, including a wider neutrality agreement among the great powers. But Romney never gained any traction. At the end of February, his pollsters expected no more than 12 percent of the New Hampshire vote. Romney left the race.[26]

Perhaps Romney's most enduring image as a presidential candidate occurred at a duckpin bowling alley in Franklin, New Hampshire. A regional variation, duckpin bowling is more difficult than the traditional tenpin game. After three tries, Romney downed only three pins. He refused to quit. After eight tries, only one pin stood. While reporters and photographers and befuddled bowlers gaped, he kept trying. He bowled and bowled and bowled, finally knocking down that last pin on his thirty-fourth try. The scene captured the ordeal of a good man, fueled by hard work and righteousness, exposed by a national spotlight that glared on his clumsy, lurching fight to reclaim the Republican Party's noble principles.[27]

Through the winter of 1968, Rockefeller felt torn. He pledged support to Romney yet undermined him by admitting that he would accept a party draft. As he spoke and wrote about the nation's pressing issues, he identified a spiritual emptiness amidst American prosperity, and he sought a reinvigorated faith in government. It enhanced his prestige. Pundits and politicians wanted him to enter the race. But if he campaigned against Nixon, he would stir the old ghosts. He would be accused of dividing the party. His personal life might also be probed, and there were new rumors of extramarital affairs, this time betraying Happy.[28]

Ten days after Rockefeller's deflating press conference on March 21, Lyndon Johnson withdrew from consideration, opening a political void. Then, on April 4, Martin Luther King was assassinated, escalating the nation's racial crisis. Rockefeller fashioned himself as the man to confront these challenges. He began reminding the public that he never rejected a candidacy; he had always maintained his availability in case of a surge in support. Business leaders, long resentful of Rockefeller's social policies, now pushed him to run. A new Rockefeller for President committee included four senators, five governors, and five former chairmen of the Republican National Committee. Opinion polls and newspaper columns flaunted his popularity. He occupied the ideal spot for attracting general voters: a rival of the exhausted Democrats, yet distant from the far-right ideologues.[29]

After hiring *Newsweek* columnist Emmet John Hughes and Harvard professor Henry Kissinger, Rockefeller planned a series of speeches on major issues. The first, a sober April 18 message to the American Society of Newspaper Editors, called for $150 billion in public and private capital to rebuild the nation's slums. It reflected his commitment to racial justice— his advisers included baseball pioneer Jackie Robinson, Wyatt Tee Walker of the Southern Christian Leadership Conference, and militant activist Charles Kenyatta. The speech further signified his larger philosophy of an activist government that harnessed the energy of free enterprise to improve society.[30]

In a remarkable twist, the most effective advocate for his candidacy was the leader of the opposing party: Lyndon Johnson. Rockefeller opened his name for a draft on April 10, right after meeting with the president. On April 23, Nelson and Happy were secret guests for dinner at the White House. The Rockefellers got the Johnson Treatment. LBJ beseeched Rocky to openly run for his job, and as he guided Happy around the White House, he melted her misgivings. Johnson preferred Rockefeller not only over Nixon, but also over any Democratic candidates, including his own vice president, Hubert Humphrey. Despite their different affiliations,

Johnson saw in Rockefeller a kindred spirit—an ambitious reformer, a forceful consensus-builder.[31]

On April 30, from the New York state capitol, Rockefeller finally entered the fray. He vowed to campaign for the Republican nomination "with all my heart, my mind, and my will." The forty days since his last announcement had upended the political status quo and intensified the feeling of social unrest. Responding to swelling cries for support, Rockefeller presented his own vision for the American future. The mood in Albany was buoyant, with exclamations of Nixon's vulnerability and Rocky's credentials. That very day, Rockefeller won the Republican primary in Massachusetts on a write-in vote, edging both Nixon and the only candidate on the actual ballot, Governor John Volpe. The surprising victory strengthened the notion that Rockefeller, alone among Republicans, could arouse voter enthusiasm.[32]

Rockefeller started giving speeches and hobnobbing with delegates around the country. Rather than criticize Nixon, he outlined his own ideas and principles. Thousands of students cheered him on university campuses in Minnesota, Iowa, and Kansas. He headed to the South, where his support was weakest, hoping to make peace with conservatives. If he allied with California governor Ronald Reagan, they could erode Nixon's support from both ends, denying him a first-ballot majority at the convention. But at a May 20 meeting in New Orleans, the conservative Reagan declined a joint photograph with his fellow big-state governor. Reagan also refused a vice president spot. He downplayed the meeting, telling reporters that "Mr. Rockefeller dropped by for a cup of coffee."[33]

Meanwhile, Nixon was determined to keep acting like a confident leader. Rockefeller had aroused his natural instinct to fight back, but he already had almost enough delegates for a first-ballot majority. The only stumbling blocks, he admitted, would be "my own mistakes." Nixon avoided confrontations with his old nemesis. In the Oregon primary, where Rockefeller's proxies engineered a small write-in campaign, Nixon ran effective television spots and gave just two speeches a day. On May 28, he won 73 percent of the vote, finishing his sweep of the contested primaries. Then he slowed down. He made the occasional radio address or delegate visit, and he got plenty of rest in Key Biscayne, Florida, with his loyal friend Bebe Rebozo.[34]

Rocky lambasted the silent front-runner, blaming Nixon for "coy evasion" and "bewildering judgments" on the Vietnam War. By nature,

Rockefeller was a traditional Cold Warrior. But as he distinguished himself from Nixon, his position on Vietnam evolved. First he placed the war into a changing global environment and warned against further "Americanization." Then he got downright dovish; in July, he unveiled a peace plan that called for a mutual withdrawal, a neutral peacekeeping force, and free elections in South Vietnam. He further contrasted himself with Nixon on the issue of third-party candidate George Wallace, the segregationist former governor of Alabama. Nixon had been strategically quiet about Wallace, since he was envisioning the South as a Republican base. Rockefeller slammed Wallace as a "racist."[35]

Rockefeller's nomination strategy revolved around Election Day. As he often mentioned, just 27 percent of voters identified themselves as Republicans, compared with 46 percent for Democrats. Meanwhile, most voters under age thirty considered themselves independents. Rocky maintained that only *he* could attract independents, forge an effective coalition, beat the Democratic nominee, carry Republican legislators on his coattails, and transcend the nation's divisions.[36]

But could he survive his own party's convention? Rank-and-file Republicans considered him a liberal, elitist outsider who betrayed them in 1964. Even moderate allies such as Charles Percy were slow to endorse him. Despite his opposition to the Vietnam War, Oregon senator Mark Hatfield supported Nixon. Rockefeller did get endorsements from Governors Raymond Shafer of Pennsylvania and Claude Kirk of Florida, who controlled their state delegations as "favorite sons." But he could not win over James Rhodes of Ohio . . . or his former booster Spiro Agnew of Maryland . . . or even the former recipient of his largesse, George Romney of Michigan, who was nursing feelings of betrayal.[37]

Rockefeller practiced his own version of the New Politics, taking his candidacy straight to the voters. Unlike Eugene McCarthy's people-powered campaign, though, Rocky relied on modern technology and the family fortune. In the months preceding the convention, he spent about $5 million on advertising, including 377 full-page ads in fifty-four newspapers. He exploited television, too. Twice a day, local stations around the country aired five-minute messages from his campaign, and three times a week, he ran glossy one-minute spots on each of the national networks, reaching 90 percent of American homes. He employed an enormous creative advertising team that sold him as a bold leader for a modern age, often emphasizing his progressive positions on issues such as Vietnam, race, and the cities.[38]

The ad blitz targeted another aspect of Rockefeller's strategy: polls. If he could show that American voters would elect him over a Democrat (unlike the "loser" Nixon), then Republican delegates might select him. The two main polling agencies, Gallup and Harris, were slow to reflect this public preference. But by late July, the Harris poll did call Rockefeller a clear winner over the Democratic nominee, unlike Nixon. Rockefeller also argued that although Nixon was stronger in the South, George Wallace would capture those electoral votes. He commissioned his own state-by-state polls to show his popularity in the big industrial states. A *Time* study predicted that Nixon would guarantee 239 electoral votes, while Rockefeller was assured 332.[39]

The final element of Rockefeller's New Politics was to travel 66,000 miles through forty-five states, schmoozing the American people. He rode a stagecoach in Idaho and a steamboat in Louisville. He chopped logs at a pancake breakfast in Oregon and danced on the streets of Cincinnati. He wore firemen's hats and posed with elephants. Wherever he went, his admirers turned out, starting with 10,000 people in the Chicago Loop. Riding through Manhattan in a pea-green convertible, he stood up, waved, grinned, and clenched his hands above his head, gathering stares from skyscraper windows and cheers of "Rocky!" from the sidewalks. He plunged into crowds, grasping hands and winking and making small talk. "Hiya . . . Best of luck and all the way . . . Hi, girls, that's the way . . . I wanna tell ya, yes, sir." His exuberance generated footage on the evening news, presenting the billionaire governor among the masses.[40]

Wherever he went, Rockefeller met with delegates for the upcoming Republican National Convention. He impressed them with his sincere belief in the principles of democracy and free enterprise but converted few to his candidacy. The nomination remained a long shot. But after dithering about one last try for the Oval Office, Rocky had poured his soul (and his money) into this improbable quest. He not only satisfied his conscience, but also fulfilled his sense of self. As the *New York Times* noted, "He clearly considered the 100-day campaign the greatest adventure of his life."[41]

There was something else, too. Through the first week of June, Rockefeller had been hesitant, worried about his place in the party, intrusions into his personal life, and the strains of another presidential run. But then the campaign changed. It was evident in how crowds pounded his back, grabbed his clothes, and shook his car. College students believed in him. Black audiences yelled out when he exhorted them. It was obvious, too, in

Rockefeller himself—in how he proclaimed his principles, railed against moral injustices like poverty and racism, promised to "heal that which divides us," demanded a new kind of politics. It was even there in how, sweating and smiling in the midst of a happy crowd, he brushed away a floppy forelock of hair. Americans were yearning for a missing feeling. They were searching for a lost hero.[42]

—5—

MAN OF THE FAMILY

ROBERT F. KENNEDY sat in the backseat of a car, lost in thought. It was the evening of April 4, 1968. Martin Luther King had just been assassinated. That afternoon, after a speech in Muncie, Indiana, the new presidential candidate had assured a skeptical young black man that most whites supported racial equality. But as he headed toward a rally in a black neighborhood in Indianapolis, reflecting on news of the tragedy, he knew that any black faith in white America was crumbling.[1]

About 3,000 people waited at a park. The cheerful admirers near the stage had not heard about King, while those on the fringes had learned the tragic news and spilled outside, full of grief and rage. It was a bizarre, explosive situation. Without any introduction, Kennedy stepped onto a truck's flatbed. The night was cold and damp. Kennedy wore a too-big black overcoat that once belonged to his brother. As the wind snarled his hair, spotlights glared upon his gaunt face. "I have some very sad news for all of you, and I think some very sad news for all of our fellow citizens and people who love peace all over the world," he began. He announced that King had been shot and killed.

Shrieks. Moans. Cries of "Oh Jesus!"

Curses and prayers and tears.

Raised fists of "Black Power!"

Kennedy acknowledged that the murder of a great nonviolent leader stirred impulses for revenge. But that would further divide a race-torn nation. Instead, "we can make an effort, as Martin Luther King did, to understand, and to comprehend, and replace that violence, that stain of bloodshed that has spread across our land, with an effort to understand, compassion and love."

OVERLEAF: Senator Robert F. Kennedy (D-NY) (courtesy John F. Kennedy Presidential Library and Museum)

And then, for the first time in five years, he publicly discussed the trauma of John F. Kennedy's assassination: "For those of you who are black and are tempted to be filled with hatred and mistrust of the injustice of such an act, against all white people, I would only say that I can also feel in my own heart the same kind of feeling. I had a member of my family killed." While he reminded the audience that most whites and most blacks wanted to live in harmony, his speech was powerful because it acknowledged suffering and loss. He quoted Aeschylus: "Even in our sleep, pain, which cannot forget, falls drop by drop upon the heart, until, in our own despair, against our will, comes wisdom through the awful grace of God."[2]

When he finished, the crowd was subdued. Some cried. Others were pensive. Unlike so many other cities, Indianapolis did not suffer a riot that evening. While Lyndon Johnson stewed in the White House and Richard Nixon demanded "law and order," Kennedy sought to empathize with African Americans. Late that night, he called Coretta Scott King and chartered the plane that flew her husband's body back to Atlanta. He listened to black leaders from Indianapolis vent their despair and fury. He canceled most campaign appearances but kept a speech in Cleveland, Ohio, where he lectured 2,200 civic and business leaders—not about assassins, not about riots, but about the "violence of institutions" that ignore the poor and the black.[3]

A few days later, Kennedy and his wife, Ethel, walked the ravaged streets of Washington, D.C., taking in the burned-out buildings, broken glass, piercing burglar alarms, and odors of tear gas. "Is that *you*?" asked one woman. "I knew you'd be the first to come, darling." Though all six announced presidential candidates attended King's funeral in Atlanta on April 9, only Kennedy walked the entire procession from Ebenezer Baptist Church to Morehouse College. Only Kennedy, clad in shirtsleeves with his jacket flung over his shoulder, won cheers from local blacks. Only Kennedy stuck around for meetings with black leaders and entertainers, listening to their ideas and their bitterness.[4]

In that moment, Kennedy emerged as the last best hope for King's dream. It was just one remarkable element in a campaign that was coated in controversy, enshrouded in myth, and blurred by Kennedy's personal evolution.[5]

It is a story framed by death.

The assassination of John F. Kennedy in November 1963 had left his younger brother in shambles. He lost a sense of purpose. His life had been oriented around Jack's aims. Now he agonized. Was his family plagued by a cosmic scourge? Was a conspiracy involving the CIA, Cuba, and/or the Mafia responsible for the death of his brother? Were his own actions as attorney general accountable? His frame shriveled. From his office at the Justice Department, he stared out the window. He wandered the streets of Washington, alone and depressed.[6]

Among the famously vigorous Kennedys, Bobby had been the runt of the litter. The seventh of nine children, he was shorter and scrawnier, more anxious and sensitive, piously Catholic, lacking natural grace or smarts. But over time, he earned the respect of his father, Joseph Sr., a dominating patriarch who made a fortune in liquor, investments, and movies. Unlike his older brothers, Bobby earned a varsity letter in football at Harvard. He was hard-driving and protective of his family. He had his father's edge, the Irish resentment of blue-blood privilege.[7]

He coordinated Jack's successful run for the Senate in 1952, selling his brother's charm and war hero credentials. He then worked for the Senate Investigations Subcommittee, associating himself with the mudslinging, ethically suspect, Red-baiting Joseph McCarthy, a choice that reflected Kennedy's moralistic conservatism. He next served as chief staffer on a congressional committee that targeted corruption in labor unions, leading to a celebrated confrontation with Jimmy Hoffa of the International Brotherhood of Teamsters. Even before managing Jack's slim victory over Richard Nixon in the presidential election of 1960, Bobby had acquired a reputation as ruthless.[8]

RFK served not only as his brother's attorney general, but also as his right-hand man. Politics had forged their bond, transforming Bobby from a scrappy upstart into a trusted counselor. For the Justice Department, he battled organized crime and handled civil rights cases, gradually developing an appreciation for the black freedom struggle. He also advised the president on cabinet appointments, met with international leaders and party officials, hatched ill-fated plots to undermine or assassinate Fidel Castro, and joined critical high-level discussions during the Cuban Missile Crisis.[9]

When the New Frontier ended in tragedy, Bobby had to find his way. His brother Joe had died in combat during World War II, his sister Kathleen died in a plane crash, his father was incapacitated by a stroke, and now Jack was dead. Bobby was the new man of the family. In 1964 he ran for Senate in New York, unseating the popular Republican Kenneth Keating. No other senator received letters asking for a lock of hair or offering lasagna recipes to fatten him up. But Kennedy was a balm for national wounds, a vessel for the romantic myth of JFK. "They're for him," he murmured as crowds cheered. "They're for him."[10]

And so the question arose: Just who was Robert Kennedy? Life as an elected official exposed his contradictions: he was charismatic but withdrawn, public-minded but ambitious, tough but sensitive. Was he a latter-day Machiavelli, or a gentle family man who melted in the presence of children? Some saw a "Good Bobby" and a "Bad Bobby."[11]

In reality he had always contained ambiguities. But he embraced change. By reading the ancient Greeks and Albert Camus, he developed a philosophy that both demanded personal growth and accepted the tragedies of fate. He tested himself with physical adventures, climbing 13,000-foot peaks and riding rickety planes into the Amazon jungle. He surrounded himself with intellectuals, celebrities, and men of action such as athletes, astronauts, and mountain climbers. He learned by listening to ideas, connecting to people, and touching and empathizing with those who needed help. He still carried a reputation as a hard-nosed political operator, but he was emerging as a moral force.[12]

Kennedy never fit in the clubby, ritualized Senate, but the office was the vehicle for his political journey. He sought a "new liberalism," flush with concerns for the downtrodden and free from the orthodoxies of the Cold War and Democratic machine politics. He went to South Africa and condemned apartheid. He championed an ambitious project for Brooklyn's impoverished Bedford-Stuyvesant neighborhood, combining government programs with private-sector initiatives to lure jobs. He befriended Cesar Chavez, the messianic leader of striking immigrant farmworkers in California. He toured the Mississippi Delta and agonized over the plight of starving black children.[13]

Kennedy became a cultural phenomenon, a "happening," a politician-cum-Beatle. His hair grew longer, his disposition more relaxed and ironic. Idealistic youth gravitated toward him. Many women were drawn to his boyish aura and moral charisma. While campaigning for his fellow Democrats in 1966, he won enthusiastic crowds. Most people assumed that he would wait until 1972, but a presidential nomination seemed inevitable. He was a rising star with time on his side.[14]

To Lyndon Johnson, Kennedy was still "that grand-standing little runt." He knew that Bobby never wanted him as JFK's vice president, and it vexed him that Bobby had been the true second-in-command, while he was the butt of jokes among the Ivy League types in the Kennedy circle. Bobby hated LBJ right back. He considered Johnson a weak-minded liar, a crude usurper of his brother's legacy. Yet he harbored some desire to be Johnson's vice president on the 1964 ticket, which would keep a Kennedy near the White House. Johnson nixed it and bragged about it. At the Democratic National Convention, after a film about his slain brother and sixteen minutes of grief-stained cheers, Kennedy quoted from *Romeo and Juliet*, suggesting that JFK should be adored like luminescent stars. "Pay no worship to the garish sun," he ended. Obviously, Johnson was the garish sun.[15]

The Kennedy loyalists of the mid-1960s were a "party unto themselves," according to David Halberstam, "a government in exile with its own shadow cabinet and with Robert Kennedy as the titular head." It darkened Johnson's streak of self-pity: his Great Society accomplished more than the Kennedys ever did, but his support was sinking, while the handsome, charismatic brothers captured the American imagination.[16]

Kennedy and Johnson split, for good, on Vietnam. RFK had supported the influx of military "advisers" in the early 1960s, but as Johnson escalated troop levels and bombed North Vietnam, Kennedy bore misgivings. In February 1966, he advocated a coalition government in South Vietnam that granted the communist National Liberation Front "a share of power and responsibility." That statement cheered the New Left, but it invited counterattacks. Vice President Hubert Humphrey likened his plan to putting "an arsonist in a fire department." Kennedy refrained from more criticism, knowing it would make him seem ambitious and treacherous.[17]

Yet he stayed on the world stage, posing an alternative to LBJ. While touring Western Europe in February 1967, Kennedy received a Vietnam peace feeler from a French diplomat. When the news leaked, Johnson exploded. "I'll destroy you and every one of your dove friends in six months. You'll be dead politically in six months," vowed the president. Kennedy spat back: "Look, I don't have to take that from you." Their cease-fire was over. That March, Kennedy called for a bombing halt in North Vietnam, political reforms in South Vietnam, phased troop withdrawals, and international monitors for free elections. While drawing attacks from establishment figures, he generated new speculation about a presidential run.[18]

Kennedy was surfacing as *the* icon of the New Politics, capitalizing on his personal charisma and modern technology to transcend the party machinery. On television, he transmitted an appealing blend of hesitating frailty and hardheaded confidence. He reached out to young people, sympathetically explaining their alienation from institutions such as government, corporations, and higher education. He advocated a conscience-driven approach to both domestic and foreign policy. Kennedy saw a national crisis of the soul. The solution was a spirit of practical hope, an acceptance of sacrifice, a call for "moral courage."[19]

Did Kennedy have the moral courage to take on LBJ? In the fall of 1967, when Allard Lowenstein started looking to "Dump Johnson," he first approached Kennedy. Bobby was cautious. He feared that he would split the Democrats, weaken the antiwar effort, and enable a Republican victory. His critics would again call him ruthless. Besides, most veterans from JFK's 1960 campaign warned that Johnson controlled too many state delegations. His brother, Massachusetts senator Ted Kennedy, counseled him to wait until 1972.[20]

Yet RFK itched to run. He ached with regret after Eugene McCarthy entered the primaries. Kennedy refused to endorse his fellow antiwar Democrat, whom he considered lazy and ill-suited to the presidency. During the early, anemic months of McCarthy's campaign, the pressure on Kennedy swelled. Meanwhile, his wife, Ethel, his young Senate staff, and some New Frontier holdovers such as Arthur Schlesinger urged him to declare. *To run, or not to run?* The Hamlet of American politics chewed it over with Senate colleagues, dinner guests, strangers, and himself.[21]

On January 30, 1968, Kennedy announced at a National Press Club breakfast that he "would not oppose Lyndon Johnson under any foreseeable circumstances." It was an Old Politics calculation, and it depressed him. It was also terrible timing. The Tet Offensive had just begun. McCarthy was building steam in New Hampshire, grabbing the college kids who once adored Bobby.[22]

Kennedy's passions stirred again. On February 12, he blasted the administration's Vietnam policy, chafing at the consideration of a further troop escalation. Then Johnson ignored the Kerner Report, signaling his indifference to the urban crisis. On the weekend of March 2–3, Kennedy loyalists swirled in and out of Bobby's Virginia estate, Hickory Hill, to relay intelligence and debate strategy. He had crossed a psychological bridge. Better to be ruthless than cowardly.[23]

Yet Kennedy fumbled into the race, tarring his image. In a final compromise effort to avoid splitting his party, Kennedy halfheartedly suggested that Johnson appoint a blue-ribbon commission to review Vietnam policy. While his adviser Ted Sorensen talked with the president, Kennedy met with Defense Secretary Clark Clifford. But LBJ dismissed the idea as a political ploy, and the leaked story made Kennedy look like a schemer. Then, early on March 13, within hours of the New Hampshire vote, Kennedy blurted to reporters, "I am reassessing the possibility of whether I will run against President Johnson." That bombshell sucked some attention from McCarthy's great showing, reviving Kennedy's reputation for ruthlessness.[24]

Kennedy did more soul-searching, made fruitless gestures toward co-operation with McCarthy, and heard warnings from fellow Democrats about the futility of a campaign. Early on Saturday morning, March 16, a team of writers tinkered with a statement at Hickory Hill while children scampered around them. The whole entourage headed to the Caucus Room at the Old Senate Office Building, where JFK had announced his campaign. This time, a Kennedy was running from behind, seeking to depose a president from his own party for the first time since 1884—a man who just happened to be his archnemesis. "These are not ordinary times," reminded RFK, "and this is not an ordinary election."[25]

Now came the "free at last" phase, when Kennedy opened fire on Johnson. Bouncing across fifteen states in fifteen days, he drew massive and passionate crowds. On college campuses in Kansas, Alabama, and Tennessee, students stomped and hollered as if he was a rock star: *"Sock it to 'em, Bobby!"* Crowds chased him through the Los Angeles airport. Blacks in Watts, Hispanics downtown, and whites in Griffith Park all cheered him with frenzy. He drew 12,000 fans at the conservative bastion of Brigham Young University. On motorcades, people charged at his open convertible, grabbing and hugging him, pulling off his cufflinks, screaming, *"Bobby! Bobby! Bobby!"*[26]

The strategy demonstrated Kennedy's unique popularity. At times, he resembled JFK, with one hand in his pocket, the other pointing a thumb, while his cadence soared, describing ills and then resolving, "We can do better!" But he was also more vulnerable, sincere. He admitted his own responsibility for Vietnam. He hit more emotional notes. He plugged into the deep frustration with Lyndon Johnson. It was Johnson, said Kennedy, who was "tearing at the fabric of our national unity" and "appealing to the darker impulses of the American spirit."[27]

Late on March 31, upon landing in New York, Kennedy heard that Johnson was withdrawing. "You're our next president!" one woman kept shouting, as RFK waded through a crowd in the terminal. "You're our next president!" Three days later, the rivals met in the White House. Johnson assured Kennedy that he would not speak out against candidates, and Kennedy managed to mutter that LBJ was "a brave and dedicated man." But the surprise announcement had stripped Kennedy of his main targets: a power-hungry president and a futile war.[28]

When Kennedy and his spokesmen started calling senators and governors, they received few commitments of support. Democratic power brokers—party officials, labor leaders, big-city bosses—feared that his candidacy could erode their clout. Indeed, Kennedy was reimagining the party constituency, orienting it along working-class interests and youthful idealism. "I think there has to be a new kind of coalition to keep the Democratic Party going, and to keep the country together," he stated. "We have to write off the unions and the South now. And to replace them with Negroes, blue-collar whites, and the kids. We have to convince the Negroes and the poor whites that they have common interests. If we can reconcile those hostile groups, and then add the kids, you can really turn the country around."[29]

For all the fervor that Kennedy generated, he aroused deep hatreds. Middle-aged, middle-class types grumbled about his floppy hair. Antiwar liberals complained that he was an opportunist. Southern whites hated his stances on civil rights and Vietnam. The business community viewed him with deep suspicion. Columnists labeled him a demagogue. Yes, his rallies generated screaming crowds, the affections of youth, and the loyalties of racial minorities. But especially on brief news clips, television audiences saw an emotional, wild-haired man rousing up the masses. To many Americans, in a time of urban rioting and campus protests, this was not enticing. This was dangerous.[30]

Though Bobby Kennedy stirred popular intensity and Eugene McCarthy projected rational restraint, both men sought to reclaim the progressive spirit of the Democratic Party. Each wanted to seek peace in Vietnam and aid the oppressed. As another indication of their political orientations, they were the only two candidates to pursue the endorsement of the National Organization for Women (NOW), a protest and lobbying organization formed in 1966. Though its leaders sought an image of respectability, NOW incorporated radical activists and called for wholesale changes in American gender relations. With the modern women's movement still in its infancy, many politicians kept their distance. Four other presidential candidates failed to even respond to NOW's questionnaire. "We couldn't be more disappointed," remarked Betty Friedan, president of NOW and author of the groundbreaking book *The Feminine Mystique*. "We hope it doesn't mean that they're not interested. We're not going to settle for any more pats on the head."[31]

Even for Kennedy and McCarthy, women's rights were not main talking points. The two candidates first competed in the Indiana primary. After King's assassination, Kennedy postponed his campaign until April 10, when he started moving in and out of the state to generate news coverage. It revealed his contradictory impact upon the American people. Radical students at the University of San Francisco called him a "fascist pig" for his complicity in Vietnam. White audiences in Oregon and Nebraska had flat responses to his calls to fight racism and poverty, while in Terre Haute, Indiana, he was taunted as a "coon-catcher." Few paid attention in South Dakota when he decried the plight of American Indians. Yet during motorcades, adoring fans rushed and grabbed at him. A mother of five in Kalamazoo, Michigan, was so overcome that she ran off with his shoe.[32]

In Indiana, Kennedy was selling liberal ideas to mostly conservative voters. Four years earlier, Alabama's George Wallace had run in the Democratic primary; especially in the industrial northwest region near Chicago, he captured "backlash" votes among the white ethnic working classes who resented liberals' emphasis on poor racial minorities. In Vanderburgh County, in the state's southwest corner, which had voted for the winning president in all but one election since 1896, majorities supported the Vietnam War and were indifferent to the racial crisis. Many of the state's residents lived in small towns and suburbs. According to stereotype, Hoosiers were inward-looking traditionalists. Kennedy's own bus driver thought he had no chance. "It's his haircut," he explained. "It's like having a beatnik run for President."[33]

The tensions between the candidates started to surface. McCarthy complained about a Kennedy campaign "fact sheet" that misrepresented his voting record. More generally, he was annoyed that Kennedy stole his thunder. "I got an A in economics and Bobby only got a C," he said, in one typical jab. McCarthy still had an army of student volunteers, though fewer than in New Hampshire and Wisconsin. But his Indiana campaign was a debacle, plagued by large debts, poor planning, competing factions, and a moody candidate who skipped appearances.[34]

There was a third Democratic candidate, too: popular Indiana governor Roger Branigin, running as a "favorite son." The honey-tongued orator, who had originally agreed to serve as LBJ's stand-in, now appealed to state pride, insisting that a Hoosier should control Indiana's votes at the national convention. He had the backing of the party's county chairmen. In a classic Old Politics practice, he controlled "donations" from about 7,000 patronage employees, who kicked back 2 percent of their salaries to the party. He also benefited from the full-throated support of the Indianapolis newspapers, the *Star* and the *News*, which disparaged Kennedy as a free-spending carpetbagger.[35]

Kennedy did have exceptional resources at his disposal. His staff included both New Frontier stalwarts and young idealists from his Senate staff. After the Wisconsin primary, speechwriter Richard Goodwin defected from McCarthy to Kennedy. Campaign maestro Larry O'Brien resigned as LBJ's postmaster general to help RFK. The Kennedy political machine was rebuilt on the fly: radio and television spots, opinion polls, district coordinators, first-class transportation and hotels, 2.5 million copies of a tabloid newspaper. Sacks of cash paid for campaign workers and get-out-the-vote efforts.[36]

As the May 7 vote approached, Bobby seemed to emerge from Jack's shadow. He was eliminating rhetorical nods to the slain president, and his moral crusade was forging his own identity. Yet he still possessed a near-mythical aura. "Oh, he's real! He's real!" screamed one teenage girl. People wanted mementos—autographs, his cufflinks, a touch of the skin. His team perfectly coordinated his events, such as the April 23 trip on the "Wabash Cannonball," an old-fashioned train ride filled with stops and speeches, winning him affection throughout north-central Indiana.[37]

Among the press corps, RFK made jokes about being ruthless, but he was charming, wry, soft. Late at night, he joined reporters for drinks, and even the hard-bitten skeptics admired his relish for shaking middle-class white America out of its complacency. When some businessmen chuckled off his mention of a rat crisis in New York City, he seethed: "Don't . . . laugh." At Indiana University Medical Center, a doctor-in-training asked how he would fund his ambitious government programs. "From you," Kennedy answered.[38]

Yet to forge a winning coalition, Kennedy tamed his image as a rabble-rouser. He trimmed his hair and spoke with more restraint. He visited historic sites, courthouse squares, and factory towns. He knew that most voters worried about crime and taxes. White audiences tended to cheer the "law and order" passages of his stump speech, when he recalled his experience as attorney general and denounced urban rioting. He also warned against an overreliance on federal welfare programs. In Vietnam, he wanted negotiations, not surrender. These centrist ideas were consistent throughout his campaign, but he was emphasizing them more, choosing practical appeals over idealistic pleas. Despite their open racial prejudices, many working-class whites liked Kennedy; he was a feisty battler, speaking to their sense of powerlessness.[39]

The frenetic campaign climaxed with a 100-mile motorcade across the northern edge of Indiana, passing through cities and rural land and tightly packed blue-collar towns. For nine remarkable hours, people lined the entire route and rushed close to the candidate. Kids ran and biked alongside him. Two young women kept waving and cheering, then leap-frogging the motorcade in their car, then getting out and waving again. At churches and factories, Kennedy shook hands and threw himself into crowds. Near the end, he roused awake some young children who had fallen asleep on a mattress on top of a car. Whether blacks or Appalachian whites or Eastern Europeans, everyone seemed enchanted by the Kennedy magic.[40]

The primary itself was more ambiguous. Kennedy won 42 percent of the vote, while Branigin got 31 percent and McCarthy, 27 percent. Kennedy neither delivered a knockout blow to McCarthy nor demonstrated that he was a surefire winner in a general election. He did win an astonishing 85 percent of the African American vote. Some journalists celebrated how he defused the "backlash," pulling majority votes in Polish American precincts, while Kennedy touted himself as "a bridge between blacks and whites." Yet in industrial Lake County, he lost fourteen of the fifteen districts carried by George Wallace in 1964. Throughout Indiana, only 30 percent of whites voted for Kennedy. Much of the other 70 percent was not just voting *for* his opponents, but *against* him.[41]

One week later, Kennedy won 52 percent of the vote in the Nebraska primary. McCarthy, who devoted little energy to the conservative farm state, got only 31 percent. Kennedy kept slicing across Nebraska by plane, car, and train. When the eastern, millionaire, Catholic politician rolled into town, his audiences were sometimes gruff and skeptical. But Kennedy charmed them with self-mocking humor ("There goes my farm program," he joked as the wind blew away a sheet of paper), and he empathized with farmers' grievances about high costs and declining prices. He was courting McCarthy supporters, intimating that the Minnesotan should drop out.[42]

Instead, McCarthy fought back. The next primary, on May 28, was in Oregon, which had a grassroots antiwar movement, few racial minorities, and general prosperity. It was fertile territory for McCarthy. Suburban liberals appreciated his quiet contrast to RFK's bombast. McCarthy seemed rejuvenated. He painted the election as a choice of character. He associated Kennedy with the administration responsible for Vietnam, and he painted the Kennedy campaign as reliant on cash, connections, and gimmicks. Kennedy declined his invitation to a televised debate. One day, the candidates almost crossed paths at the Portland Zoo, but Kennedy's entourage sped away. "Coward, coward, coward!" cried the McCarthy camp.[43]

Nothing went right for Kennedy. His local campaign organization was weak. Columnist Drew Pearson revealed that RFK, while attorney general, had sanctioned a wiretap on Martin Luther King. Most important, Kennedy resonated with the "have-nots," and Oregon was full of "haves." "Sometimes I wished they'd booed me or kicked me or done something," he lamented. "I just couldn't get much response." He was grumpy, snapping at campaign aides. No son of Joe Kennedy had ever lost an election.[44]

McCarthy beat him, capturing 43 percent to his 37 percent. Kennedy already had allowed that if he lost a primary, he might not be a viable candidate. Now McCarthy had revived his own standing among liberals. Democratic officials sighed with relief, as the split support for two challengers cleared the path for the administration's new contestant, Vice President Hubert Humphrey. "I'm not the same candidate I was before," Kennedy admitted.[45]

His last best chance was the June 4 primary in California, with 174 winner-take-all delegates. The state magnified all the affluence and turbulence of modern America: huge population growth, the urbane Bay Area and the chaotic paradise of Los Angeles, sprawling suburbs and vast farmland, Hollywood and Watts, political radicals on both the Right and the Left. Jesse Unruh, the state's premier Democratic power broker, supported Kennedy, but the party lacked cohesion. Yet California possessed a vibrant liberal tradition that furthered social and economic justice, as well as a media-driven culture of celebrity politics. It was perfect for RFK's mass-market style of New Politics.[46]

Freed by defeat, Kennedy confronted McCarthy head-to-head, blasting his opponent for ads that distorted his foreign policy record. He agreed to appear with McCarthy on an ABC program to answer questions from a panel of news reporters. Despite the huge television audience, however, it was a boring affair. McCarthy was dull, but his calm demeanor seemed presidential, while Kennedy showed few flashes of his old pugnacity.[47]

Kennedy poured unprecedented resources into a primary election. He launched a blitz of television and radio advertisements, recruited intellectuals to speak before liberal groups, and flaunted endorsements from glitzy movie stars. He staged another whistle-stop tour, delighting voters at train stations in the San Fernando Valley. Rallies and motorcades across the huge state led to constant scenes of frenzied crowds flocking to him. "Don't tell me people in this country don't love me," he smiled upon boarding the campaign plane. His tie was gone, his cufflinks had been ripped off, and his shirt was matted to his chest. He put a socked foot on the armrest. "On the other hand, perhaps all they wanted was a shoe."[48]

Before his last rally, in San Diego, Kennedy dropped to the stage and covered his face. He found a bathroom and vomited. For eighty-four days, he had campaigned with few breaks and little sleep. His eyes were hollow. His skin was sunburned. His throat was raw. His hands were bloodied by scratches. But he had shaken up the presidential race and given the nation's discontents a political voice. Now what? Hubert Humphrey was inheriting LBJ's delegates. The personal animosity between Kennedy and McCarthy crippled the possibility of uniting their liberal, antiwar campaigns against the Democratic establishment.[49]

On June 4, Kennedy won with 46 percent of the vote. McCarthy got 42 percent. The California primary had amplified RFK's status as America's most loved and most hated politician. He was a celebrity candidate with slick media appeals, evoking deep passions and winning the prodigious loyalty of blacks and Hispanics. Yet his hectic crowd scenes drew associations with the nation's disorder, and his rhetoric exposed a stinking underbelly of troubling inequalities. McCarthy—with his cool demeanor on talk shows and the evening news—controlled the white suburban vote. It seemed unlikely, moreover, that Kennedy could win over the party bosses. But on that same day he also won the South Dakota primary, and the New York primary was still to come, and maybe he could cement an alliance with McCarthy by offering him secretary of state. Just past midnight, at the Ambassador Hotel in Los Angeles, his mood was jubilant. "On to Chicago and let's win there," he ended his victory speech.[50]

Kennedy usually exited straight through the crowd, but on this night, he slipped out the side and headed through the pantry, where he shook hands with kitchen workers. As he kept walking into a hallway, Sirhan Sirhan, a mentally unhinged twenty-four-year-old Palestinian American who objected to Kennedy's support for Israel, moved in from the fringes and fired a snub-nosed pistol. *Pop pop pop pop!* Campaign aides wrestled Sirhan to the ground and pried away the gun. Kennedy lay on the ground. Throughout his chaotic campaign, the Kennedy staff had felt quiet dread at the sound of a popped balloon or a bursting firecracker. But at this moment, Bobby seemed to accept his fate. "Jack," he whispered, "Jack."[51]

It is a story framed by death.

Robert F. Kennedy was pronounced dead on June 6, 1968. "Doom was woven in your nerves, your shirt, woven in the great clan," wrote Robert Lowell. Kennedy was remembered for his spirit of self-growth, his stimulation of love and loathing, his public combativeness and private gentleness. His memorial service in New York City ran on the fumes of this last campaign: the massive logistical accommodation of politicians, celebrities, and television was given true meaning by the people who lined the blocks outside St. Patrick's Cathedral, waiting to pay their respects.[52]

One last time, Kennedy rode a train, and people flocked to him. Over 1,000 members of his circle boarded a train with the casket, heading to Washington, D.C., for his burial at Arlington National Cemetery. An estimated 2 million people waited along the route. In cities, people watched from the roofs of shabby apartment buildings. Young boys stopped playing baseball and held their caps to their hearts. In an open field, a girl sat bareback on a horse. They were white and black, cops and nuns, kids and old people. They cried, put hands to their hearts, or saluted. They placed coins on the tracks. They tossed roses at the last car. They held signs: "GOODBYE BOBBY."[53]

As Kennedy's body was laid to rest, the American people grappled with questions. Why did Sirhan kill him? Or was it us? Had we created a violent society that murdered its prophets of hope? Some called for significant gun control legislation; others, for attention to the nation's poor. Yet the political mood was despondent. Without Kennedy to build liberal support, Eugene McCarthy lacked enough sway with Democratic delegates. Without Kennedy to stir conservative fears, Nelson Rockefeller lost his argument that the Republicans needed a popular moderate. The nominations of established, Old Politics candidates such as Richard Nixon and Hubert Humphrey now seemed inevitable. This, wrote James Reston, was "the final and bitter irony in the murder of Robert Kennedy."[54]

—6—

FAVORITE SON

R ONALD REAGAN sat down for lunch and asked if he should run for president. On August 5, 1968, just hours before the opening of the Republican National Convention, the governor of California had been hustling around Miami Beach, charming delegates with presentations of his conservative policies. For much of the Republican right, Nelson Rockefeller was abominable, while Richard Nixon failed to inspire enthusiasm. Reagan was their star.[1]

Reagan hosted the lunch in his fancy suite at the Hotel Deauville. His guests were the state party chairmen from South Carolina, Mississippi, Florida, and Alabama. These key figures were trying to push the Republican Party to the right, leveraging the South's influence as a conservative bloc. But three of the four leaders counseled Reagan to stay out. "We liked him more than Nixon and did not want to see him hurt," recalled South Carolina's Harry Dent. Nixon had the nomination sewn up.[2]

On cue, William Knowland burst into the room. The former senator announced that the California delegation was about to caucus. "The feeling that you should run, for the sake of the country and the sake of the party, is very strong," he told Reagan. The Californians sought a resolution imploring their governor to openly campaign for the nomination. Reagan had already agreed to this plan, but for the sake of the drama, he played his role. He said that if the resolution passed, he would run. After the California meeting, Knowland called an impromptu press conference, while Reagan arrived from another delegate pitch. "As of this moment I am a candidate before this convention," proclaimed Reagan.[3]

A jolt of excitement shot through Miami Beach. Reagan left to make more rounds, where he kept cajoling delegates to have an "open conven-

OVERLEAF: Governor Ronald Reagan (R-CA) (courtesy Ronald Reagan Presidential Library and Museum)

tion." Some started drifting to Reagan. The Mississippi chairman said that his delegation "is loose and it could go either way." Despite months of careful groundwork, Reagan portrayed the cause as the will of the people. "Gosh, I was surprised," he said among the raised eyebrows of the cynical press corps. "It all came out of the blue."[4]

Rockefeller was thrilled: while he attacked Nixon from one end, Reagan would pull support from the other. But Nixon's campaign proclaimed that "the Reagan declaration changes nothing." The front-runner had the 667 votes necessary to win on the convention's first ballot.[5]

Two days later, Nixon captured the nomination. To a national audience, the Republican National Convention would appear a dull affair, rife with stale rituals. But it masked a hidden drama. Miami Beach was buzzing with discussions about the nature of the Republican Party. These backroom dealings, which shaped the course of American political history, were sparked by the last-minute challenge of a new conservative hero.

Ronald Reagan told stories. He spun them with sincerity and humility. He illustrated big, clear ideas with human anecdotes and little jokes. He also coated his own life in myth, filtering out unpleasant details, treating his narrative as pure and idyllic. As a young man in small-town Illinois during the Depression, he worked as a radio announcer, re-creating baseball games based on telegraph reports. He moved to Hollywood, where he played nonthreatening, good-natured types in light comedies, romances, westerns, and war flicks. While those roles dried up in the 1950s, he was undergoing a political baptism. As president of the Screen Actors Guild, he championed the fight against communist infiltration. As a spokesman for General Electric, he allied himself with big business. By the early 1960s, the former New Deal liberal was a loyal Republican.[6]

But Reagan did not emerge as a significant political figure until 1964, when a national television audience heard "The Speech." It was a campaign talk for Barry Goldwater. Reagan shared Goldwater's right-wing views, but he was a spellbinding orator with television experience, and he had honed this speech for years, stirring conservative Republicans. In a serious but genial tone, while sprinkling in vivid examples, he decried the "soup kitchen of the welfare state," the accommodation of communist enemies, and the dangers to individual freedom. Reagan was flooded with praise, even as Goldwater lost in a landslide. Conservatives saw Reagan as their hope for the future.[7]

In 1966 Reagan ran for governor. He crisscrossed California, winning over voters with versions of The Speech, selling his image as a "citizen-politician." The Democratic incumbent, Pat Brown, was saddled with the state's ills: high taxes, crowded schools, pollution, antiwar demonstrations at Berkeley's University of California campus, and race riots in Watts. Reagan modeled a formula for Republican success. He never expressed personal anger or overt prejudice, blurring any association with Goldwater-style extremism. Yet he tapped into voters' resentments, particularly among white, middle-class suburbanites. While calling for limited government, he decried a morality gap—an all-encompassing way to depict radical hippies, black rioters, welfare moochers, and snooty eggheads as the spoiled brats of liberalism.[8]

In his first executive position, Reagan slashed budgets for universities and public health, filled administrative positions with conservative businesspeople, and proposed a 10 percent across-the-board spending cut. The needs of California's surging population, however, demanded more government revenue. To balance the budget, he approved the largest state tax increase in American history.[9]

Reagan was a popular governor. His conservative base considered him a strong executive who welcomed tough decisions. It appreciated his patriotic pride, calls for social order, and rhetorical digs at the Left (a standard joke described a hippie as "a fellow who has hair like Tarzan, who walks like Jane, and who smells like Cheetah"). There was something comforting, too, about his simple, down-home style. He wore boxy, old-fashioned suits. He loved mac-and-cheese and vanilla ice cream. He said "Jeez!" and "Holy Toledo!" His wife, Nancy, lovingly smiled at him throughout every rendition of The Speech.[10]

Critics dismissed him as a pop confection, an actor playing the role of governor. But that also explained his appeal. He was made for the television age. His warm, avuncular style smoothed the edges on his far-right opposition to popular liberal programs such as civil rights legislation, federal aid to education, and Medicare. "He is compelling, romantic even," described the writer Jim Murray. "If you're a forty-year-old precinct worker, Ronald Reagan is an event in your life."[11]

Reagan's rise was propelled not just by his political personality, but also by a grassroots movement rooted in the conservative principles of economic liberty, social order, and moral righteousness. In the swelling suburbs of southern California's Orange County, for instance, white migrants from the South and Midwest brought along their evangelical Christianity and small-town ideals. They adapted their traditionalism to the modern sprawl of California. Huge majorities in Orange County championed laissez-faire capitalism, aggressive anticommunism, and demonstrative patriotism. While bemoaning liberal elites who encouraged government dependency and cultural decay, they elected officials who satisfied their vision of a decent community.[12]

In the 1950s, the conservative movement had lacked coherence. There were intellectuals seeking a traditional moral order, virulent anticommunists such as Wisconsin senator Joseph McCarthy, and critics of New Deal liberalism such as Ohio senator Robert Taft and *National Review* editor William Buckley. But right-wingers were cast to the margins, dismissed as hateful and zany. The John Birch Society combined rabid anticommunism with conspiracy theory; its leader, Robert Welch, even smeared Republican president Dwight Eisenhower as a communist agent.[13]

Yet those Birchers were often the same practical activists participating in local politics. In the 1960s, with Democratic presidents in place, the John Birch Society built its numbers, while the Young Americans for Freedom organized conservative college students around principles of strong foreign policy and limited government. Republican women's clubs promoted family values in living-room meetings and local fundraisers. Conservative publishers attacked the liberal bias of the mainstream media. One committee established a national network of party leaders, dedicated to refashioning the Republican Party as the voice of true conservatism.[14]

Phyllis Schlafly was one key activist in the New Right. A mother of six married to a prosperous lawyer, Schlafly wore pearls and high heels, and she espoused the virtues of traditional womanhood. She saw no contradiction between those values and her public life; rather, she considered it her patriotic duty to engage in conservative politics. She ran for Congress in Illinois in 1952 and worked for various anticommunist and Catholic organizations. In 1964, Schlafly assumed the vice presidency of the growing, right-wing National Federation of Republican Women. She also penned a short book titled *A Choice Not an Echo*. It blasted the elite Republican "kingmakers" who kept stealing the presidential nomination from the conservatives. It sold 3.5 million copies. Among its readers were the delegates to the Republican National Convention, who would nominate Barry Goldwater for president.[15]

On the surface, Goldwater's presidential campaign looked like a fiasco: the Arizona senator was a listless campaigner, moderate Republicans shunned him, and his campaign was infected with extremist kooks. "Barry Goldwater not only lost the presidential election yesterday but the conservative cause as well," opined the *New York Times*. But underneath that surface, the campaign laid the foundation for the modern conservative movement. Goldwater's dedicated supporters learned the craft of politics: knocking on doors, hosting coffee klatches, circulating free paperbacks, printing bumper stickers, talking to reporters, mastering party rules, and packing conventions. This army of activists was bound by common cause and infused with a forward-looking spirit.[16]

Without question, a racial "backlash" helped drive the New Right. Conservatives opposed civil rights legislation, and black delegates at the 1964 Republican convention endured nasty bigotry. Goldwater's campaign included many open racists. The Republican Party carried the Deep South despite the region's tradition of Democratic dominance. Increasingly, however, these conservatives claimed to be "colorblind," submerging racist resentment under the rhetoric of free enterprise and social order. And this movement was sweeping west, across the Sunbelt. The growing southern suburbs of Atlanta or Dallas resembled the vast, prosperous, mostly white tracts of Orange County, Scottsdale, or Colorado Springs. They fought similar local battles around issues such as taxation and schools. The politics of the Sunbelt was pushing the Republican Party to the right, into the arms of Ronald Reagan.[17]

Even before Reagan assumed the governor's office in early 1967, he considered a run for president. He hired F. Clifton White, the mastermind behind the Draft Goldwater movement, to explore his presidential prospects. White had been gathering a circle of right-wing power players called the "Hard Core," working with the Young Americans for Freedom and the new American Conservative Union, and compiling poll data that indicated popular support for conservative ideas. White believed in Reagan, as both a man and a political commodity. In White's chats with party officials, Reagan's name kept surfacing as a dark horse candidate.[18]

But Reagan was ambivalent. He lacked experience. Nancy was unenthusiastic. Moreover, Californians would resent a new governor who was campaigning for president. Reagan thus staked a middle ground: he ran in the state primary as a "favorite son." This way, he controlled the eighty-six votes of the California delegation and ensured that his name was placed in nomination at the Republican National Convention. But he avoided open competition with Richard Nixon.[19]

Instead, in late 1967, he launched a cross-country speaking tour, thrilling loyal Republicans at $100-a-plate dinners with his denunciations of the welfare state, leavened by one-liners ("If we don't win this one, this will be the regular price for dinner"). He launched a charm offensive at governors' conferences and even jousted with liberal students at Yale University. Meanwhile, young aide Tom Reed ran an underground campaign that courted conservative citizens' groups. His thirty-minute biographical film packaged Reagan as the triumphant vote-getter, a contrast to Nixon the loser.[20]

Reagan's strategy was to avoid the primaries, win party support, and wait to see if Nixon faltered. "We don't want to antagonize Nixon," said one anonymous confidant. "If he fails, we will want every delegate he has." Reagan kept crafting a national profile by criticizing the Johnson administration's caution in Vietnam, its weak response to the seizure of the *Pueblo*, and the Kerner Report's failure to blame black militants for urban riots.[21]

By April 1968, Reagan was offering a charismatic contrast to Robert Kennedy, who terrified conservatives with his rabble-rousing among the poor and minorities. Following reports of growing grassroots support for his nomination, Reagan avoided endorsing Nixon. "The job seeks the man," insisted Reagan. He soon embarked on a five-state tour through the Midwest and South—ostensibly to raise funds for the party, but really to stir more enthusiasm for a Reagan nomination. Yet during a May meeting in New Orleans with southern state chairmen, he downplayed his presidential ambition *too* much, and party leaders started reconciling themselves to Nixon.[22]

Reagan kept on. He denounced liberal spending and radical lawlessness as "a grand design for the Apocalypse." He condemned the "climate of violence" on college campuses. He likened antiwar protestors to the "jack-booted young monsters" of the Hitler Youth. He defended the surge in gun ownership, because people were losing faith in government's ability to protect them. In the aftermath of Martin Luther King's assassination, the Poor People's Campaign staged an encampment on the National Mall to demand antipoverty legislation; Reagan insisted on its forcible removal once the federal permit expired.[23]

Reagan never campaigned in either Nebraska or Oregon, where eager citizens' groups had entered his name on primary ballots, but won over

22 percent in both states. He rebuffed Nelson Rockefeller, who hoped to win the nomination by recruiting Reagan as his running mate. And in the final month before the Republican National Convention, Reagan delivered a prime-time address on national television and gave speech after speech in the South, winning fevered cheers from faithful conservatives. "Ron Turns Me On," proclaimed an ever-present button.

"Son," drawled South Carolina senator Strom Thurmond, "you'll be president someday." Just not in 1968.[24]

Miami Beach, a ten-mile stretch of sand off the Florida coast, was packed with hotels that featured gaudy replica architecture and overlooked an endless beach. By day, poolsides were thick with the aroma of suntan lotion, and by night, clubs glittered with fleshy delights. It was a bubble of indulgence; a dreamy dip into pastrami sandwiches, cherry cheesecake, flamboyant cocktails, and burlesque revues; a sun-drenched oasis from the crises of race and crime and poverty and Vietnam.[25]

The 1,333 delegates to the Republican National Convention mixed vacation delights with political duty. They were 80 percent male and more than 95 percent white, with an average age around fifty. About one-third were businessmen, and the majority made comfortable incomes. They were clean shaven and well scrubbed. Many shared a sense of moralism and propriety, a faith in traditional family, and a romantic vision of an ideal American past. These delegates earned their place through their dedicated service to the party. They skewed more conservative than the average Republican voter.[26]

As Richard Nixon arrived in Miami Beach, he cultivated an aura of certainty. He had already received an endorsement from Dwight Eisenhower, and he had just crafted his acceptance speech in near-isolation at a beach house in the Hamptons. His campaign marshaled enormous resources for the convention, including a staff of 300, three floors of the Hilton Plaza, fleets of cars and speedboats ("Nixon's Navy"), and communications trailers. The convention was full of ridiculous pomp: pretty "Nixonaires," elaborate receptions for delegates, an overabundance of balloons, and even a baby elephant. Nixon sought to project confidence that he would win the majority of delegate votes on the first ballot, and thus become the Republican nominee for president.[27]

Nelson Rockefeller held out hope. The New York governor's late, frenetic campaigning that summer had won over many independents, women, and college-educated suburban types. Reporters liked him. Rocky kept touting that only he could beat a Democratic rival. His momentum sputtered when a Gallup poll gave Nixon a slight edge over the Democratic contenders, while calling Rockefeller even with them. Then a Harris poll showed Rockefeller as a clear winner—and Nixon as a loser—in the general election. This discrepancy led to a rare joint statement from the polling agencies. The statement clarified that Gallup had polled from July 20 to 23, and Harris from July 25 to 29. Taken together, the results demonstrated that Rocky was gaining on Nixon.[28]

But national polls were different from party politics. Many of the Republican delegates hated Rockefeller's liberal policies, divorce, and attacks on Barry Goldwater. Rockefeller had between 250 and 350 committed delegates, mostly from the Northeast. He hoped to sway more delegates and some "favorite son" governors. He staged a lavish effort. Over seventeen-hour days, he spread smiles, handshakes, winks, and exhortations for the Republican Party to cast a wide net. Young "Rocky Girls" toured lobbies in straw boaters and lemon-yellow miniskirt dresses. He spent $50,000 on a huge party at the Americana Hotel.[29]

Rockefeller's strategy hinged on Reagan. Together, they might keep Nixon under 600 votes on the first ballot. Then the balloting would continue until a candidate won a majority. Both Rocky and Reagan thought they could pull it off. Reagan was gaining support. On an early visit to Miami Beach to testify before the platform committee, he thundered for law and order, fanning the ardors of his audience. He had about 175 commitments, and every time he visited another state caucus, he won more conservative hearts.[30]

When Reagan returned for the official convention, a phalanx of citizens' groups held a cheering, patriotic display at the airport. The scene repeated itself in various hotel lobbies. Reagan responded with an aw-shucks demeanor, still playing the role of modest good guy. Despite his fifty-seven years, he exuded a fresh-faced sincerity. There was a sense of propriety to the whole endeavor. The "Reagan girls," older than the Nixonaires or Rocky Girls, were clad in red-white-and-blue outfits with longer hemlines. They wore old-fashioned hairdos, nodding to nostalgia.[31]

After Reagan declared his candidacy on Monday, August 5, he moved from hotel to hotel, selling himself to state delegations. On that Wednesday, former U.S. treasurer Ivy Baker Priest Stevens formally nominated him. "Destiny has again marked this man," she orated, "a man steeped in the glorious traditions of the past, a man with a vision of the unlimited possibilities of a new era." On Thursday, he rejected overtures for the vice president slot: "Even if they tied and gagged me, I would find a way to signal by wiggling my ears." That evening, right up until the balloting, Reagan lobbied four delegations just off the convention floor. He, not Rockefeller, posed the most serious threat to Nixon.[32]

Yet conservatives feared that by switching to Reagan, they were opening the door for Rockefeller. Campaign manager F. Clifton White knew better: he had arranged many secret promises to vote Reagan on the second ballot. But to stop Nixon on the first ballot, he needed those conservative southern delegations. Alabama, Mississippi, and Florida all adhered to the unit rule, whereby the delegates voted as one bloc. They adored Reagan but were pledged to Nixon. White believed that if one state split, the others would follow. "He's on the wire, I know he's on the wire," he agonized after huddling with one bigwig. "There were tears in his eyes when he said goodbye, he agrees with everything we say—but he can't get off his commitment to Nixon." Reagan put cracks in the dam, but it just would not break.[33]

"The essential problem was Strom Thurmond," rued a Reagan aide. "I don't think anyone knew the extent to which Thurmond had a hold on the South." The senator from South Carolina was a giant in southern politics. Like most white southerners of his era, he had started as a Democrat. In 1948, after the Democratic Party adopted a pro–civil rights plank, Thurmond ran for president on the independent States Rights ticket. In 1956 he helped draft the Southern Manifesto, which protested federal enforcement of racial integration. He aligned himself with a broader Sunbelt conservatism that attacked labor rights and federal regulation. In 1964 he crossed party lines to campaign for Barry Goldwater, and then he switched to the Republicans himself.[34]

Thurmond's career coincided with a southern population boom, especially in modern suburbs of cities such as Atlanta, Charlotte, Dallas, and Houston. In the 1950s, Dwight Eisenhower did well among the region's white-collar professionals, slackening the Democratic grip on the "Solid South." In the 1960s, the civil rights agendas of John F. Kennedy and Lyndon Johnson alienated white southerners from the Democrats, redrawing the nation's electoral map. And after Goldwater won five Deep South states in 1964, those states were apportioned more delegates for the

1968 Republican National Convention. By switching parties, Thurmond had positioned himself as an essential southern Republican. His "law and order" conservatism touched both the upwardly mobile suburbs and the traditional white base.[35]

Nixon had long courted Thurmond. With the southerner in his corner, he could stave off challenges from the party's right wing. But Nixon first had to prove his conservatism. On June 1, 1968, after meeting in Atlanta with southern party chairmen, he laid out his views for Thurmond. Nixon told the senator that he sought conservative judges for the Supreme Court, opposed proposals to integrate schools by busing students into different districts, and refused to pick a liberal vice president. Most important, Nixon pledged a strong military response to communism. Shrewdly, he conveyed respect for Thurmond's entire profile as a conservative, rather than as just a segregationist. On the ride to the airport, Nixon lauded how Thurmond could deflect a third-party challenge from George Wallace. Thurmond soon endorsed Nixon.[36]

But at the convention in Miami Beach, Nixon heard reports of southern defections to Reagan. It unnerved him. His laugh got a little too calculated, his mannerisms a little too sharp. Here and there, he stuttered a word. But he righted the ship by continuing to pursue a "southern strategy." If he defended those delegates from Reagan, he controlled the nomination.[37]

At a late-night meeting, Nixon reiterated his right-wing positions for Thurmond: "strict constructionists" on the Supreme Court, strong national defense, quelling of domestic protest. For vice president, he would not "cram anyone down anyone's or any section's throat." He would adhere to federal guidelines for school desegregation, but he disapproved of busing programs to integrate schools. The next day, in meetings with southern delegates, he proclaimed, "I don't believe you should use the South as the whipping boy." He also dispatched aides to connect with southern leaders, promising to "bring peace" on civil rights and "lay off pro-Negro crap."[38]

Meanwhile, Thurmond stanched leaks. Whenever a Reagan representative spoke before a state delegation, Thurmond followed. "We have no choice, if we want to win, except to vote for Nixon," he lectured. "I love Reagan, but Nixon's the one." He reassured southern conservatives. "Senator Thurmond's the greatest man living in this country today," said delegate Bobbie Ames of Alabama. "When he said Nixon satisfied him, you could hear the sighs of relief all over the room."[39]

Hours before the roll call, Thurmond wandered the convention floor with a megaphone, warning that a vote for Reagan equaled one for Rockefeller. He gave interview after interview to the press. He buttonholed individual delegates, sometimes even compelling Reagan defectors to switch back. These actions had enormous import. Thurmond's partnership with Nixon foretold the South's transition to the Republicans, and it hardened the party's conservative identity.[40]

As another element of that summer's Poor People's Campaign, Ralph Abernathy, Martin Luther King's successor in the Southern Christian Leadership Conference, led demonstrations in Miami Beach. The 1964 Goldwater movement had driven many African Americans from the Republican Party. Only twenty-nine delegates—less than 2 percent—were black. Rockefeller's faltering candidacy signaled the decline of moderate Republicanism. As many whites mixed racial hostility with distaste for urban violence and government programs, black leaders grew disaffected with the GOP. The politics of race was shifting. While on assignment in Miami Beach, Norman Mailer realized his fatigue with the black struggle for equality. "It was a miserable recognition," he reflected. If a progressive writer felt like this, "then what immeasurable tides of rage must be loose in America itself?"[41]

On the evening of August 7, as the convention voted for its presidential nominee, a riot broke out in Liberty City, a black ghetto about six miles away. The violence reflected the discontent festering within poor black communities, especially after the King assassination. Local black leaders explained their grievances: a lack of job opportunities, poor housing, and this "lily-white" convention. After a "vote power" rally, some blacks looted stores, threw rocks and bottles, set fires, and flipped over cars. About 100 people were arrested. Police contained the mayhem, but if it had spread, they had planned to raise the drawbridge connecting Miami Beach to the mainland.[42]

The Republican National Convention stayed insulated from Liberty City, from the ills of the nation, and from dramatic tension of any sort. These gatherings were relics of another time, replete with long-winded oratory and hotheaded conflicts. But in the age of television, with a national audience watching, parties tried to project unity. The Republicans drafted a platform with no particular position on Vietnam or anything else. Then, over four days, they staged introductions and welcomes and orations, followed by cheers and balloons and more cheers. There were Star Spangled Banners and Pledges of Allegiance, choral groups and marching bands, a tape-recorded message from ailing Dwight Eisenhower, and hyperpatriotic bluster from the actor John Wayne. In an age of turmoil, the convention depicted a reassuring blandness.[43]

Early on the morning of August 8, Nixon officially won the nomination. He received 692 first-ballot votes, just enough for a majority. In line with initial predictions, Rockefeller had 277; Reagan, 182; and various minor candidates, another 182. For all the back-room intrigue, there were no surprises.[44]

The surprise arrived later that day, when Nixon announced his running mate of Spiro Agnew. *Spiro Agnew?* "It's some kind of disease," guessed a man on the street during a TV news segment. "It's some kind of egg," guessed another. Reporters and delegates were shocked, too. Agnew, in fact, was the governor of Maryland. His selection reflected the emerging Republican character.[45]

Agnew was a man of the suburbs, the key distinguishing characteristic of the American landscape, full of detached single-family dwellings that bred a certain comfort and conformity. He played golf and watched football. No one ever considered him destined for greatness. But he was brooding and serious, with an upright manner and good managerial skills. Also, he liked power. In 1960 he ran for Baltimore County judge and finished last among five candidates. Two years later, he won election as county executive. Certain to lose reelection in 1966, he instead ran for governor, and he triumphed over a divided Democratic Party that nominated a blustery race-baiter named George Mahoney. Thanks to a solid record on civil rights, Agnew had a reputation as a moderate Republican.[46]

In 1968, however, racial conflicts transformed Agnew's image. In early spring, after protests at all-black Bowie State College, he closed the campus and ordered hundreds of arrests. Then, in the aftermath of King's assassination and riots in downtown Baltimore, he gathered the city's black leaders. Backed by state troopers, Agnew sanctimoniously rebuked these community pillars for failing to denounce black radicals such as H. Rap Brown and Stokely Carmichael. Many of the leaders walked out. One called Agnew "as sick as any bigot in America." Yet many whites applauded his hard line, and in the coming months, Agnew echoed

Ronald Reagan in calling for law and order and blasting the Poor People's Campaign.[47]

Agnew had once been an enthusiastic, even fanatical, backer of Nelson Rockefeller. He admired the New York governor's style and vision, and he kept pushing Rocky to run. But when Rockefeller decided on March 21 to avoid the election, his choice blindsided and humiliated Agnew. When Rockefeller later entered the race, Agnew was critical. Sensing an opportunity, Nixon flattered Agnew with private meetings and phone calls. As a favorite son, Agnew controlled Maryland's votes. Soon after arriving in Miami, he endorsed Nixon. He then gave the speech that put Nixon's name in nomination.[48]

Speculation had run rampant over the vice presidential pick. This generation had seen both Harry Truman and Lyndon Johnson enter the Oval Office upon a president's death. Moreover, the choice might signal the party's ideological direction. Most press accounts assumed Nixon would balance the ticket with a moderate such as Illinois senator Charles Percy or New York City mayor John Lindsay. Just before the presidential nomination roll call, the *Miami Herald* reported that Nixon would choose Oregon senator Mark Hatfield, a critic of the Vietnam War. Southern delegates, tempted by Reagan, got nervous.[49]

But Nixon sought to unify the party. Beginning at 2:00 A.M., soon after his nomination, and continuing past noon that day, Nixon held four meetings with different advisers and party leaders, culling the list of names. Eventually, it got down to four people: Mark Hatfield, California's lieutenant governor Robert Finch, Massachusetts governor John Volpe, and Spiro Agnew. The Vietnam hawks objected to Hatfield. Finch, a close friend of Nixon, withdrew from consideration. After one meeting, Strom Thurmond handed Nixon a list of "acceptables" and "unacceptables," with Agnew and Volpe in a separate "no objection" category.[50]

Only Nixon had kept Agnew in the discussion. In the end, he alone chose Agnew. Volpe had lost his own state primary to Rockefeller, and Agnew hailed from a Border State, which would help Republicans in the South. Also, Nixon considered Agnew a centrist, tolerable to all Republicans. But the party's moderate wing was furious. Agnew derived his sole notoriety from his stiff response to black protest. It was a final insult to Nelson Rockefeller, the former apple of Agnew's eye. Rocky fumed that he was more popular among the general population than within his party. When asked why he lost, he tapped his fingers on a podium, fuming. "Ever been to a Republican convention?" he snapped.[51]

Ronald Reagan was more cheerful, and even a little relieved. After the balloting, he had stepped to the podium and moved to make Nixon's nomination unanimous. He also praised Agnew: "It's a good choice. It will be acceptable to the South and to all sections of the country. Governor Agnew has a good record for dealing firmly with rioters." Reagan moved too late in 1968, but he had enshrined himself as the conservatives' champion, just as the Republican Party was tilting to the right. He was set up for the future.[52]

Yet in his later recollections, Reagan ignored his own fervent efforts to win the nomination. He claimed that he never really campaigned in Miami Beach. As always, Ronald Reagan spun stories.[53]

———

By the convention's final evening, it was impossible not to marvel at the careful, crafted comeback of Richard Nixon—"a phoenix risen from the ashes," according to the *Wall Street Journal*. Four years after splitting over Goldwater, the Republicans put forth a unified front. Nixon appeared more confident and sincere. He lacked Rockefeller's assets or Reagan's allure, but in an age of riots and hippies and inflation and a confusing, depressing war, he was solid and durable. "I like Nixon," said one delegate. "He wipes his butt the way I do."[54]

Nixon's triumphant speech fit the temper of Middle America. "Let's win this one for Ike," he said, evoking the dying war hero and popular ex-president. He defended a tough response to urban crime and rioting, and he ended on an emotional note, shading back to his own childhood, when he heard distant train whistles and dreamed of better possibilities, celebrating the national spirit. Most important, however, was his call to "the great majority of Americans, the forgotten Americans, the nonshouters, the non-demonstrators." They were factory workers and businessmen and soldiers. "They're not racist or sick, they're not guilty of the crime that plagues the land," he said. "They are good people; they are decent people. They work hard and they save and they pay their taxes and they care."[55]

Nixon was finding the language that tied himself to average Americans. They felt dismissed by intellectuals and elites, and they shuddered at rioters and radicals. They worked hard, acted respectably, strove for something better. They saw a society in chaos, and they yearned for order. Nixon was like them. He was their man.[56]

—7—

HIS OWN MAN

HUBERT HUMPHREY caught the stench of tear gas. From the twenty-fifth floor of Chicago's Conrad Hilton, the vice president of the United States gazed down upon a nightmarish scene. On the evening of Wednesday, August 28, 1968, thousands had gathered outside the hotel, intent on marching toward the Chicago Amphitheatre and disrupting the Democratic National Convention. They cried, "Dump the Hump!" and "Pigs!" and "Peace now!" and "Fuck you, LBJ!" Some carried rocks, sticks, and other makeshift weapons. About 300 Chicago policemen and national guardsmen in riot gear blocked their passage down Michigan Avenue.[1]

That day, Humphrey should have been enjoying his greatest triumph: the presidential nomination of the Democratic Party. Instead, while hosting a rotating cast of power brokers, he worried about delegate defections and antiwar protests. At one point, a stink bomb detonated in the lobby and fumes wafted through the hotel's air-conditioning vents, forcing him to retreat into the shower.[2]

That night, down on the street, a wedge of policemen charged into the crowd. "The police attacked with tear gas, with Mace, and with clubs," described Norman Mailer, who was watching from six floors below Humphrey. He likened the scene to "a chain saw cutting into wood . . . a scythe through grass . . . a wind blowing dust." Panicked screams and angry curses were punctuated by dull thuds, as the police clubbed heads. Officers broke formation and targeted individual protestors. Some beat the helpless, wounded victims lying on the street. Some attacked reporters. When a crowd of terrified bystanders pressed against the Hilton, the huge plate-glass window cracked open. The police stomped over the glass

OVERLEAF: Vice President Hubert Humphrey (D-MN) (courtesy Minnesota Historical Society)

shards and into the hotel lounge, swinging nightsticks. Outside, cops were yelling, "Kill, kill, kill!"[3]

The outraged activists chanted back: *"The whole world is watching! The whole world is watching! The whole world is watching!"* The action made for riveting television. Later that evening, the networks kept flipping from live feeds of the political convention to the bedlam on the streets. While delegates watched on portable sets and shuddered at the wanton brutality, protestors raged at the nomination of Hubert Humphrey, the man of the Democratic war machine. From the rostrum, Connecticut senator Abe Ribicoff condemned "gestapo tactics in the streets of Chicago." Chicago mayor Richard J. Daley shouted at the stage; according to both amateur and expert lip-readers watching on television, it looked like Daley hissed, "Fuck you, you Jew son of a bitch, you lousy motherfucker, go home."[4]

Back at the Hilton, Humphrey bristled that the networks were airing footage of the rioting instead of a seconding speech for his nomination. He fussed as the New York delegation, which supported Eugene McCarthy, donned black armbands and sang "We Shall Overcome." He nervously emptied ashtrays and tidied the room. At a press conference, he claimed to have been too busy to watch the carnage. His eyes were still moist from the tear gas.[5]

Just after midnight, Humphrey had the votes necessary for a first-ballot majority. "Boy, I feel like really jumping," he exclaimed, and in his hokey way, he kissed the television screen when it showed his wife, Muriel. But underneath that ebullience, his smile was tight, his manner forced. He was one step from the presidency, but as the Chicago violence illustrated, his party was torn asunder by the Vietnam War, split by different visions of American democracy. At one point during the balloting, he fled into the bedroom and cried.[6]

Tears of joy? Tears of pain? For Hubert H. Humphrey in 1968, it was tough to tell.

Tears had spilled down Humphrey's crimson face five months earlier, when he read Lyndon Johnson's speech withdrawing from the election. "You don't mean it," he protested. "You *can't* mean it." The president put his finger to his lips, demanding secrecy. Humphrey soon left for a diplomatic trip to Mexico City. That whole day, he was uncharacteristically terse. He did not even tell Muriel the news. When Johnson read his surprise ending that night, it discombobulated his loyal vice president. A chapter in his political life closed, and a new one opened.[7]

Humphrey hailed from tiny Doland, South Dakota, where his father ran a drugstore. He was the type of do-gooder kid who was valedictorian, the lead in the school play, and a three-sport letterman. Politics enchanted him. At age thirty-four, he won the office of mayor of Minneapolis. A cyclone of action, he united Minnesota's feuding Democratic and Farmer-Labor Parties, scrubbed the city of organized crime, and helped found the liberal group Americans for Democratic Action. In 1948, his impassioned speech defended a civil rights plank in the platform at the Democratic National Convention, compelling the exodus of Strom Thurmond's segregationist "Dixiecrats."[8]

That same year, he won election to the Senate. Humphrey had a national name—he was passionate, smart, hardworking, earnest, and principled. But he was also a brash, long-winded upstart in a tradition-bound, go-it-slow institution. Over time, he learned at the foot of Majority Leader Lyndon Johnson, who used Humphrey as a bridge to the party's liberal wing. Humphrey transformed from an idealistic mouthpiece to a deft, pragmatic politician. As Democratic whip, he brilliantly orchestrated the passage of the Civil Rights Act of 1964.[9]

Humphrey yearned for the presidency. John F. Kennedy crushed his bid in 1960. By 1964, he saw his only route to the White House through the vice president's office. He lobbied for the job. Johnson drew out the process for drama: rejecting Bobby Kennedy, toying with Eugene McCarthy, and stringing along Humphrey right until his selection at the Democratic National Convention.

Humphrey embraced a breathtaking variety of responsibilities, whirling from task to task. He served at times as a point man on civil rights, the Peace Corps, the space program, and urban affairs. He made the diplomatic rounds from Asia to Africa to Europe. He evangelized for the administration before party officials, business executives, schoolkids, and anyone else who would listen. He had a real human touch. He was open, simple in his tastes, and curious about people. He called his sweet and supportive wife, Muriel, "Momma," and he publicly doted on his granddaughter Vicky, who had Down syndrome. And yet, he was so agreeable, so empathetic, so emotional, and so entranced by so many causes that he seemed to stand for nothing in particular. He lacked the commanding presence that many Americans expected of a president.[10]

Lyndon Johnson tormented his eager-to-please understudy. In one moment, the president fluffed him with praise. In the next, he berated Humphrey or embarrassed him or stripped him of responsibility. Humphrey felt vulnerable. While the press speculated that Bobby Kennedy was the true Democratic heir, Humphrey kept his wagon hitched to LBJ. He showered the president with ebullient tributes, reflecting not only his loyalty, but also his insecurity. His advisers had once cautioned against the vice presidential slot, warning that "Johnson would cut his balls off." But Humphrey was resolute. He called his relationship with LBJ a "marriage with no divorce." He was the "wife."[11]

Vietnam sharpened the Johnson-Humphrey dynamic. In February 1965, amidst inner-circle debates about bombing North Vietnam, Humphrey wrote a memo arguing that without an open discussion before the American people, support for the war would erode. The dissenters would be "more Democratic than Republican," especially "at the grassroots." Humphrey advocated a peace settlement that would highlight the president's political ingenuity. LBJ was annoyed. He dismissed Humphrey's opinion; he just wanted support. From that point, Humphrey was omitted from the critical meetings that led to military escalation.[12]

Humphrey responded with effusive demonstrations of his loyalty. In fact, he emerged as the war's peppiest cheerleader. He took morale-building trips to South Vietnam, and he sold the war to Congress and the public with trademark fervor. Despite his lack of access to confidential intelligence briefings, he insisted that the United States was beating despotic communists. This salesmanship repaired his standing with the president, but it destroyed his progressive reputation. By 1967, with LBJ bunkered in the White House, Humphrey's speeches became targets of public protest. Once a paragon of liberal ideals, he now personified liberal hypocrisy.[13]

"Has Bobby got it locked up yet?" worried Humphrey as he stepped off the plane in Washington, D.C., one day after Johnson's withdrawal. While the Kennedy forces worked the phones and sought endorsements, Humphrey resisted pleas to immediately declare his own candidacy, reasoning that he would look too ambitious. In meeting after meeting, he assessed his level of support. The April 4 assassination of Martin Luther King further slowed his political clock. Meanwhile, the Kennedy avalanche never happened, thanks to the wariness of party and business leaders.[14]

Humphrey envisioned his boss launching the campaign with a back-slapping, "he's my boy" endorsement. But when Humphrey visited the White House, Johnson deflected him, claiming that to negotiate peace in Vietnam, he needed to transcend party politics. (That same month, he privately urged Nelson Rockefeller to run.) During his presidential tenure, moreover, Johnson had stripped the Democratic National Committee of personnel and resources. This choice kept the power of party leadership in the White House. But as Johnson's personal prestige declined, this network of party officials grew feeble.[15]

Still, in a race against Kennedy and McCarthy, Humphrey represented the Democratic establishment. He buttered up mayors, governors, senators, and representatives. His energetic travels as vice president endeared him to party loyalists, and his traditional base included northern liberals, farmers, and labor unions. He won generous pledges from business magnates, who dreaded Robert Kennedy as president, and even won the backing of southern Democrats, who had long despised Humphrey's stance on civil rights. "I'm not happy about Hubert," stated one southern governor, "but I'd certainly go along with him before I'd come within a mile of Bobby." Finally, on April 27, Humphrey declared his candidacy, promising to unify the party and the nation, sprinkling in an exuberant ad-lib about "the politics of happiness, the politics of purpose, and the politics of joy."[16]

The "politics of joy" line was the first blunder of Humphrey's campaign. His critics blasted him: how could he be so sunny amidst the deaths in Vietnam, murder of King, riots in ghettoes, and chaos at Columbia? His second mistake was a loose organization. While liberal senators Fred Harris and Walter Mondale served as campaign cochairmen, his vice presidential staff members jockeyed for power, and old political cronies kept whispering in his ear. Humphrey lacked the steel to enforce a disciplined team. He was trying to unify the country, and he could not even unify his campaign.[17]

Humphrey entered too late to mount effective primary campaigns, but he remained the favorite. Most states apportioned their delegates through state organizations and party conventions. Democratic officials such as county chairmen, who could select and sway delegates, preferred a party man like Humphrey. In Pennsylvania, for instance, Eugene McCarthy was the only name on the April 23 primary ballot. But Humphrey had the endorsement of party leaders, including the mayors of Philadelphia and

Pittsburgh and the president of the United Steelworkers of America. In June, he gained the huge majority of Pennsylvania's 130 delegates. State by state, the party apparatus gave Humphrey a commanding lead. "Favorite son" governors and senators favored Humphrey, as well.[18]

That spring, Humphrey seemed to restore order to the Democratic Party. He was the candidate who promised to maintain the party's New Deal coalition, including labor unions, intellectuals, African Americans, white southerners, and city bosses. Humphrey belonged, moreover, on the old-fashioned campaign trail. He just loved shaking hands, smiling, and kissing babies. During long and passionate speeches, he bounded with incurable optimism. He gushed with empathy, whether around work-ers, housewives, or executives. He sang "We Shall Overcome" in a black church and did the boogaloo with James Brown in Watts ("Oh my good-ness, Jimmy," he gushed). Whether on the stump or in close conversation, he might say, "By golly, it's great to be an American." He was impossibly, sincerely corny.[19]

To contrast himself with the passions of Kennedy and McCarthy, Humphrey forced a pause before answering questions. He set time lim-its on his speeches. He stressed his maturity and experience. If no longer the principal of prairie progressivism, he became, according to the *New York Times*, "the favorite of the middle-of-the-road forces: middle-aged, but still potent, organized labor; the moderate South; middle-aged liber-als who have not been quite consumed by war passion, pro or con; and middle-class Negroes." In national polls, he dominated his Democratic opponents.[20]

Then, in early June, Robert Kennedy was assassinated. It assured Hum-phrey the nomination. But it shook him personally, and it enfeebled his campaign. He lost his foil. Without the specter of Kennedy, Johnson felt no pressure to shift his Vietnam policy or help Humphrey. The big-money donations dried up. Campaign activity halted. The murder had poisoned the polluted waters of 1968 America. It further disillusioned the Ameri-can voter about politics, about Democrats, about old-fashioned establish-ment liberals who toed the line on Vietnam.[21]

That summer, Humphrey was an icon of national malaise. His poll num-bers dropped. At a rally in Cleveland, Mayor Carl Stokes implored, "Who's gonna be the next President of the United States?" "Stokes!" the crowd responded. The mayor had to coach them to name the vice president. Even worse, Humphrey's campaign appearances became sites of antiwar protest, dotted by signs such as "HHH Hell No," "Hollow-Hypocrite-Hawk," and "RFK Is Gone—No One's Left." Everywhere he turned, he heard, "Dump the Hump!"[22]

Was Hubert Humphrey his own man? That was the bigger question looming over the entire enterprise. In a party split by war, he was tied to the administration's policy. Some suggested that he resign his office, so that he could articulate his own position, but Humphrey resisted that idea. In the spring of 1968, peace talks had begun in Paris. He stayed loyal to Johnson.[23]

Humphrey gave one speech that actually stated, "I am my own man." He never mentioned Johnson, though he included an awkward metaphor about fathers and sons. It was a little pathetic. Clearly, Humphrey had beliefs distinct from those of his boss, but in order to win the nomination, he spoke in vague platitudes. What did he stand for? "In the eyes of many of his old allies," suggested the *Atlantic*, "the new Hubert is but a vestige, morally and ideologically diminished by his years of faithful service to the Great Emasculator."[24]

Eugene McCarthy was the only real obstacle to Humphrey's nomination. That summer, McCarthy won the New York primary, and he packed stadiums from Fenway Park to Madison Square Garden. His army of zealous followers called for public demonstrations at the Democratic National Convention, along with revised procedures for delegate selection, so that the nominee represented the popular will.[25]

But after Kennedy's death, McCarthy entered a deep funk, as if resigned to an inevitable tragedy. He cultivated his aura of intellectual detachment. While feuding plagued his ever-changing campaign team, he listlessly courted state delegates and former Kennedy supporters. Americans were disenchanted. His party was in crisis. Soldiers were dying. And yet McCarthy hid behind his poetry and his pithiness, spurning the crown of true leadership.[26]

George McGovern joined the race just two weeks before the Democratic National Convention. The South Dakota senator—a former World War II bomber pilot and history professor—was an early critic of the Vietnam War. A progressive idealist with a reputation for personal character, he regretted not declaring for the nomination in 1967, which had freed McCarthy to challenge Johnson. McGovern had been a friend and fan of

Robert Kennedy. After announcing on August 10, he sought to bring Kennedy's delegates under his banner. Though the actual nomination was a long shot, McGovern hoped to shape a peace plank for the Democratic platform, as well as bolster his own national standing.[27]

One week later, a final candidate entered the fray, this time from the party's conservative southern faction. Georgia's governor Lester Maddox had once refused to serve black customers at his restaurant, in defiance of the Civil Rights Act. He controlled few delegates, but his candidacy allowed racist hard-liners to avoid voting for a liberal. Though the "Solid South" had long been a key part of the Democratic coalition, that day was ending. Before the convention, the credentials committee seated an interracial delegation from Mississippi, ousting the all-white segregationist group headed by the governor. Maddox himself left Chicago in the middle of the convention, denouncing a party of "misinformed socialists and power-mad politicians."[28]

Vietnam continued to preoccupy the Democrats. As the convention approached, the Paris peace talks stalled, and the United States still bombed portions of North Vietnam. Both McCarthy and McGovern called to end that bombing and create a coalition government in South Vietnam, which would include the communist National Liberation Front. Lyndon Johnson maintained that a bombing halt would cede a bargaining chip and endanger American soldiers. A coalition government, moreover, would admit American failure. Before the convention began, Hubert Humphrey needed to appease the antiwar liberals, satisfy the Cold War imperatives of the Democratic establishment, and assert his own independence.[29]

By late July, Humphrey had drafted a statement that called for a bombing halt. Instead of issuing it, he took it to the White House. Johnson shot it down, not only arguing on strategic grounds, but also claiming, in Humphrey's words, "he'd destroy me for the Presidency." Johnson chafed at Humphrey's perceived disloyalty. The weight of Vietnam was again burdening the president. "I haven't worked all my life just to have my own party repudiate me at the last minute," he vowed.[30]

Johnson sometimes mentioned that party leaders urged him to run in Humphrey's place. The convention had been scheduled to coincide with his sixtieth birthday, and he entertained the fantasy of a popular groundswell for him, capped by his triumphant appearance in Chicago. Maybe he just wanted to be asked. Maybe he just wanted to yank Humphrey. In any case, he allowed the rumors to swirl. Finally, just before the convention, he stated, "I am not a candidate for anything, except maybe a rocking chair."[31]

But Johnson kept undercutting Humphrey. "He cries too much," complained LBJ. "That's it—he cries too much." In early August, Humphrey flew to Johnson's Texas ranch, where he presented his Vietnam plank for the official Democratic platform. The president, hinting at a diplomatic breakthrough, persuaded him to stick with the White House version. The next day, LBJ had a friendlier meeting with Richard Nixon, the man who most benefited if the war was prolonged through the election. Later, on the phone, Johnson coached the Republican candidate, lending him talking points on Vietnam. It appeared that Johnson might not want his own vice president to succeed him.[32]

Humphrey's predicament worsened on August 20. Soviet tanks rolled into Czechoslovakia, where the government had been instituting political reforms and encouraging cultural freedom. The Soviet invasion earned international condemnation. It also hardened the anticommunist resolve among establishment Democrats, and it derailed Johnson's proposed East-West summit, which he envisioned as a solution for Vietnam. On the night of the invasion, after a National Security Council meeting, Johnson questioned Humphrey's toughness, accusing him of yielding to peaceniks like McCarthy.[33]

Humphrey had one more chance. His proposed plank stated qualified conditions for a bombing halt, which mollified much of the antiwar faction. Yet it omitted any mention of a coalition government, which satisfied the staunch anticommunists. He ran it by Secretary of State Dean Rusk and White House National Security Advisor Walt Rostow, who both approved. But in Chicago, while Humphrey's camp met with leaders from the platform committee, Johnson barked his objections through an intermediary on the phone. Hours later, LBJ aide Marvin Watson relayed the president's firm refusal of the wording.[34]

Humphrey buckled. Though he called Johnson to complain, he accepted the White House position. He was too afraid that Johnson would pull support from the party's power brokers. In the aftermath, Humphrey realized the cost. "I should have stood my ground," he later reflected. "I told our people I was still for the plank, but I didn't put up a real fight." In the moment, he cowered under the president's shadow.[35]

Throughout 1968, antiwar activists had been planning to disrupt the Democratic National Convention. They fell into two main camps. Each, in its own way, challenged an American liberalism rooted in pragmatism and consensus. For the radicals on the Left, this stance lacked authenticity. It was stripped of human value. It resulted in such travesties as Vietnam.[36]

One peace faction was the National Mobilization to End the War in Vietnam (the Mobe), an umbrella organization for many antiwar groups. Seeking a radical reorientation of American values and priorities, the Mobe invited a confrontation with the Democratic establishment. The other group was the Youth International Party, or Yippies. Not really a political party, the Yippies specialized in absurd street theater that attracted television cameras. During the Democrats' "National Death Convention," they planned a "Festival of Life" in Grant Park, replete with music and drugs and meditation. They also flung out a hodgepodge of outrageous threats, such as dumping LSD in the water supply and having "hyper-potent" Yippies seduce the delegates' wives and daughters.[37]

Due to Lyndon Johnson's withdrawal and the Mobe's slowness to organize for Chicago, the protestors never assembled a massive contingent. City authorities rejected permits for demonstrations and encampments in public parks. They even denied the permit to the pro-McCarthy group, Coalition for an Open Convention, which wanted to hold a rally at Soldier Field. Fearing "unintended violence," McCarthy urged protestors to avoid Chicago.[38]

Mayor Richard J. Daley nevertheless prepared for an invasion. "We won't let anyone come to Chicago and take over our city, our streets and our convention," he vowed. He placed the 12,000-man police force on twelve-hour shifts, with over 10,000 national guardsmen and 7,000 army troops on alert. The Chicago Amphitheatre was ringed by a seven-foot chain link fence topped with barbed wire. Manhole covers were sealed. Delegates entered the convention hall through military-style checkpoints.[39]

Daley was among the last of a dying breed, the big-city "boss" who maintained order and ruled politics. The mayor since 1955, he was also chairman of the Cook County Democratic Party, which empowered him to dispense patronage jobs and political favors. As the controlling force for the 118-vote Illinois delegation, Daley was a kingmaker in the Democratic Party.[40]

Each of Chicago's ethnic enclaves had its own representatives in the Daley machine. Daley himself still lived in his own childhood neighborhood, the working-class Irish district of Bridgeport. A stubby man with simple tastes, he had a common appeal. His administration revitalized the downtown Loop and delivered good city services. In exchange it demanded order. The mayor had difficulty empathizing with the city's black population, who were confined into teeming ghettoes and brutalized by police. After the riots following Martin Luther King's assassination, Daley demanded that police "shoot to kill" any arsonist and "shoot to maim or cripple" any looter.[41]

Daley was determined to showcase his city during the convention, despite crisis after crisis. Chicago's huge hall, McCormick Place, burned down in 1967, forcing the relocation to the Amphitheatre, miles from downtown hotels and near the stinking stockyards. Electrical workers went on a long strike. One week before the convention, the two major cab companies also went on strike. Meanwhile, fears brewed of another black uprising on the South Side, near the Amphitheatre.[42]

By the weekend prior to the convention, thousands of protestors had gathered in Lincoln Park. At the Festival of Life, the Yippies nominated their own presidential candidate: a swine named "Pigasus." The crowd included anarchists, revolutionaries, peaceniks, and young toughs bent on a fight. The police demanded adherence to the 11:00 P.M. curfew. On the night of Saturday, August 23, the poet Allen Ginsberg led a calming Buddhist chant—*Ommmmmmmmmmmm*—and the park cleared without incident. But on Sunday night, August 24, the police charged in, swinging nightsticks and deploying tear gas. Protestors fought back, toppled garbage cans, and spat insults. As the slaughter spilled beyond the park and into the nearby Old Town neighborhood, policemen clubbed every target they could hit.[43]

The next afternoon, in Grant Park, hundreds had gathered around a statue of a Civil War general on horseback, taunting policemen with cries of "Ho, Ho, Ho Chi Minh." A few climbed onto the statue. Police waded into the crowd and attacked. While the convention kicked off at the Amphitheatre, rallies at Grant Park called to end the war and revolutionize American politics. In Lincoln Park, police overran the hippies' futile barricade of picnic tables and trash cans.[44]

In the days leading to Hubert Humphrey's nomination, Chicago remained the scene of protest after protest: clergymen's vigils, a mule train from the Poor People's Campaign, picketers chanting "Dump the Hump!" The streets and parks were filled with raging battles, invited by alienated activists who tossed rocks and sticks and cries of "Pig!" and all-too-welcomed by policemen who bashed heads, sprayed tear gas, and yelled, "Get the fuckers!"[45]

The officers often removed their badges before the beatings. Resenting their media role as villains, they also targeted reporters. These cops were frustrated by high crime rates and urban riots, and they chafed at civilians who imposed limits on them. Now they raged at these white, privileged kids who demanded revolution with filthy language and disgusting tactics, such as tossing human feces. As a theater for the politics of confrontation, Chicago was exposing the deeper cleavages in American society.[46]

"This convention is Hubert Humphrey's bar mitzvah," promised one of his aides. "This is where he finally breaks his dependency on Lyndon Johnson and becomes his own man." He had 1,400 to 1,500 delegates in his favor, more than the 1,312 necessary for a first-ballot majority. Given his ties to organized labor and Democratic officials, he had locked up many northern, industrial states. But his support was softer among some conservative delegations, especially in the South. So Humphrey tried to straddle the party's rifts. It guaranteed the nomination, but it diminished his stature.[47]

From his arrival in Chicago, Humphrey felt vulnerable. A tiny crowd greeted him at the airport. Humphrey met with the Illinois caucus, but Daley gave no official endorsement. Then Texas governor John Connally raged that Humphrey supported the liberals' call to abolish the "unit rule." Southern governors had been cementing their authority through this Old Politics maneuver, whereby an entire delegation voted for one candidate. Humphrey apologized to Connally, weakly explaining that he had intended the reform for 1972. It nevertheless passed in 1968. The party leaders were as grumpy as the peace activists. "Wherever there was alcohol and peanuts," wrote Jeremy Larner, "Democrats were talking about whom they could get instead of Humphrey."[48]

Eugene McCarthy squandered his last chance. His legitimacy eroded after he dismissed the invasion of Czechoslovakia, stating, "I do not see this as a major world crisis." In his one joint appearance with Humphrey and George McGovern, before the California caucus, McCarthy stayed flat, failing even to state his position on Vietnam. He still envisioned himself as a vessel for an idealistic people's movement. When Humphrey took his temperature on the vice presidency, McCarthy coldly replied,

"Don't bother to offer it." He also rejected a devilish notion to make John Connally his vice president. When he told reporters that Humphrey had the nomination wrapped up, McCarthy demoralized his supporters and crippled the peace effort.[49]

One hope remained: that old Kennedy magic. In 1962, at age thirty, Edward M. "Ted" Kennedy had filled JFK's seat as senator from Massachusetts. He was a natural senator: patient and respectful, a gregarious consensus builder, a rational balance to the impetuous Bobby. A trip to Vietnam in early 1968 confirmed his gnawing suspicions about the war. When Robert Kennedy was killed, the youngest Kennedy brother heard the calls to assume the cause. But the assassination had crushed his soul. Instead of working, he took long, solitary night excursions on his sailboat.[50]

That summer, Humphrey kept invoking Bobby and lauding Ted. He wanted to unite the party with Ted as his vice president. "For me, this year, it is impossible," said Kennedy in late July. "My decision is final, firm, and not subject to further consideration." He reemerged one week before the Democratic National Convention with a nationally televised speech, calling for American withdrawal from the "bottomless pit" of Vietnam. Humphrey then visited Kennedy, urging him to reconsider the vice presidential slot. Humphrey promised a stronger position on Vietnam after the convention. To Ted, that seemed like a betrayal of Bobby's crusade.[51]

What about the presidency itself? Party leaders such as California's Jesse Unruh and Illinois's Richard J. Daley predicted disaster if Humphrey led the ticket in November. With Kennedy, Democrats would win more offices down the ballot. So on the Sunday of convention week, Mayor Daley refrained from endorsing Humphrey for forty-eight hours, giving Ted time to decide. Kennedy was still mourning his brother. He also lacked experience, feared getting trapped into running as Humphrey's vice president, and worried about seeming too ambitious. But a romantic atmosphere still wafted around the Kennedy name. His brother-in-law Steve Smith went to Chicago as his emissary. Kennedy was not running, but he might not resist an outpouring of grassroots support.[52]

"Draft Ted" stickers decorated lapels on the convention floor. On Tuesday morning, August 27, Smith met with Eugene McCarthy, who controlled over 500 delegates. McCarthy proposed a plan: he would let himself be nominated, which would acknowledge his supporters' sacrifices, and then dramatically withdraw in favor of Kennedy. He added a thorny qualifier: "I am doing this for Ted Kennedy, but I would never have done it for Bobby." But in the end, Ted was not ready to declare. Perhaps, too, he distrusted McCarthy. The Kennedy boom deflated.[53]

Now there were no plausible alternatives to Hubert Humphrey, who remained unable to unite the Democratic Party. During the Tuesday debate before the California caucus, Humphrey was asked to distinguish his Vietnam policy from Johnson's. "I did not come here to repudiate the President of the United States," he asserted before launching into another long-winded oration. While disappointing the liberal Californians, he reassured John Connally and other southern governors, who released their delegations for Humphrey. Mayor Daley did the same for Illinois.[54]

On the night of Tuesday, August 27, Daley led the convention's celebration of Lyndon Johnson's sixtieth birthday. The president had planned a surprise trip to gloriously defend his record, but he ultimately stayed in Texas. He had already annihilated any middle ground that Humphrey might have occupied. Well after midnight, while America slept, convention leaders tried to hold the debate on Vietnam. The howls of antiwar delegates echoed through the Amphitheatre. Finally, an enraged Daley ordered a postponement, signaling to Chairman Carl Albert by slashing his finger across his throat.

The debate took place during the afternoon of Wednesday, August 28. The majority plank got 1,567 votes, and the minority plank 1,041. Heading into the general election, the Democratic Party remained tied to Johnson's war.[55]

Violence infected Chicago. Tear gas wafted through a mass demonstration in Grant Park. Police tried to contain the protest, but people kept spilling out, taking their grievances to the streets. On the convention floor, where signs proclaimed "We Love Mayor Daley," officers roughed up reporters and antiwar delegates. And that night, the savagery reached its crescendo in front of the Hilton Hotel, as Humphrey looked on. Disillusion ran deep. Eugene McCarthy tried to calm the passions by withdrawing his name from nomination, but it was too late. Hubert Humphrey represented a party in chaos, and the whole world was watching.[56]

In the black early morning of Thursday, August 29, Humphrey's Hilton suite had the mood of a morgue. Chicago's bloodshed had stained him. Hundreds of peace delegates staged a silent, candlelight march from the

Amphitheatre, and when they filed into Grant Park, a protestor with a bullhorn proclaimed, "Those candles mark the wake of the Democratic Party."[57]

Humphrey had to pick a vice president. The right choice might pave over some cracks in a fractured party. Despite some Democratic overtures, Nelson Rockefeller resisted leaving the Republicans or taking the number 2 job. Richard J. Daley favored Sargent Shriver, an architect of the Peace Corps and the War on Poverty, as well as a brother-in-law to the Kennedys. John Connally vetoed liberals such as New Jersey governor Richard Hughes. Lyndon Johnson recommended North Carolina governor Terry Sanford. Humphrey liked Oklahoma senator Fred Harris, but he really wanted Ed Muskie, a sensible and subdued senator from Maine. Still, Humphrey waffled. He stayed on the phone, searching for advice, and delayed his press conference from 12:00 to 2:00 to 2:30 to 4:00. Finally, at 4:30, he adhered to his instinct, choosing Muskie.[58]

Chicago's chaos continued. That evening, national guardsmen stopped a march led by comedian-activist Dick Gregory and arrested seventy-nine people, including convention delegates such as former presidential aide Harris Wofford and renowned columnist Murray Kempton. Other marchers endured the all-too-familiar pain of tear gas and nightsticks. Early the next morning, in a grotesque conclusion to Chicago's turbulent week, the police responded to reports of debris tossed out the windows of the Hilton by raiding the McCarthy headquarters on the fifteenth floor. In a sign of the times, staffers of a major presidential candidate raged at "motherfucking pigs."[59]

By then, Humphrey had delivered his acceptance speech. Though schmaltzy, it won applause, resonating with the party faithful in the Amphitheatre. He acknowledged the violence on Chicago's streets. He thanked Lyndon Johnson. He yearned for peace, both at home and abroad. And he pleaded to revive the national spirit, summoning the dreams of Martin Luther King and Robert F. Kennedy. But it was not enough. For all his oratorical gifts, he said nothing new about Vietnam. At the end, George McGovern showed support by joining him onstage, but Eugene McCarthy was nowhere in sight. In that moment, perhaps no one—certainly not Hubert Humphrey—could have united the Democratic Party.[60]

_____

"We ought to quit pretending that Mayor Daley did something that was wrong," said Humphrey in the convention's aftermath. "He tried to protect lives." While unnerved by radical theatrics and reports of assassination plots, the Democratic nominee was also gesturing to a powerful boss. His statement further alienated the party liberals. As later documented by the "Walker Report," an extensive investigation by a federal commission, the protestors had provoked law enforcement, but the most blame lay with city authorities. The report termed Chicago's carnage a "police riot."[61]

The Democrats were in disarray. "It was a convention of delegates who smelled defeat, and many of them didn't seem to care," stated one postmortem. The Democratic coalition was disintegrating. Instead of showcasing the party's achievements, the convention exposed the party's wounds. Saddled with the burden of Lyndon Johnson, Humphrey left Chicago as both the violent perpetrator and the pitiful victim.[62]

The radicals had dramatized their call for a political revolution. They had unmasked the hypocrisies of the Democratic Party, the true costs of the Vietnam War, and the sinister violence of the establishment. For many participants, observed the writer Jean Strouse, "it was a taste of fascism, reminiscent of Stalin, Hitler, Prague, and a warning that it *can* happen here."[63]

The Republicans were delighted. Their rival party had reinforced its association with urban chaos. While Mayor Daley exaggerated the revolutionary threats, assassination schemes, injuries to policemen, and biased media accounts, the House Un-American Activities Committee investigated radical conspiracies during the convention. The Justice Department later prosecuted prominent New Left figures, known as the "Chicago 8," in a trial rendered ridiculous by the antics of the Yippies.[64]

The national mood drifted rightward. The television networks and national columnists thought that they were portraying the gross aggression of a police state, but to their amazement, public opinion polls and letter-writers favored Daley and his cops. Few Americans seemed to care about police brutality. More resented these radical hippies and their liberal coddlers. They wanted law and order.[65]

—8—

THE LITTLE MAN

G EORGE WALLACE stomped across the stage at Madison Square Garden, giving jagged salutes to 15,000 roaring supporters at a campaign rally. It was October 24, 1968, just weeks before Election Day, and the former governor of Alabama was staging a history-making third-party challenge. At the iconic New York arena, his fans tossed fake-straw "Wallace" hats into the air, bobbed to a brass band playing "Dixie" and "Yankee Doodle Dandy," and waved signs that read "Wallace Friend of the Workingman" and "Liberalism is Responsible for the Degeneracy in America." He stepped behind his bulletproof podium, a strutting bantam rooster, sporting a gold watch and a big gold Masonic ring, with slicked-back hair and bushy eyebrows. He buzzed with cocky energy.

The joyous frenzy turned into jangled rage. Some anti-Wallace protestors in the crowd had raised their fists in a mock Nazi salute. "Nigguh lovers!" bellowed a man from the balcony. Wallace's fans charged in, swinging signs and fists. Women spat upon the beaten hippies. After tensing for a moment, the candidate settled down. "Y'all just got George Wallace some more votes," he said, blowing his hecklers a kiss.[1]

Outside Madison Square Garden, thousands of police officers manned the barricades. Radical activists flung rocks and bottles at the cops, banged on a bus carrying Wallace voters from Long Island, and snatched and burned Confederate flags. Wallace-lovers relished the fight. One man smashed a liquor bottle into the face of a Trotskyist woman, leaving a bloody hole, with her eyeball dangling from the socket.[2]

In the arena, small cadres from revolutionary organizations such as Students for a Democratic Society and Workers World disrupted the rally, even booing throughout the Lord's Prayer. Wallace fed off the conflict,

OVERLEAF: Governor George Wallace (I-AL) (courtesy Alabama Department of Archives and History)

trotting out his classic one-liners. "Hi ya, sweetie," he greeted one long-haired critic. "Oh, I thought you were a she." His admirers loved it. They had strapped into a roller-coaster of political emotion—screaming with fervor, laughing at barbs, quieting with reverence, and stirring with rage. Wallace blasted the snobby media, "pointy-headed" bureaucrats, "communist professors," haughty Supreme Court judges, lying pollsters, and weak-kneed politicians who coddled special interests. "Why do the leaders of the two national parties kowtow to these anarchists?" he scowled. He recalled how a radical had lain down in front of President Johnson's limousine. "The first time they lie down in front of my limousine it'll be the last one they'll ever lay down in front of," he thundered. "Their day is *over!*"[3]

White supremacists dotted the crowd, including but not limited to the Ku Klux Klan, the American Nazi Party, and the Minutemen, a white Protestant militia prepared to battle uprisings by blacks and communists. Wallace supporters beat a small group of African American attendees, while others shouted, "Hey niggers, get out of here, niggers." Yet Wallace was not just gathering fringe groups. His campaign had wanted to book Shea Stadium, anticipating up to 60,000 people. New York City was torn by labor and racial strife. Madison Square Garden was filled with off-duty policemen, factory workers, and other blue-collar whites who saw their society in decay. Looking for answers, they found George Corley Wallace.[4]

Wallace was tapping into the long political tradition of American populism, whereby charismatic leaders claimed to represent common, hard-working Americans against the elite class. But no American politician had ever harnessed these impulses to such reactionary ends. "Wallace is the ablest demagogue of our time, with a bugle voice of venom and a gut knowledge of the prejudices of the low-income class," wrote Richard Strout in the *New Republic*. Accounts of Hitler's rise in the 1930s no longer seemed so distant, he thought. If Wallace could tap such deep veins of resentment, "something is wrong in America."[5]

In 1958, after losing the contest for Alabama governor to a race-baiting rival, George Wallace had mashed his cigar and vowed, "No other son-of-a-bitch will ever out-nigger me again." He was a political battler, befitting a scrappy former state boxing champion who served during World War II as a flight engineer in the Pacific. He had no personal interests or relationships outside politics. A state representative by age twenty-six and circuit court judge by thirty-two, he began as an acolyte of "Big Jim" Folsom, a gregarious populist who, while governor, fought for liberal state programs and racial moderation.[6]

When he ran for governor again in 1962, Wallace won as a tub-thumping racist. During his 1963 inaugural address, he proclaimed, "Segregation today! Segregation tomorrow! Segregation forever!" Appealing to the "Great Anglo-Saxon Southland," he condemned communist activism and federal tyranny. While the 1963 Birmingham campaign and 1965 Selma-to-Montgomery march spotlighted the oppression of African Americans, the governor milked the sense of victimhood among white voters, intensifying racial hatreds. Most memorably, during the 1963 integration of the University of Alabama, Wallace "stood in the schoolhouse door," symbolically resisting the federal government's enforcement of the legal registration of two black students. Assuring his constituency's loyalty and the national media's disgust, the governor embraced the white southern tradition of doomed defiance.[7]

Yet Wallace had national ambitions. In 1964, he entered Democratic primaries in three northern states. Deftly, he tied himself to the "common man," who faced the threat of big-government tyranny. His flamboyant verbal jousts were tailor-made for television sound bites. Working-class voters, particularly the white ethnics who lived and worked close to African Americans, cheered him. Despite an impromptu campaign with few resources, he won more than 30 percent of the votes in Wisconsin and Indiana. He won 43 percent in Maryland, where an intense civil rights campaign on the Eastern Shore had spurred a backlash. His brand of us-against-them politics stretched beyond the South.[8]

When Barry Goldwater won the Republican nomination, Wallace bowed to pressure from wealthy southern conservatives by leaving the Democratic race. He considered a headline-grabbing party switch, but Strom Thurmond beat him to the punch. Meanwhile, right-wing columnist John Synon was arguing that a third-party candidate could sweep the Deep South, prevent a majority for any party in the Electoral College, and force the election into the House of Representatives. Wallace loved the idea of both Republicans and Democrats pleading for his swing votes. The only problem was that the Alabama constitution prevented a governor from succeeding himself. If out of office after 1966, he would lack the staff, resources, and notoriety for an outsider bid to the presidency.[9]

Legislators rebuffed his plan to change the state constitution, so Wallace hatched another bold scheme: he ran his wife for governor. Lurleen Wallace was a private, restrained woman who preferred fishing to politics, and she had just been diagnosed with uterine cancer. But she remembered the dark times after her husband lost the 1958 election, so she acquiesced. Throughout the campaign, the couple toured together, with Lurleen reading a two-minute speech, followed by George launching long attacks on the federal government and national media. Lurleen crushed the opposition in both the Democratic primary and the general election. As everyone understood, George remained in power.[10]

On Lurleen's inauguration day in January 1967, George led a secret meeting at a Montgomery country club to plan his third-party campaign for president. Organized by Klansman speechwriter Asa Carter and notorious Selma sheriff Jim Clark, it gathered powerful white supremacists from Texas, Louisiana, and Missouri. Though he delayed a formal announcement, Wallace established headquarters and publicly discussed his election strategy. That spring he toured northern industrial cities such as Pittsburgh, Cleveland, and Syracuse. Downplaying the issue of racial segregation, he presented himself as a champion of "this man in the textile mill, this man in the steel mill, this barber, the beautician, the policeman." Despite its revulsion for his crass politics, the national press marveled at Wallace's torrential energy and daring ambition.[11]

Wallace needed to get on state ballots around the country. That effort began in California, which required 66,059 people to register for his American Independent Party by January 2, 1968. A hired firm collected only 2,000 signatures, so Wallace took about twenty-five state-salaried Alabamians to the West Coast for six weeks, including the governor's staff and state troopers, along with "volunteer" citizens who relied on state contracts. Up and down the Golden State, Wallace gave over 100 versions of his stump speech, railing against the "perfessers, liberals, social engineers and all those people who want to tell the rest of us how to live." Most audiences were just 80 or 100 people. They were white, older, and working-class, and many were transplants from the South. They gravitated to Wallace. Californians established at least twenty campaign offices, and over 100,000 people registered for his party.[12]

By June 1968, Wallace had qualified for twenty-two state ballots, with at least ten more on the horizon, under names such as the American Independent Party, American Party, Independent Party, and George Wallace

Party. He was demonstrating something fundamental about the American electorate: the South was everywhere. But he avoided an explicit talk about race. Instead, as one southern reporter described, Wallace would castigate federal bureaucrats and celebrate principles such as property rights and then instruct "those who don't understand me" to "ask the little man," such as a cab driver or police officer. "They know what I'm talking about!"

"He means *niggers*," someone would explain. "He means niggers moving next door or trying to buy into your neighborhood."[13]

On February 8, 1968, Wallace made the official announcement of his presidential run. No party outsider had influenced an election since Strom Thurmond and Henry Wallace in 1948. George Wallace was the most important third-party candidate since 1912, when Theodore Roosevelt ran under the Progressive Party, taking votes from Republican William Taft and helping elect Democrat Woodrow Wilson.[14]

At first, most pundits figured that Wallace would help the Democrats by siphoning away conservative southerners from the Republicans. But that winter, Wallace went north, enticing not only right-wing Goldwater loyalists but also industrial workers who traditionally voted Democrat. In three days across Pennsylvania, he nearly doubled the 10,551 signatures necessary to get on the ballot. "Wallace is a new Messiah!" exulted one happy admirer. When Lyndon Johnson dropped out, southern Democrats got ornery about the liberal alternatives, and some drifted to Wallace. When riots erupted after Martin Luther King's assassination, many whites approved Wallace's angry demands for tough police responses. It was a national campaign. As governor, he campaigned on the slogan "Stand Up for Alabama." His new slogan was "Stand Up for America."[15]

The campaign halted on May 7, when Lurleen died of cancer. When she ran for governor, George had proclaimed that doctors issued a "clean bill of health." But she soon needed surgery to remove tumors in her pelvis and colon, and she underwent radiation treatments after the discovery of another pelvic tumor. After an emergency operation to remove an intestinal obstruction, she shriveled down to seventy pounds. When she died, her devastated husband stopped campaigning for a month. He also lost the privileges of the governor's office, such as state troopers and administrative workers. His poll numbers dipped.[16]

Lurleen's death heightened George's sense of isolation. There were ruptures among his advisers, as some sought to conserve funds for a gubernatorial run in 1970 and others wanted to win every possible vote in
1968. Wallace was solitary and nervous by nature, traits sharpened by his
combat experience. Toward the end of World War II, he had endured a
nervous breakdown. He still hated flying. While in the air, he stared out
the window, without a book or magazine, until bursting into the cockpit
to check on the conditions. He was also growing deaf, which hampered
genuine conversations. Some suspected that it made him more stubborn,
more obsessive.[17]

Returning to the campaign trail lifted Wallace's mood. Starting on
June 11 in Memphis, he launched an eight-state, eleven-day swing through
the South, rebuilding his base while stuffing the campaign coffers. Then
he journeyed north again to reach more white, blue-collar voters. In six
days in Massachusetts, he gained the 61,238 signatures to get on the ballot; borrowing from Eugene McCarthy, he even imported college student
volunteers from Alabama. Protestors often jeered him, but that just kept
his name in the news. After protestors disrupted Wallace's event in Minneapolis, Lyndon Johnson issued a statement defending Wallace's right
to free speech.[18]

In April, Wallace was at 9 percent in national polls. By July, he was at
16 percent. It looked like he would appear on forty-eight ballots and win
five Deep South states. President Johnson gave him a foreign policy brief-
ing, just as he did for the major party candidates. Yet he possessed little
support from established politicians, whether Republican or Democrat.
Before the Republican National Convention, Nelson Rockefeller and Ronald Reagan each argued that they could best defuse the Wallace threat.
After the convention, Wallace bragged that he forced Nixon to pick a "law
and order" vice president in Spiro Agnew. "They're talking like we do,"
he gloated.[19]

Then, at the end of August, Hubert Humphrey emerged from the Democratic National Convention as a battered candidate, amidst swelling discontent about Vietnam and urban rioting. The conditions had ripened.
George Wallace was set to rise.

––––––––––

The Wallace campaign was built on the resources of the racist, antigov-
ernment "Radical Right." Henry Seale, owner of Dallas Aero Services, let

Wallace use his planes for free, explaining, "He's like us on the nigger situation." Another early backer was archsegregationist Leander Perez, a millionaire political boss from southeastern Louisiana. Robert Shelton, Imperial Wizard of the United Klans of America, was a political ally in Alabama. J. B. Stoner of the National States Rights Party hatched the slogan "Governor George C. Wallace—Last Chance for the White Vote." Other ultra-right-wing supporters included Texas billionaire H. L. Hunt and his son Bunker, disgraced general Edwin Walker, and notorious anti-Semite Gerald L. K. Smith. State-level Wallace organizations often were staffed by members of the John Birch Society or the White Citizens Council.[20]

But over the course of 1968, the campaign was fueled by what Wallace called the "little folks." Over 75 percent of his official campaign contributions were under $100, an unprecedented level of grassroots fundraising in modern presidential elections. "I am only a factory worker and I wish I could send more," read one typical letter, accompanied by a $15 check. Wherever Wallace went, he held $25-a-plate dinners. At rallies, his supporters stuffed cash into yellow plastic buckets circulated by "Wallace Girls." Unlike just about every other campaign in American history, Wallace voters *bought* millions of bumper stickers, hats, posters, and buttons— not to mention souvenir coins, phonograph albums, and red-and-white satin neckties emblazoned with "WALLACE."[21]

The rallies were cornpone with a knife edge. His devotees carried homemade signs with slogans like "Keep America Free" and "Support Your Police." Confederate flags draped behind the stage. The proceedings began with the national anthem and the Lord's Prayer. An Alabama country-rock band played tunes such as "Dixie" and "When the Saints Go Marching In," followed by a harmony duo, Mona and Lisa Taylor, who sang "Are You for Wallace?" to the tune of "Are You from Dixie?" A spokesman with a preacher's cadence beseeched the crowd for funds, and Wallace Girls brandished their yellow buckets. A good crowd got excited, angry, even spiritually moved or sexually aroused.[22]

Feverish cheers greeted Wallace as he took the stage. His stump speech jumped from point to point, but he had great timing and simple language, perfect for the mass-television age. Early in his speech, he deflected accusations of racism, insisting only that states should handle issues such as school desegregation and housing discrimination. He regularly cited how, in 1966, Lurleen won the most black votes in Selma (omitting that African Americans voted a straight Democratic ticket to support a moderate senator and defeat racist sheriff Jim Clark). If they called him "racist and a hate-monger and a fascist," he argued, they were just ignoring his popular politics.[23]

"Washington is a jungle," he cried, summoning apocalyptic images of stabbings and rapes in the shadow of the White House. He exploited popular fears of black and hippie violence. While liberals described a "sick society" to explain this unrest, Wallace stoked the conservative conviction that higher crime rates, radical protests, and urban riots derived from a lack of discipline. He celebrated the actions of the Chicago police at the Democratic National Convention. He wanted armed troops to protect American cities, if necessary. "Proper use of the police force is the only thing left now to curtail anarchy in the country," he said. "Let the police stop it like they know how to stop it."[24]

Like Huey Long in the 1930s or Joseph McCarthy in the 1950s, Wallace practiced what historian Richard Hofstadter called "the paranoid style in American politics," blaming elite conspirators for cultural unrest and casting himself as the people's champion. Often, in this dark strain of American political history, the villains were greedy financiers, suspect Catholics and Jews, or leftist radicals. The good guys were the white, Protestant common folk.[25]

Wallace blasted federal institutions, such as the Supreme Court and the Department of Justice, and attacked "over-educated, ivory-tower" opinion makers such as newspaper editors, television newscasters, college professors, and government bureaucrats. "They don't ask the cab drivers anymore," he thundered. "They ask some fellow writing guidelines—some fellow with a pointed head who can't even park a bicycle straight." He blamed these soft-brained intellectuals for Vietnam, too—it was a stupid war to enter, but even stupider to retreat like cowards.[26]

Wallace was not a traditional fiscal conservative; as the Democratic governor of Alabama, he had boosted spending for many social programs. Rather, as a populist, he appealed directly to his audience's cultural resentments. The United States in 1968 faced complex social, economic, and diplomatic problems; Wallace created easy enemies (liberal elites and radical troublemakers) and simple solutions (states' rights and brute force). While whetting a sense of alienation, he celebrated a romantic vision of blue-collar whites as upholders of American democracy.[27]

To his followers, he was both hero and outlaw. He promised order while delivering chaos, dismissed charges of racism while associating with bigots, and championed traditional morality while crushing dissent. Slipping back and forth from the country preacher to the macho bad boy, he applied the modern tools of a national movement to the rituals of an old-fashioned barnstorming tour. In the process, he forged a near-mystical connection to his followers. The New Politics was most associated with liberals, such as Eugene McCarthy and Bobby Kennedy. But no one in 1968 better led a bottom-up, mass-participation challenge to the political establishment than George Wallace.[28]

By September, Wallace was surging. A Gallup poll gave him 19 percent of the popular vote. A Harris poll indicated that 86 percent admired him for "having the courage to say what he really thinks" and only 41 percent classified him as "racist." Wallace proclaimed that he would sweep the seventeen southern and Border States, which contained 177 electoral votes, and target eight big northern states with 180 more electors. Some experts predicted that he would fare better than the floundering Humphrey.[29]

He was a star in the South. In Montgomery, he filled a 15,000-seat arena despite charging $10 admission. He played on the region's prideful resentment: "Both national parties look down their nose, calling us rednecks," he proclaimed in New Orleans. In Kentucky, Confederate flags waved as he celebrated southern pride. At a "national convention" in Dallas, he told Texans to "assert their manhood" by voting for him. In another sign of the South's divorce from the Democrats, Governors John Bell Williams of Mississippi and Lester Maddox of Georgia abandoned Humphrey to endorse Wallace.[30]

In guarded quarters, Wallace still spoke like a demagogue. On one late-night flight, he suggested that state police might "physically" take over schools to halt federally mandated integration. On that same ride, an aide told him about fights between black and white students at two high school football games in Florida. "See? A white school is playing a nigger school," he said. "They're having a race riot. The courts are making them play!"[31]

The frenetic schedule took a toll. "I am so tired these days," he said. "I'm just counting the days until this campaign is over." He admitted that the burden of the presidency was frightening. He kept getting sick. His wife had just died, and he endured an embarrassing controversy involving Ja-Neen Welch, a curvy blonde commercial actress from Indiana who joined some campaign rallies. Welch announced that she would marry Wallace after the elections. Staffers dismissed her as a liar. "I just wish that the Governor and I could be alone," sighed the exiled woman. "He's so sweet."[32]

In early October, Wallace again charged into industrial northern states. An estimated 50,000 supporters cheered his motorcade through downtown Chicago, followed by another 10,000 screaming admirers in the all-white suburb of Cicero. In one day in Michigan, he attracted 8,000 in Grand Rapids, 5,000 in Kalamazoo, and 5,000 more in Lansing. Approximately 20,000 packed Boston Common on a cold, windy day. Wherever he spoke, protestors chanted "Pig!" and "Fascist!," while Wallace voters jeered back, "Hippies go home!" Fights often broke out. Wallace fed off the violent energy—he needed it. "These anarchists are the kind of folks that people in this country are getting sick and tired of," he proclaimed.[33]

Factory workers defected to Wallace. Labor unions had been a critical component of the Democratic coalition since the New Deal. This alliance had boosted the well-being of white workers, but they bore little benefit from the liberal measures of the 1960s, such as antipoverty programs and civil rights legislation. Although union leadership stuck to the Democratic Party, straw polls of locals revealed enthusiasm for the outsider candidate. "I like Wallace," explained a lift truck operator in Garden City, Michigan. "He sounds like a man who'll do something about the rioting." By September, Wallace was polling at 50 percent with union workers in the South and 15 percent with organized labor nationwide. Humphrey was at 42 percent, the first time since the Great Depression that the Democratic nominee lacked a majority of union voters.[34]

Wallace appeared on the cover of *Time* and *Newsweek*. In mid-October, he got an ironic assist from one of his professed enemies, the U.S. Supreme Court, which ruled that Ohio's notoriously prohibitive ballot laws were unconstitutional. Now Wallace's name would appear on all fifty state ballots.[35]

The politics of the white South—a politics that mixed resentment of federal authority, black progress, and liberal elites—was spreading nationwide. "Governor, I've never been south of South Milwaukee," confessed a Polish American man in Wisconsin, "but I am a Southerner." Wallace voters were typically lower middle class, with steady jobs and home mortgages. But they felt like victims of the Great Society. Taxes and inflation squeezed their disposable income. Racial integration came at their expense. Open housing laws placed blacks in their neighborhoods. Hippies were defaming God and country, and black people were asking too much, too fast.[36]

Wallace's great political gift was summoning those resentments and rendering them legitimate. His admirers testified that he was the strong, forthright man to return America to greatness. "We will see Wallace elected because he will bring tranquility," said one woman in Lake County, Indiana. "He will put everyone in their place—the colored, the students, the people on welfare, anyone who is causing so much trouble."[37]

Could Wallace foment an election crisis? According to the Constitution, if no candidate won a majority in the Electoral College, the election would go to the House of Representatives, with each state having one vote. Wallace hoped to force this scenario and then enact "a solemn covenant" with another candidate, which would ensure policies and appointments that satisfied his agenda. To combat this threat, Republican Charles Goodell and Democrat Morris Udall rallied fellow representatives to a plan first proposed by political science professor Gary Orfield, whereby each state pledged its vote to the candidate with the most popular votes.[38]

Yet the Wallace threat fizzled before Election Day. One reason was his pick for vice president. During the early campaign, he satisfied various state ballot requirements by naming former Georgia governor Marvin Griffin, but both men understood it as a temporary measure. In September, he settled on Kentucky politician A. B. "Happy" Chandler. But as commissioner of Major League Baseball, Chandler had overseen Jackie Robinson's integration into the National League in 1947. As governor of Kentucky, he had acceded to school integration in 1956. Telegrams poured into Wallace headquarters, fuming about Chandler's racial moderation. One day before the announcement, Wallace aides intimated to Chandler that wealthy donors had nixed him. "I don't know who Mr. Big is," fumed Chandler. He appeared a voice of maturity and practicality. Wallace looked more racist than ever.[39]

Five weeks before the election, Wallace still had no running mate. Then he found retired air force general Curtis LeMay, the brilliant, single-minded architect of air campaigns into Germany and the firebombing of Japan during World War II. During the Cold War, he organized the Strategic Air Command into a dominant security force, and from 1961 to 1965 he served a frustrating stint as air force chief of staff. LeMay believed that once a nation commits to war, it must use all its resources to crush its enemy. Upon retirement, he criticized the limited war strategy in Vietnam. His memoir included a notorious line about bombing North Vietnam "back into the Stone Age."[40]

After first resisting Wallace's entreaties, the general worried that Richard Nixon was aligning himself with Rockefeller-style moderates. In early October, LeMay joined the ticket. But instead of boosting Wallace among Cold War conservatives, LeMay crippled the campaign. Before LeMay's first press conference, Wallace cautioned LeMay that reporters would try to trap him into making warmongering statements. In his first answer, the general criticized Americans' "phobia" about nuclear weapons. A squirming Wallace interjected that LeMay preferred negotiation to war. But LeMay refused to discount the possibility of nuclear warfare, adding a bizarre digression about the Bikini atoll, site of nuclear tests: "The fish are all back in the lagoons; the coconut trees are growing coconuts; the guava bushes have fruit on them; the birds are back." However, "the land crabs are a little bit 'hot.'"[41]

"LeMay Casts Mushroom Cloud on Wallace Presidential Drive," blared one headline. Wallace had picked a running mate who stoked fears of nuclear Armageddon. "America is indeed in danger," shuddered one columnist, "when a man with this kind of all-out military thinking becomes the running mate of a man with far-out racial and political thinking, to form one of three major teams in the presidential campaign." LeMay's pathological bluntness kept derailing the campaign. In Irish Catholic Boston, he defended abortion. In southern Florida, he bragged about the racial integration of the air force. Just weeks before Election Day, the campaign sent LeMay to Vietnam, an ocean away from most reporters.[42]

Even more damaging to Wallace was an all-out public relations campaign staged by union leaders. The labor movement was plagued by organizational rivalries and diminishing influence, but Wallace's inroads threatened its alliance with the Democratic Party. "We've got to convince our people who are swayed by Wallace's speeches," said AFL-CIO president George Meany, who realized the threat to his own political influence. "We've got to see that our people know the facts." The AFL-CIO spent an estimated $10 million to attack Wallace. It took out radio and television ads, mobilized speakers, and circulated millions of pamphlets that denounced his record on labor rights, education, and public health, while also highlighting his racist bedfellows. The blitz eroded Wallace support in states such as Michigan, Pennsylvania, Ohio, and New York, where organized labor was strongest.[43]

As Wallace attracted more attention, he invited more vocal resistance from establishment figures. A *New York Times* editorial called a vote for Wallace "an incredibly thoughtless expression of what is worst in American life and an invitation to disaster." Ted Kennedy pleaded with supporters of his slain brothers to reject the "dark" and "extremist" Wallace movement. Moderate Republicans such as Michigan governor George Romney and Massachusetts senator Ed Brooke lambasted Wallace for encouraging political extremism and spreading racism.[44]

African Americans generally abhorred Wallace. Ralph Abernathy of the Southern Christian Leadership Conference implored black people to vote against Wallace, vowing that "we are not going to let this country be turned into a fascist type state." The activist comedian Dick Gregory cracked, "George Wallace would be the ideal president of the U.S.A.—Union of South Africa."[45]

The Democratic ticket saw an opportunity. Vice presidential candidate Ed Muskie often targeted Wallace, and Hubert Humphrey suggested that the Wallace stink was masked by "the perfumed, deodorized, detergentized campaign of my Republican opponent—a man who has deliberately courted the most radical extremist elements in his own party—who continues this appeal in his speeches—and who will be fully in their debt should he win the Presidency."[46]

Richard Nixon conceded the Deep South to Wallace, but he craved the surrounding states. His selection of Spiro Agnew reflected his quest for suburban, New South voters. For most of 1968, he spoke neither good nor ill of Wallace. After Wallace's September surge, Nixon appealed to backlash voters, not by attacking Wallace, but by co-opting him. He told crowds that he shared their concerns about crime, taxes, and Vietnam. Unlike Wallace, he could actually address those concerns. Where Wallace aroused their wrath, Nixon offered experience and stability. Meanwhile, Republicans from Nelson Rockefeller to Barry Goldwater warned that a vote for Wallace would only help the Democrats.[47]

Wallace's momentum dwindled. A nine-day tour through the West rendered him tired and cranky. With few exceptions, the crowds were smaller and less combative. His poll numbers dropped back to 15 percent by late October. He got irritated at rallies and snapped at aides in private. Contrary to the evidence, he insisted that his audiences remained huge and adulating. He whined of unfair media treatment. And he suggested a nefarious conspiracy of professional pollsters, political big shots, and the "Eastern money interest crowd." "They lie when they poll," he cried. "They are trying to rig an election."[48]

George Wallace did not win the presidential election of 1968, but he shifted the entire trajectory of American politics. He exposed the nation's foul underbelly of racism, violence, and fear, and he linked those impulses to a romantic nostalgia for the American past, a celebration of self-reliance, and an antipathy toward federal power. Amidst the turmoil of 1968, he forged a language of populist conservatism that never went away.[49]

—9—

DOWN TO THE NUT-CUTTING

ON THE EVENING before the election, the candidates took to television. Hubert Humphrey staged a telethon on ABC. Richard Nixon did the same on NBC. In this final mass appeal to American voters on November 4, 1968, they showcased the styles of their campaigns.

Humphrey rambled across the dais, holding a microphone, flanked by Ed Muskie. He presided over a loose affair. The television audience could see cue cards, wires, cameras, and folding chairs. Humphrey fielded some questions directly from viewers. Hollywood stars such as Paul Newman, Joanne Woodward, Burt Lancaster, and Kirk Douglas manned the phones. He laughed at Buddy Hackett and gabbed with Frank Sinatra. Eugene McCarthy called in support. A filmed tribute from Ted Kennedy evoked his family's mystique. A sentimental documentary showed Humphrey playing with his granddaughter. Humphrey was having fun. After the four-hour marathon, he danced the Charleston at a Hollywood party.

Nixon ran a tighter show. He did one hour for the eastern market and one hour for the western audience. He sat alone on a pedestal chair, in the middle of a blue-carpeted stage. Spiro Agnew was nowhere in sight. A phalanx of "Nixon Girls" answered phones and wrote down questions, which staffers then selected, edited, and delivered to the friendly moderator, former Oklahoma football coach Bud Wilkinson. Nixon responded with restrained, practiced answers, projecting an image of statesmanlike competence. He slipped only once, using a crude expression about castrating bulls, a job for the toughest cowboys; it was time, he said, to "get down to the nut-cutting."

At the end, Nixon raised his arms in his trademark V salute, then walked offstage with a stoic glare. Back at his hotel, he ate a sandwich,

OVERLEAF: Richard Nixon before a television audience (courtesy Richard Nixon Presidential Library and Museum)

drank a glass of milk, and got in bed. If he exercised discipline, he could stay confident. This time, his enemies would not steal the presidency. He would do whatever it took.[1]

The Nixon campaign had been crafted with meticulous precision. After the Republican National Convention that August, Nixon held a retreat at a seaside resort in San Diego. His team planned a strategy. He would concentrate on California, Texas, Illinois, Ohio, Michigan, Pennsylvania, New Jersey, and New York, which together delivered 227 electoral votes. He would hit three major themes: inflation, "law and order," and Vietnam. And he would limit his public appearances to well-organized events, tailored to television. His first stop was Chicago, scene of the recent Democratic disaster. An estimated 400,000 people cheered Nixon's nineteen-block, confetti-showered motorcade though the Loop. Even the police were polite.[2]

Campaign manager John Mitchell, a naval commander during World War II, enforced the sober, white-shirt-and-briefcase style of a corporate law office. John Ehrlichman coordinated travel with military diligence. H. R. Haldeman kept the candidate rested and relaxed, while holding the press hordes at bay. The first-class operation was powered by $1,000-a-plate dinners and copious contributions from corporate leaders (as well as from illegal foreign sources, it was later learned). The planes ran on time. Advance copies of speeches were always available. Volunteers received four-page booklets about how to distribute handbills. Reporters had little access to Nixon, but they ate, drank, and traveled in style.[3]

From San Francisco to Philadelphia to Houston, from airport speech to downtown motorcade to arena rally, Nixon drew crowds of well-mannered admirers, vetted to exclude black militants, bearded hippies, and other suspicious types. He kept to his well-rehearsed stock speech. "My friends," he intoned, "I am proud that I served in an Administration in which we had peace in the United States, in which we did not have this problem of violence and fear which pervades this nation and its cities today." Most important, he transmitted confidence. Veteran reporters contrasted the snippy, aloof candidate of 1960 with the cordial, professional executive of 1968. Polls ranked Nixon the most likable and experienced candidate. He seemed like a president-in-waiting.[4]

Television shaped the fall campaign. In 1960, during his first debate with John F. Kennedy, the medium had shown Nixon at his sweaty, grumpy worst. Eight years later, television presented a composed New Nixon. A creative team led by Harry Treleaven, Leonard Garment, and Frank Shakespeare used TV to bypass a skeptical press corps and directly engage the American people. They sought to convey *feelings*, visual associations with a man's character. Their advertisements displayed compelling montages over Nixon's voice: calling for new leadership in Vietnam over shots of wartime devastation, appealing to "forgotten Americans" over scenes of hardworking people, demanding law and order over pictures of black criminals and bloody radicals. In a more lighthearted vein, Nixon also made a cameo on the quirky comedy show *Laugh-In*, popping on-screen to utter a version of the show's catchphrase: "Sock it to *me*?"[5]

Instead of debating other candidates, Nixon did ten one-hour television question-and-answer sessions, expertly staged by Roger Ailes, a former talk show producer. Though not a natural entertainer, Nixon thrived in the controlled environment. The ice-cold studio kept him sweat-free. Makeup smoothed his floppy jowls. For each show, a panel of local citizens represented a cross section of backgrounds and viewpoints. It was okay if some questions were hostile; it added dramatic punch, and the candidate could twist any question toward a well-rehearsed set piece, which landed well with friendly studio audiences imported by state Republican committees. Nixon came off warmer, steadier, more genuine.[6]

He was not cool like Kennedy or elite like Rockefeller. Rather, he was almost painfully "square": awkward around strangers, resentful of the wealthy and graceful, defined by his work, and clad in sober suits. His favorite snack was cottage cheese with ketchup. But a lot of voters were square, too. They admired Nixon's battle for respect. They liked his wife, Pat, a seasoned campaigner and hard worker with basic tastes but just the right touch of glamour, a voice for American women who wanted "peace at home and peace abroad." They were reassured by his fresh-faced adult daughters, Tricia and Julie. The bubbly Julie was engaged to David Eisenhower, grandson of the former president, and together they charmed Republicans across the generation gap.[7]

And yet, who was the *real* Richard Nixon? Reporters kept probing, playing armchair psychologist, seeking the true person. He had been the anticommunist gut-puncher, the maudlin hero of Middle America, the loser. By 1968, he had proven himself a master craftsman of politics. Every speech hit the same applause lines, with the same studied gestures. Every answer started with a thoughtful pause, even for the same old questions. Every action, every word, every moment was calibrated to gain another vote. But for all his intelligence and ambition, Nixon never seemed to enjoy himself. His shyness and insecurity lurked just beneath the surface. The campaign had packaged a man of confidence and substance—but it had no soul.[8]

In September 1968, the modern feminist movement had its coming-out party with a protest of the Miss America pageant in Atlantic City, New Jersey. About 100 activists from a group called the Women's Liberation Movement tossed girdles, bras, and beauty products into a "freedom trash can" while picketing a contest that celebrated "the degrading mindless-boob-girlie symbol." They further objected to the pageant's exclusion of African Americans (one block away, another beauty pageant crowned the first Miss Black America). In an era before the mainstream media or the general public understood the basis for the women's movement, the press cast the activists as kooky bra-burners. The demonstration also inspired a small counterprotest led by Terry Mewsen, a former Miss Green Bay, Wisconsin. Her placard proclaimed, "There's Only One Thing Wrong with Miss America. She's Beautiful." The button that pinned the sign to her dress advertised Nixon for president.[9]

To support Nixon was to drop anchor in the turbulent waters of 1968. The Republican held a huge lead. He could run out the clock until Election Day, avoiding controversial policies, instead offering such banalities as "peace with honor abroad" and "order with progress at home," keeping himself between the hateful Wallace and the hapless Humphrey. Nixon sensed the nation's great anxieties. In such times, voters gravitated toward a firm-handed father figure. He offered leadership, experience, discipline. "The next President must unite America," he pronounced. "He must calm its angers, ease its terrible frictions, and bring its people together in peace and mutual respect. He has to take *hold* of America before he can move it forward."[10]

He maintained his silence on Vietnam, arguing that talking about it would undermine the Paris peace talks. This tactic gathered a wide spectrum of voters unhappy with the war. On the domestic front, while Democrats highlighted the economic progress of the 1960s, Nixon emphasized that rising prices and higher taxes threatened the welfare of the American people. Finally, Nixon called for "law and order." He described escalating crime rates. While blasting liberal Attorney General Ramsey Clark, he rejected the Kerner Report's notion that poverty caused crime.

He demanded a "moral and civic order" rooted "in the family, the church, the school, and the community."[11]

Nixon also promised to appoint "strict constructionists" to the Supreme Court. That summer, Chief Justice Earl Warren had announced his retirement. Conservatives despised the Court under Warren, which had promoted liberal expansions of constitutional rights while eroding state power. It had not only ruled to enforce racial equality, but also stressed individual liberties, including the rights of criminals. By 1968, large majorities of Americans deemed the courts "too soft" on crime.[12]

Nixon's impending election derailed the nomination of Abe Fortas as chief justice of the Supreme Court. While an associate justice, Fortas had served as an informal adviser to Lyndon Johnson. Conservatives wanted the next president to appoint the new chief justice. During confirmation hearings, senators accused Fortas of "cronyism," arguing that his political ties compromised his judicial impartiality. In a dubious ethical choice, Fortas had also accepted a $15,000 salary from private donors to teach a summer course at American University. Most luridly, Strom Thurmond fulminated against Fortas for siding with the 5–4 majority in a decision that allowed an exhibitor to show pornographic movies. In darkened Senate offices, Thurmond hosted screenings of raunchy films while describing the liberal judge as a promoter of smut. That October, amidst a Senate filibuster, Fortas withdrew from consideration. The episode injected a conservative social morality into Republican politics, a movement that intensified in the coming years.[13]

Nixon further foreshadowed this trend through his public association with the Baptist evangelist Billy Graham. A spiritual adviser to presidents, Graham had enormous public influence, particularly in the South. Through television and mass revivals, he spread a doctrine that focused on individual faith and social decency. Graham had been friends with Nixon since the Eisenhower administration; in the early Cold War, government and religious leaders forged a new public consensus that the United States was a "Christian nation" rooted in free enterprise, in contrast to godless communists. By 1968, though, public religiosity had become the domain of conservatives. Graham maintained official neutrality during the election; but he was troubled by America's social discontent, and he clearly favored Nixon. He advised Nixon during the Republican National Convention, attended a Nixon television special, stated similar "law and order" viewpoints, and shared a stage during a

September crusade service. "I've known Richard Nixon intimately for 20 years," he said. "I can testify that he is a man of high moral principle."[14]

Graham appealed to those upwardly mobile, socially conservative, suburban voters at the heart of Nixon's "southern strategy." But as George Wallace climbed the polls, Nixon fretted about losing Texas, Florida, and the Border States. Wallace owned the hard-core racists. Nixon craved the swing voters embittered by liberalism. If he attacked Wallace, he alienated that audience. Instead, he acknowledged their shared concerns about riots, Vietnam, and federal intrusion, while suggesting that a third-party vote helped only Humphrey. Strom Thurmond spread a similar message, airing TV spots in southern markets that vouched for Nixon's conservatism.[15]

On issues of race, Nixon danced with delicacy. An effective president could not be perceived as racist. Yet there were few black faces at his rallies, and in his best-case scenario he counted on about 15 percent of the black vote. He pushed "black capitalism" initiatives to spur business ownership and jobs, campaigned with Massachusetts senator Ed Brooke, and insisted that his anticrime policies would benefit black communities. Still, Nixon spoke the language of the New South. His calls for law and order heightened racial fears, and he sought to strip War on Poverty programs. When federal agencies withheld funds from southern school boards to enforce school integration, he said, "I think we are going too far. In my view, that kind of activity should be very scrupulously examined and in many cases I think should be rescinded." To many African Americans and other liberal critics, Nixon was dressing Wallace's raggedy ideas in a respectable suit.[16]

More damning was his vice presidential pick, Spiro Agnew. The governor of Maryland was a right-wing attack dog, albeit a three-legged one that kept tripping down the campaign trail. "If you've seen one city slum, you've seen them all," said the alleged expert on urban affairs. After declaring Humphrey "soft on communism," Agnew claimed he was unaware of the phrase's poisonous association with the 1950s Red-baiting of Joe McCarthy. He used the term "Polack," oblivious that it was an anti-Polish epithet. On his campaign plane, he called a dozing Asian American reporter "the fat Jap." The *New York Times* reported that while a Maryland public official, Agnew illegally profited from partnerships with land speculators. He was a national punchline, a second-rate bumbler, a mediocre bigot.[17]

Agnew embarrassed the campaign. Paradoxically, he also comple-
mented it. Agnew wrestled in the dirt for those Wallace votes, taking pot-
shots at "pseudo-intellectuals" and the "effete corps of impudent snobs"
in the national press. He crowed that the *New York Times* failed to prove
its allegations of financial impropriety. Everywhere he went, in blustery
impromptu speeches, he hammered on law and order: student radicals
were "spoiled brats who never had a good spanking," part of a spreading
"unconscious anarchy." If he lacked judgment and restraint, so what? He
had simple values: hard work, patriotism, discipline. Agnew reverberated
with the voters whom Nixon was chasing. "This guy is made for 1968," said
a Nixon aide. "He's Joe America. Follows the Colts. Drinks beer. Comes
across honest."[18]

Nixon was not really leading a political movement. Rather, he was
tapping into the anxieties of the broad middle class, "the silent center"
that feared the erosion of its personal and national prestige. "He can rely
on no great charisma, no emotionally involved shock troops, no lead in
party loyalty," stated the *Wall Street Journal*. "He can rely only on the diffuse sentiments of a great mass of quiet voters, and if he succeeds it will
be because he senses those sentiments better than his opponents do. It
will be because, just like he tells it, the election will be decided by the
forgotten Americans."[19]

Meanwhile, Hubert Humphrey bore the stench of the Chicago slaugh-
terhouse. His poll numbers plummeted. His fundraising floundered. He
lacked a real campaign plan. The scheduling of the Democratic convention for late August—to coincide with Lyndon Johnson's birthday—left
him with little time. His advisers had different visions, and his longtime
staff was unexceptional. Larry O'Brien, the talented party official, agreed
to stay as campaign manager, but he termed it a "hopeless task."[20]

Humphrey kept trying to evoke Harry Truman's underdog triumph
in 1948. Twenty years later, however, the Democratic Party had lost the
"Solid South," union workers were defecting to Wallace, and liberals
were disgusted by Vietnam—some even supported Nixon, figuring that
he could end the war. To have any chance, Humphrey needed critical big
states such as California, Illinois, New York, and Pennsylvania.[21]

A small, dispirited crowd watched his opening event in Philadelphia.
Humphrey scurried around the country, talking to whoever would listen,

always running late, devoid of any organization or theme, plagued by loose lips. He suggested that the United States could soon start removing troops from Vietnam; the next day, President Johnson gave a speech in New Orleans that contradicted him. Then, in Houston, after skimming a newspaper article, Humphrey mistakenly proclaimed that American troops were drawing down. That blunder made him seem feeble. He had become the embodiment of a bloated and directionless party, the butt of national anguish. As one columnist chronicled, his image toggled from a "toady" to a "warmonger" to a "cynical practitioner of the 'old politics'" to "a bit of an ass."[22]

No modern candidate had ever endured such abuse. Antiwar radicals massed wherever he appeared, chanting through his speeches: "Dump the Hump!... Saigon, Prague, Chicago... Two-four-six-eight, we don't want a fascist state!... Write in McCarthy." The demonstrations dominated press accounts of his campaign appearances. At a rally in Boston Common, Humphrey scolded an organized horde of 500 dissenters: "Your actions here are going to disgust the American people."[23]

Humphrey pleaded for support from his fellow Minnesotan Eugene McCarthy. "It is inconceivable to me that we wouldn't be together when the choice is between Nixon and Wallace and myself," he said. After the Democratic National Convention, McCarthy vowed to wait a few weeks before giving any endorsements. His idealistic adherents were rejecting Humphrey. McCarthy mused about a fourth-party candidacy, though he declined to run for the antiwar "New Party." Instead, he vacationed in the French Riviera. Upon his return, he still withheld an endorsement. In his mind, his candidacy had set voters free. By staying aloof from the race, he preserved that ideal, along with his own pride. But he further destroyed his party's prospects.[24]

At this stage, the Democrats' only asset was Ed Muskie. The tall, quiet vice presidential candidate had a basic likability; the Catholic, Polish American Democrat had served as governor and then senator in Protestant, Republican Maine. His pragmatic, low-key style made him popular among all party factions. The general election introduced him to a national audience. When antiwar college students in western Pennsylvania heckled him, Muskie invited one to the microphone. It defused the tension, and his profile soared. In contrast to the blathering Humphrey, calculating Nixon, bristling Agnew, and raging Wallace, Muskie appeared cool and dry, soothingly old-fashioned, a unity builder in a fractured party.[25]

Humphrey tried to sell himself and Muskie as a package deal: "I'm going to have Ed Muskie serve as a Special Assistant President, a super Cabinet official, a coordinator of domestic programs." The campaign sent Muskie to every college campus, union hall, ethnic convocation, and inner-city venue that it could schedule. He often portrayed Nixon as slick and manipulative, especially for his soft-shoe shuffle to steal Wallace voters.[26]

But Muskie was put into the extraordinary position of justifying the party's choice for president. In the *New York Times*, columnist Tom Wicker portrayed Humphrey as "the weakling puppet of the White House . . . a burnt-out case who left his political manhood somewhere in the dark places of the Johnson administration." Muskie had to defend Humphrey. "I mean, a man is a man in many ways," he said. Humphrey was compassionate, courageous, public. "I think he is a man. And I think he has proven it."[27]

Humphrey still worried about Lyndon Johnson's approval. He grew glum and fatalistic. In late September, the campaign hit rock bottom. Protestors were ruining his events. Local Democratic candidates treated him like a contagious disease. A Gallup poll gave him only 28 percent of the vote; Nixon had 43 percent, and Wallace was up to 21 percent.[28]

The campaign spent its last significant funds on a nationally televised, September 30 speech in Salt Lake City. It would address Vietnam. Advisers circulated competing drafts, illustrating Humphrey's trap: some wanted to run on the administration's record, and others clamored for a clean break from Johnson. "You have to prove you are your own man," insisted Larry O'Brien. The night before the speech, the debate lasted into the wee hours, with exhausted aides drifting in and out of the hotel room, while a testy Humphrey, clad in his bathrobe, penciled in changes. Finally, he kicked out his staff and brought in secretaries. By 5:00 A.M., he had dictated a full draft. Humphrey then slept a few hours, campaigned all day, and taped the speech. Just before it aired, he called a grumpy President Johnson with advance warning.[29]

The Salt Lake speech was a turning point. Most important, Humphrey stated, "As President, I would stop the bombing of the North as an acceptable risk for peace." He said that a bombing halt would foster peace negotiations that led to withdrawals of American troops, an internationally supervised cease-fire, and free elections in South Vietnam. The speech stayed somewhat close to the administration's position; the bombing halt would occur only with evidence of the communists' good faith, such as a restored Demilitarized Zone between North and South Vietnam. In tone and spirit, however, Humphrey staked his independence. It annoyed Lyndon Johnson. On the phone with Republican senator Everett Dirksen, the president picked the speech apart. Richard Nixon later echoed those exact criticisms.[30]

"I feel good inside for the first time," enthused Humphrey. Over the course of October, he emerged, once again, as the exuberant crusader. Absent his rival's resources, he practiced a "lunch-bucket" brand of politics: taking his case to the people, bounding into crowds, pressing hands and smiling. His rolling, loquacious speeches mixed fire and hokum. He trumpeted Ed Muskie—"I ask you to contemplate a President Agnew"— while blasting George Wallace as an "apostle of hate." He defended the fight for true racial equality. Contributions rolled in. Crowd sizes grew. Hecklers dissipated. Party officials came on board. Poll numbers crept upward. Finally, Humphrey was his own man.[31]

Hitting a chord with voters, Humphrey demanded a television debate against "Richard the Chicken Hearted." He teased Nixon for sidestepping or straddling every controversial issue. Unlike his Republican opponent, Humphrey gushed with affection for his wife, gabbed with reporters, and craved human contact. "It's easier to sit around a TV studio," he said, but the American people wanted the authentic candidate, to "look at him, feel him, touch him, smell him." He sincerely believed that he could beat Nixon. "Give 'em hell, Hubert," one supporter shouted. "Well, it may be too good for them," he cracked back.[32]

Humphrey remained a long shot. In mid-October, a Harris poll placed him five points behind Nixon, while Gallup had him eight points behind. Due to the slow start and party split, he raised half as much money as Nixon. His haphazard campaign still broke schedules and forgot materials. In some states, party officials seemed resigned to a loss. Among the electorate, "law and order" remained a consuming issue. Though he acknowledged the widespread frustrations with crime and violence, Humphrey never effectively separated the quest for racial justice from the stigma of rioting.[33]

Throughout October, Eugene McCarthy kept his distance. While attending the World Series, he mused about baseball to *Life*. He made some appearances for antiwar candidates in state elections. The Salt Lake speech, he sniffed, was "good openers for twenty-five cent poker."

McCarthy wanted a new government in South Vietnam, draft reforms for conscientious objectors, and more democratic procedures for party delegates. Fellow liberals such as George McGovern and Ted Kennedy endorsed Humphrey, given his domestic track record and peace over-tures. But McCarthy chose his principles—and his ego—over the prag-matic fight against Nixon. Finally, one week before the election, in a late and understated gesture, he said that he was voting for Humphrey and recommended the same of his supporters. "I'm voting for Humphrey," he wryly cracked the next day. "And I think you should suffer with me."[34]

Lyndon Johnson was both Humphrey's ally and enemy. With an eye on history, he knew that a Republican victory would scar his reputation. He thus offered the occasional endorsement. "From what I have observed of Vice President Humphrey over more than 20 years," he stated in a radio address, "I believe that he has—in a unique measure—the understand-ing, the imagination, the commitment to freedom that this responsibility requires." Privately, however, he questioned Humphrey's fortitude. As he told Clark Clifford, Humphrey would get more respect if he "showed he had some balls."[35]

Meanwhile, Billy Graham was visiting the White House on behalf of Nixon. Graham assured the president that Nixon admired Johnson, val-ued his advice, and "will do everything to make you . . . a place in his-tory because you deserve it." LBJ knew that if Humphrey won, he would make big concessions for peace in Vietnam, besmirching the Johnson legacy. Johnson thus refrained from an all-out effort to elect Humphrey. He did not lean on party officials or open the taps on party funds. He did, however, keep twisting Humphrey's nipples. On the final weekend of the campaign, Humphrey was ten minutes late for a meeting. When he got to the White House, an aide informed him, "The President is not going to see you. The meeting is canceled." Humphrey prickled upon this final humiliation.[36]

And yet, the very next day, Johnson lauded Humphrey in front of 58,000 roaring partisans at the Houston Astrodome: "That man, my friend and co-worker for twenty years, is a healer and a builder and will represent all the people all the time." Humphrey thanked his boss and gave a rousing, touching speech. It was a critical moment in a critical state, fueling the sense of momentum heading toward Election Day. The most recent Gal-lup poll had him just two points behind Nixon, 42–40.[37]

"Yeow!" exclaimed Humphrey after his final campaign appearance, a fervent, confetti-strewn, open-air motorcade through Los Angeles. "We might just do it!" In the last week, he had touted the "upsurge," gathered the McCarthy endorsement, zigzagged across the battleground states, and claimed 251 electoral votes—enough to deny Nixon a majority. He promised to revive the Democratic coalition: union workers would spurn Wallace, liberals would get to the ballot box, Americans would remember the party's ideals. At the end, he hammered, again and again, on one theme: "Whom do you trust with the most powerful position on earth? Whom do you trust?"[38]

The Humphrey comeback highlighted the missing elements in Nixon's operation. After a restful long weekend in Key Biscayne, Florida, Nixon had staged a final, three-week blitz that included more radio spots, a short book that stated his positions on issues, and continued concentration on the big swing states. He advanced his image as the steadier, more competent choice. The campaign gears kept grinding.[39]

But that polished, prepared stump speech failed to inspire people. Now the hecklers moved to his events, which exposed glimpses of the old Nixon, flustered and cross. He dodged a television debate, because federal "equal time" provisions mandated the participation of George Wallace. When Humphrey offered to help buy time for a one-on-one debate, Nixon still refused. As Humphrey climbed in the polls, Nixon worried that the House of Representatives would decide the election. With a tinge of desperation, Nixon urged Humphrey to adhere to the results of the popular vote. Humphrey nixed that deal.[40]

Would this election slip away, too? Was Nixon still a loser? The anxiety stirred his insomnia. Often, late at night, John Ehrlichman fed him a sleeping pill and a stiff cocktail, then called Nixon's friend Leonard Garment. Nixon would recount the day, worry about losing, summon old resentments, and bare his self-pity. Finally, the muttering would drift off as he fell asleep.[41]

———————

Nixon's scariest nightmare was a peace deal in Vietnam. It would portray the Democrats as the good guys, lending Humphrey a vital edge. Into October, the situation had been perfect: the Paris peace talks stalled, and the United States bombed North Vietnam. Nixon was content to let LBJ engage in frustrating diplomacy and attack Humphrey's Salt Lake speech as a political ploy.[42]

Then, on October 9, the peace talks gained momentum. Soviet diplomats, fearing a "Nixon-Wallace-LeMay deal" that would intensify American military efforts, pressured their communist allies in Hanoi to work with President Johnson. Over the coming weeks, the negotiators reached basic agreements: the United States would stop bombing North Vietnam, both sides would respect the Demilitarized Zone, and communist forces would cease attacking South Vietnamese cities. The South Vietnamese government and National Liberation Front would sit at the bargaining table, though without official recognition from the opposing side. A still-skeptical Johnson reviewed every possible contingency with his advisers, demanding personal assurances from military commanders that a bombing halt would not endanger American soldiers.[43]

Since September, Nixon had received secret reports about the Paris peace talks from Henry Kissinger, who had served as Rockefeller's foreign policy adviser and now angled to join a Nixon administration. The back-channel news fed Nixon's paranoia. He stewed that Johnson's bombing halt would steal the election for Humphrey. On October 16, the president briefed Nixon, Humphrey, and Wallace via conference call. While updating the candidates on the negotiations, Johnson assured Nixon that it was a genuine effort for peace. Nixon distrusted him; he was receiving more secret reports of White House machinations.[44]

On October 26, as rumors spread of the impending possibilities for peace, Nixon undercut Johnson. He announced that he had learned about "a flurry of meetings in the White House and elsewhere," pushing toward a bombing halt. "I am also told that this spurt of activity is a cynical, last-minute attempt to salvage the candidacy of Mr. Humphrey. This I do not believe." The maneuver was classic "Old Nixon," simultaneously accusing an enemy and professing a pious distance.[45]

Now the election took its darkest turn, toward a storm of diplomatic chicanery. Standing in the eye was Anna Chennault. The alluring widow of a heroic general and member of the influential anticommunist "China Lobby," Chennault was a Republican fundraiser renowned for cocktail parties at her posh penthouse in the Watergate apartment complex. That July, she and South Vietnamese ambassador Bui Diem had held a clandestine meeting with Nixon and John Mitchell. They established that Chennault would serve as a liaison between the Nixon campaign and the South Vietnamese government. By late October, with expectations of the bombing halt, Chennault was relaying information to John Mitchell every day. Mitchell, who obsessed about bugged phone lines, kept switching his number.[46]

Through Ambassador Diem, Chennault relayed Republican urgings that South Vietnamese president Nguyen Van Thieu "stand firm" in peace negotiations. Originally, Thieu had accepted the negotiating terms. But in late October, he balked, objecting that the National Liberation Front could not be an equal participant in Paris. Thanks in part to CIA bugs of Thieu's office, Johnson suspected that this abrupt shift in South Vietnamese policy was due to Nixon, or at least his "agents." He presumed that Nixon was secretly promising to better protect the interests of the weak, corrupt regime in Saigon.[47]

The Logan Act of 1799 stated that if an American citizen interfered with diplomatic negotiations, it was treason. Johnson had no direct proof of Nixon's involvement, but the National Security Administration was intercepting Ambassador Diem's cables to President Thieu, and FBI surveillance on Chennault and the South Vietnamese embassy confirmed that Republicans were steering Thieu. On October 31, Johnson held another conference call with Nixon, Humphrey, and Wallace. He jabbed at the Republican nominee, alluding to interference from "some of the old China lobbyists." But, he added, "I know that none of you candidates are aware of it or responsible for it."[48]

That same evening, in a nationally televised address, Johnson announced the new bombing halt. The Nixon team panicked. "I listened that Hallowe'en night, and heard the goblins of defeat echoing in LBJ's words," recalled speechwriter William Safire. "With the 'war over,' the nation wouldn't need Nixon to bring peace, and could turn the Democrats on pocketbook issues." Polls revealed a Humphrey surge. Peace-seeking voters, especially women, were flocking to the Democrats. But the next day, President Thieu announced that South Vietnam refused to join the Paris negotiations. In twenty-four hours, the burst of hope fizzled. In those last critical days before the vote, the state of peace negotiations was awash in confusion.[49]

Had either Humphrey or Johnson exposed Nixon's role in the "Chennault Affair," it might have altered the election. Humphrey later expressed some mild regrets for not attacking his opponent. But Johnson never showed his vice president the reports of the National Security Administration, CIA, and FBI that most tarnished Nixon. The election, ultimately, was not the president's priority. Johnson wanted to burnish his legacy with a cease-fire in Vietnam. And if this diplomatic intrigue became public, then the American public might have turned against Saigon, and Hanoi might have abandoned the Paris talks.[50]

Moreover, no "smoking gun" proved Nixon's knowledge of the scheme. On November 2, the FBI reported that Chennault contacted Ambassador

Diem with a personal message from her unidentified "boss," saying, "Hold on, we are gonna win." It drew Nixon closer to the crime. "They oughtn't be doing this," Johnson told Republican senator Everett Dirksen. "This is treason." Still, despite the mounting evidence, he resisted airing the information, since he lacked definitive proof of Nixon's personal involvement. On November 3, when Johnson spoke on the phone with Nixon, he avoided a direct accusation. Nixon sidestepped any affirmation or denial.[51]

When Johnson hung up, Nixon and his advisers burst out laughing. He had survived the crisis. In his mind, he had been bold. He thought that the Democrats were stealing the election. When it came "down to the nut-cutting," he did what had to be done.

Did he commit treason? If so, the evidence is in the shadows. Yet the recently discovered notebook of Nixon aide H. R. Haldeman shines another sliver of light. In the entry from October 22, 1968, it describes Nixon's orders. "Keep Anna Chennault working on" South Vietnam, it states. "Any other way to monkey wrench it? Anything RN can do."[52]

—10—

BRING US TOGETHER

RICHARD NIXON soaked in a hot bath. It was Election Night, November 5, 1968. His supporters partied in the ballroom downstairs at the Waldorf-Astoria Hotel in New York. His wife and daughters waited in a separate suite. His staff counted votes. He knew it could be close. All year, he had run a campaign of discipline and precision. The voters never saw his anxieties, his torments, his fears. Now, with all the votes in, he spent forty minutes in a steaming tub.[1]

Hubert Humphrey had a roiling stomach and jangly nerves. That morning, he had cast his vote in the tiny hall in Marysville Township, Minnesota. Then he took a nap, got his suit cleaned, sipped hot chocolate at a diner, and puttered around his house. After dinner, he arrived at Election Night headquarters, the Leamington Hotel in Minneapolis. His supporters cheered, but Humphrey lacked his usual pep. He flitted around the hotel: plopping into a chair, staring at the television, tapping his finger against his teeth, then breaking from his trance into the ebullient, sociable Humphrey of old. The odds were long, but he was winning New York, Pennsylvania, Michigan. "I swear to God," he proclaimed, "I'm going to bust a gut."[2]

George Wallace whirred around his den, flipping channels. While staffers, friends, and General Curtis LeMay had gathered at the TraveLodge Motel in Montgomery, Alabama, and thousands of supporters waited for one last rally at the Garrett Coliseum, Wallace stayed at his brick, ranch-style house. His children and their friends poked their heads in. The candidate fetched sodas for the occasional visitor. He won Alabama, Georgia, Louisiana, Mississippi, and Arkansas; but Nixon grabbed the Outer South

OVERLEAF: Richard Nixon and Hubert Humphrey, three days after Election Day (courtesy Richard Nixon Presidential Library and Museum)

and Border States, while Humphrey took Texas. "George Wallace has gone down to ignominious defeat," proclaimed Walter Cronkite of CBS. Wallace mashed his cigar. "A deep Southerner getting that many votes is not ignominious," he scoffed, switching the channel again.[3]

Past midnight, three big states remained in doubt: California, Ohio, and Illinois. If Humphrey won two of those, Nixon would lack an Electoral College majority, and the election would go to the House of Representatives. Nixon's vast information-gathering operation assured him that he won all three states. But in the wee hours of November 6, with the results not yet official, his inner demons stirred. Breaching protocol, he made an adviser call Humphrey's headquarters to demand a concession. "Lay it on the line. Don't fool around," he commanded. "We've won Illinois, so let's get this thing over with." Humphrey's campaign missed the call, avoiding the awkwardness. Not until dawn did the television networks confirm that Richard Nixon was the next president of the United States.[4]

In a year defined by radical protest, rebellious youth, and racial upheaval, the election was determined, in the words of analyst Richard Scammon, by the "unpoor," "unyoung," and "unblack." The typical American voter was white, middle aged, well educated, suburban, and relatively prosperous. These people fretted that taxes and inflation would erode their hard-earned status. They worried less about racial inequality than about racial violence. The Vietnam War concerned them, but not as much as dirty hippies spitting at police. By Election Day, they felt malaise. In the face of great challenges, Wallace had aroused primal hatreds, while Humphrey flailed in pursuit of the old liberal spirit. Nixon stayed steady.[5]

It was just enough. Nixon took 301 Electoral College votes and 43.4 percent of the popular vote. If the election had been held a few days later, surmised pollster George Gallup, Humphrey might have won. "It wasn't that Humphrey had become more appealing," added Louis Harris. "Rather, at the end, the electorate was casting around for a mooring in a tempestuous and emotionally exhausting political year." Humphrey managed enough votes from union workers, racial and ethnic minorities, public sector employees, young professionals, and peace-seeking liberals to capture most of the Northeast, while Johnson's support helped deliver Texas. He finished with 191 electors and 42.7 percent of the popular vote. Though the loss was razor-thin, he got 12 million fewer votes than Lyndon Johnson won in 1964.[6]

Wallace won 46 electors and 13.5 percent of the popular vote. He bled enough white working-class votes from Humphrey to tilt states such as New Jersey, Ohio, and Illinois toward Nixon. But by dominating the Deep South, which had abandoned the Democrats, Wallace hurt Nixon, too. Nixon nevertheless won by maintaining the Republican stronghold in the West and Midwest, capturing enough big battleground states, and staving off Wallace in the Border States.[7]

Through the Nixon campaign, the Republican Party presented a united front. Its appeal to the "silent center" tapped the nation's mood. The Republicans envisioned a future as the dominant party. The old Democratic coalition had enjoyed one last hurrah, but southern whites had already left, and the party was losing the broader white working class. In 1968, Wallace took many of those votes. In the election's immediate aftermath, he adopted a triumphant air, bragging that he had made the South respectable, while Nixon won by parroting his message. His movement had folded into the new conservative majority. "When you add his vote to our vote," crowed Wallace, "there are more of us than there are of them."[8]

Even before Lyndon Johnson departed the Oval Office, historians and journalists grappled with his legacy. His Great Society produced an impressive legislative record in civil rights, education, health care, immigration, housing, and more. His leadership affirmed the federal government's responsibility to protect its citizens' welfare. Yet he left Washington as a tragic, forlorn figure. It was not just Vietnam. It was his compulsion to manipulate, to dissemble, to conceive of political power based entirely on what you could get and what you could deliver. Johnson towered over the 1960s, but a new generation of liberals demanded idealism and honesty, while a movement of conservatives objected to his basic doctrines. In an age when modern politicians needed television to enhance mass appeal, LBJ seemed like a man from another time.[9]

Hubert Humphrey again cried. On November 8, at a coast guard airport north of Miami, he met with Richard Nixon, and Humphrey's tears flowed. In defeat, the public esteem for Humphrey had swollen. He had reclaimed his old mantle as "The Happy Warrior," fighting for liberal causes with stubborn optimism. But he had no obvious future. Upon emerging for a joint public appearance on the tarmac, the outgoing vice president was smiling and gracious. Nixon, the longtime loser, commiserated: "I know exactly how you feel."[10]

In 1970 Humphrey won back a seat as senator from Minnesota, and in 1972 he ran again for president, but he withdrew before the convention. The publication of the Pentagon Papers, exposing the high-level decisions that escalated the Vietnam War, had revived Humphrey's image as LBJ's puppet. He flirted with another run in 1976, but his health was failing, and he died in 1978. He stands as one of American history's great progressive statesmen, brimming with ideas and energy, a true public man. Still, his reputation is scarred by his subservience to Lyndon Johnson.[11]

With the erosion of the New Deal alliance between middle-class progressives and blue-collar workers, the Democratic Party needed vision and leadership. None of the candidates from 1968 met the challenge. Eugene McCarthy's campaign had trained a new generation of liberal organizers, but they never again rallied around him. McCarthy grew only more quixotic. He left the Senate in 1970, ran a poor challenge for the Democratic nomination in 1972, and staged a halfhearted third-party campaign in 1976. To the end, he was bound to his own sense of self, distant and private, a better poet than politician.[12]

Two Democratic stars had risen in 1968: Ted Kennedy and Ed Muskie. Kennedy had resisted a last-minute campaign at the Chicago Democratic National Convention; he had a bright future, given his inheritance of the family mantle. But in 1969, after a drunken barbecue on the Massachusetts island of Chappaquiddick, he drove off a bridge, and the young woman in his car, Mary Jo Kopechne, drowned. Kennedy, who was married, failed to report the accident until the next morning. His presidential prospects faded. By 1972, Muskie was the party favorite, despite his cerebral and plodding style. But during the New Hampshire primary, Richard Nixon's campaign manufactured a fake letter that accused him of insulting the state's French Canadians, and the right-wing *Manchester Union Leader* smeared his wife as "unladylike." In front of cameras, Muskie raged with tears. "It changed people's minds about me," he reflected. "They were looking for a strong, steady man, and here I was weak." He soon withdrew from the race.[13]

After the Chicago disaster in 1968, the Democratic Party had enacted dramatic reforms for delegate selection, including open processes such as primaries or caucuses, as well as proportionate representation for racial minorities, women, and youth. The liberal, antiwar George McGovern— a short-lived candidate in 1968—exploited these reforms to capture the party nomination in 1972. That year's convention featured a kind of chaos different from that of 1968—and a different kind of Democrat. The long-winded convention floor fights featured old-line party officials along-side hippies in tie-dye, blacks in dashikis, and gay activists. The Democrats had expanded participation in the nation's political institutions, but those "unpoor," "unyoung," and "unblack" voters saw a party out of touch with the nation's major concerns.[14]

Liberalism has persisted as a significant strain in American politics. The federal welfare state still provides essential security in realms such as finance and health care, while the government has expanded opportunities across lines of race, gender, and sexuality. Yet the 1968 election had exposed a rupture that never really healed: the party remains torn between the old, centrist "class" Democrats and the new, left-liberal "conscience" Democrats. Just as important, the party lost its affirmative, wide-armed, muscular vision of progress. For most of the 1960s, Democratic leaders had vowed to improve the fortunes of ordinary Americans, to combat ills of poverty and racism, to foster order both at home and abroad. That liberal optimism was stifled by the chaos of 1968.[15]

George Wallace's third-party movement splintered into fifty crumbling state organizations, while the campaign staff feuded over the disappearance of millions in contributions. Yet Wallace himself remained a potent force. He maintained a busy headquarters in Montgomery, producing a monthly newsletter that fulminated against spineless intellectuals, weak Supreme Court justices, and politicians of both parties. In 1970 he won a tight, dirty race for governor of Alabama. He not only promised to increase state services, lower taxes, and combat drugs and pornography, but also cast his opponent as the darling of black militants. In the words of one aide, the plan was to "promise them the moon and holler 'nigger.'"[16]

Richard Nixon feared another Wallace challenge in 1972, since they mined similar anxieties over morals, drugs, crime, radicalism, and race. The White House snuck $400,000 to Wallace's opponent in Alabama, while the IRS launched a probe into illegal campaign financing and government bribes that focused on his brother Gerald Wallace. Perhaps not coincidentally, as the IRS dropped its investigation, George Wallace entered the presidential race—as a Democrat. He won five primaries and captured 325 delegates, flustering the more liberal candidates. Meanwhile, agents for Nixon and Wallace conferred in secret, trading political intelligence.[17]

On May 15, 1972, at a shopping center rally in Maryland, a mentally ill man shot Wallace. Paralyzed from the waist down, Wallace lost his chance at the nomination. He tried again in 1976, finishing third in the Democratic race, and served two more terms as Alabama governor. He started identifying as an evangelical Christian and gesturing at racial reconciliation. Whatever lurked in the man's heart, his legacy is nefarious. The presidential campaigns of George Wallace had unleashed forces of rage, resentment, and racism for a new era. American politics still bears the stain.[18]

On the morning after Election Day, when Richard Nixon greeted his loyal supporters in the Waldorf-Astoria ballroom, he recalled riding a campaign train through Ohio. He saw a thirteen-year-old girl named Vicki Cole holding a sign. It read, "Bring Us Together."[19]

That challenge stood before Nixon. He had wanted a convincing majority, a popular mandate to lead with strength. Instead he eked out a victory, and Democrats still controlled both houses of Congress. Nixon realized the national disquiet, the anxiety over Vietnam, the crisis of race. In the months after the election, he maintained his air of steady competence. He worked long hours and assembled his cabinet. While supporting Lyndon Johnson on foreign affairs, he avoided much personal contact with the press. With the presidency in hand, he was shedding his image as the divisive, partisan "Old Nixon."[20]

For Inauguration Day, young Vicki Cole got an all-expenses-paid trip from Ohio to Washington, D.C., where she held the "Bring Us Together" sign in a triumphant parade. The press learned that she had not made the original sign. Nixon's advance team had spray-painted the slogan, so that it looked like grassroots enthusiasm. Vicki had not even read the sign; she had plucked it off the ground as Nixon's train approached. Anyway, her favorite candidate had been Bobby Kennedy.[21]

A metaphor lay within the tale of Vicki Cole: Nixon manufactured his support but inspired little passion. As president, he first sought to position the Republicans in the center, backing progressive measures on issues such as the environment, workplace safety, and health care. But in such a divided political environment, neither liberals nor conservatives cheered him. So he sharpened the national mood of backlash, exploiting the cultural divides. The "forgotten Americans" were now a "Silent

Majority," disgruntled with hippie protestors, black militants, and indulgent elites. He manufactured a cynical "War on Drugs," while Vice President Spiro Agnew lambasted the mainstream media and "radical liberals," or "radiclibs." To win in 1972, Nixon would not "bring us together" but widen the nation's rifts.[22]

As president, Nixon made a historic visit to China and negotiated an arms-limitation treaty with the Soviet Union. But he also prolonged the bloodshed in Vietnam, seeking a political cushion before the inevitable fall of Nguyen Van Thieu's regime. Criticism of the war fed his paranoia. To ensure reelection, he succumbed to his darkest impulses. The resulting Watergate scandal—a saga of wiretaps, burglaries, bribes, investigations, denials, and trials—led to disgrace. Agnew resigned in 1973, after revelations of his financial improprieties. Nixon resigned in 1974, rather than endure impeachment. The 1968 campaign had projected what Nixon might have been: a statesman, a unity-builder. But his presidency revealed the traits that he had masked in 1968: self-doubt, cheating, hating, dividing.[23]

In the end, he was a loser.

If Richard Nixon tainted his reputation, his election nevertheless foretold the revival of the Republican Party. With the growing suburbs, conservative South, and white working class in its fold, Nixon capitalized on what strategist Kevin Phillips called "the emerging Republican majority." The party had long stood for principles of limited government and staunch foreign policy. After 1968, it increasingly fused those ideas with "gut-level" issues that appealed to cultural conservatives: opposition to abortion, busing, gun control, feminism, and affirmative action. If someone considered voting for George Wallace in 1968, they probably had voted for Democrats in the past. They would vote for Republicans in the future.[24]

During the 1970s, the moderate Republicans lost influence. Even Nelson Rockefeller, the longtime champion of progressive Republicanism, veered to the right. As governor of New York, he enacted new measures of fiscal austerity, supported harsh drug laws that multiplied the prison population, and sanctioned a murderous police invasion of Attica State Prison. He got one more frustrating sniff of the White House, when Gerald Ford appointed him vice president in the aftermath of Watergate. But when Ford ran for reelection in 1976, he appeased conservatives by boot-ing Rocky off the ticket.[25]

Ronald Reagan challenged Ford for that nomination. As in 1968, he fell short, but this time he fought through a dramatic open convention, fur-ther enshrining himself as a right-wing hero. Through the decade's eco-nomic troubles, foreign policy humiliations, and cultural cracks, he put forth his principles, which he bathed in sunny optimism and gee-whiz nostalgia. He appealed to an imagined past of moral order and national power. To win the Oval Office in 1980, he forged a New Right coalition that included anticommunist hard-liners, free-market advocates, evangelical Christians, and working-class whites. His presidency then shaped an era of conservative dominance in American politics that has stretched into the twenty-first century. The foundation was laid in 1968.[26]

APPENDIX

1968 ELECTION TIMELINE

January 2: George Wallace finishes successful effort to get his name on ballot in California

January 3: Eugene McCarthy announces entry in New Hampshire Democratic primary

January 12: George Romney begins campaigning in New Hampshire

January 17: Lyndon Johnson delivers State of the Union address

January 23: North Korea seizes U.S. naval vessel *Pueblo*

January 30: Robert Kennedy states that he has no plans to run against Lyndon Johnson

January 30: Tet Offensive begins

February 2: Richard Nixon officially declares candidacy and begins New Hampshire campaign

February 8: George Wallace announces his third-party candidacy

February 29: George Romney withdraws from race for Republican nomination

February 29: Release of report by the National Advisory Commission on Civil Disorders (Kerner Report)

March 1: Clark Clifford replaces Robert McNamara as secretary of defense

March 10: Nelson Rockefeller meets with Republican leaders to discuss possible candidacy

March 12: Eugene McCarthy gets 42 percent in Democratic primary in New Hampshire; Richard Nixon wins Republican primary

March 13: Robert Kennedy states that he is reassessing candidacy, meets with Eugene McCarthy

March 15: Edward Kennedy meets with Eugene McCarthy in Green Bay, Wisconsin

March 16: Robert Kennedy announces candidacy for the Democratic nomination

March 21: Nelson Rockefeller declares that he is not campaigning for the Republican nomination

March 25: Advisers known as the "Wise Men" urge Lyndon Johnson to seek diplomatic solutions in Vietnam

March 31: Lyndon Johnson announces bombing halt in much of North Vietnam and adds that he will not seek reelection in 1968

April 3: Eugene McCarthy wins Democratic primary in Wisconsin; Richard Nixon wins Republican primary

April 4: Martin Luther King is assassinated

April 4: Robert Kennedy gives speech in downtown Indianapolis

April 9: Funeral of Martin Luther King

April 23: Lyndon Johnson privately urges Nelson Rockefeller to run for president

April 23: Student protest begins at Columbia University

April 27: Hubert Humphrey announces candidacy for Democratic nomination

April 30: Nelson Rockefeller enters campaign for Republican nomination and wins Massachusetts primary as write-in candidate

May 7: Robert Kennedy wins Democratic primary in Indiana; Richard Nixon wins Republican primary

May 7: Lurleen Wallace dies of cancer

May 14: Robert Kennedy win Democratic primary in Nebraska; Richard Nixon wins Republican primary

May 20: Ronald Reagan and Nelson Rockefeller meet in New Orleans

May 28: Eugene McCarthy wins Democratic primary in Oregon; Richard Nixon wins Republican primary

June 4: Robert Kennedy wins Democratic primary in California; Richard Nixon wins Republican primary

June 5: Robert Kennedy is shot by Sirhan Sirhan

June 6: Robert Kennedy is pronounced dead

June 8: Funeral of Robert Kennedy

June 11: George Wallace relaunches his campaign

August 5: First day of Republican National Convention in Miami Beach; Ronald Reagan declares his candidacy

August 6: Second day of Republican National Convention; Strom
  Thurmond urges southern delegates to support Richard Nixon

August 7: Third day of Republican National Convention; balloting
  begins for presidential nomination while a riot takes place in nearby
  Liberty City

August 8: Fourth day of Republican National Convention; Richard
  Nixon wins nomination in early morning, selects Spiro Agnew as vice
  presidential candidate, and delivers acceptance speech that evening

August 10: George McGovern announces candidacy for the Democratic
  nomination

August 17: Lester Maddox announces candidacy for the Democratic
  nomination

August 20: Soviet Union invades Czechoslovakia to suppress political
  reforms

August 25: Chicago police violently clear Lincoln Park of protestors in
  advance of Democratic National Convention; Lyndon Johnson rejects
  last version of Hubert Humphrey's proposed compromise plank on
  the Vietnam War

August 26: First day of Democratic National Convention; police attack
  protestors in Grant Park and Lincoln Park

August 27: Second day of Democratic National Convention; momentum
  builds for candidacy of Edward Kennedy until he refrains from
  declaring; continued violence on streets of Chicago

August 28: Third day of Democratic National Convention; debate on
  Vietnam plank takes place, and voting begins on presidential
  nomination; police beat protestors in downtown Loop

August 29: Fourth day of Democratic National Convention; Hubert
  Humphrey wins Democratic nomination just after midnight,
  selects Edward Muskie as vice presidential candidate, and delivers
  acceptance speech that evening; national guardsmen arrest
  protesting antiwar delegates

August 30: Chicago police launch early morning raid of Eugene
  McCarthy's campaign headquarters at Conrad Hilton Hotel

September 30: Hubert Humphrey gives nationally televised speech
  in Salt Lake City that somewhat distances him from the Johnson
  administration's Vietnam policy

October 1: Abe Fortas withdraws his name for nomination to chief justice of the Supreme Court in the midst of a Senate filibuster

October 3: George Wallace announces Curtis LeMay as his vice presidential pick

October 9: Initial momentum toward breakthrough in Paris peace talks

October 15: Supreme Court rules that George Wallace's name must be placed on ballot in Ohio, ensuring his place on all fifty state ballots

October 16: Lyndon Johnson briefs Nixon, Humphrey, and Wallace on Vietnam negotiations

October 24: George Wallace rally in Madison Square Garden

October 29: Eugene McCarthy offers late and flat endorsement of Hubert Humphrey

October 31: Lyndon Johnson announces bombing halt in North Vietnam on national television

November 1: Nguyen Van Thieu announces South Vietnam's refusal to join Paris peace talks

November 3: Lyndon Johnson speaks with Richard Nixon about his campaign's possible interference in the Vietnam negotiations, but avoids any direct accusations

November 4: Hubert Humphrey and Richard Nixon hold telethons in final push for voters

November 5: Election Day

November 6: Richard Nixon confirmed as the winner of the presidential election

NOTES

CHAPTER ONE

1. "Johnson Wrote Last of a Dozen Drafts of Speech," *New York Times*, January 18, 1968, 17; Hugh Sidey, "Thoughts on the State of the Man," *Life*, January 26, 1968, 30D.

2. "The Crucible," *Time*, January 26, 1968, 11–12; "Somber & Spare," *Time*, January 26, 1968, 13–14; "LBJ and the Restlessness," *Life*, January 26, 1968, 4; Kenneth Crawford, "State of the Audience," *Newsweek*, January 29, 1968, 26; Kyle Longley, *LBJ's 1968: Power, Politics, and the Presidency in America's Year of Upheaval* (New York: Cambridge University Press, 2018), 23–29.

3. "A 'New' LBJ? Why Many People Thought So," *U.S. News & World Report*, January 29, 1968, 16; "The Look of Leadership," *Time*, November 24, 1967, 21–22; "Live and in Color—The Real LBJ," *Newsweek*, November 27, 1967, 23–24; Myra McPherson, "The President and His Changing Image," *New York Times*, March 26, 1968, 34; "The State of the Nation," *Los Angeles Times*, January 19, 1968, A4; "As the Other Side Sees It," *U.S. News & World Report*, January 29, 1968, 30–32; "Republicans Report on the State of the Union," *U.S. News & World Report*, February 5, 1968, 78–84; "The 'New' Lyndon," *Newsweek*, January 22, 1968, 19–20; "The State of LBJ," *Newsweek*, January 29, 1968, 16–24.

4. Max Frankel, "Johnson Pullout Conceived in '65," *New York Times*, April 2, 1968, 1; Hugh Sidey, "A Surrender of Power . . . and a Burst of Hope," *Life*, April 12, 1968, 30–33; Drew Pearson, "The Ghosts That Haunted LBJ," *Look*, July 23, 1968, 25–29; Lyndon Baines Johnson, *The Vantage Point: Perspectives of the Presidency, 1963–1969* (New York: Holt, Rinehart and Winston, 1971), 429–30.

5. "Too Much for One Man," *Look*, August 20, 1968, 29–31; James Deakin, "The Dark Side of LBJ," *Esquire*, August 1967, 45–48; Larry L. King, "My Hero LBJ," *Harper's*, October 1966, 51–61; Harry McPherson, *A Political Education* (Boston: Atlantic Monthly Press, 1972), 445; George Reedy, *Lyndon B. Johnson: A Memoir* (New York: Andrews and McMeel, 1982), 6–9, 52–53, 157–59; Hugh Sidey, *A Very Personal Presidency* (New York: Atheneum, 1968), 99–100, 214–16.

6. Robert Dallek, *Lone Star Rising: Lyndon Johnson and His Times, 1908–1960* (New York: Oxford University Press, 1991); Robert Dallek, *Flawed Giant: Lyndon Johnson and His Times, 1961–1973* (New York: Oxford University Press, 1998), 3–53; Theodore H. White, *The Making of the President, 1964* (New York: Atheneum, 1965), 41–42.

7. James T. Patterson, *Grand Expectations: The United States, 1945–1974* (New York: Oxford University Press, 1996), 524–92; Julian E. Zelizer, *The Fierce Urgency of Now: Lyndon Johnson, Congress, and the Great Society* (New York: Penguin, 2015); G. Calvin Mackenzie and Robert Weisbrot, *The Liberal Hour: Washington and the Politics of Change in the 1960s* (New York: Penguin, 2008), 1–227.

8. Gareth Davies, *From Opportunity to Entitlement: The Transformation and Decline of Great Society Liberalism* (Lawrence: University Press of Kansas, 1996);

Allen J. Matusow, *The Unraveling of America: A History of Liberalism in the 1960s* (New York: Harper and Row, 1984), 217–71; Dallek, *Flawed Giant*, 411–18; "Washington," *Atlantic*, November 1967, 4–14.

9. *Wall Street Journal*, August 1, 1968; "Power of a President—Too Much, or Too Little?," *U.S. News & World Report*, November 11, 1968, 48–51; "LBJ's Mood in Time of Trouble," *U.S. News & World Report*, April 8, 1968, 68–70; Harris Wofford, *Of Kennedys and Kings: Making Sense of the Sixties* (1980; reprint, Pittsburgh: University of Pittsburgh Press, 1992), 317–18; Richard Goodwin, *Remembering America: A Voice from the Sixties* (Boston: Little, Brown, 1988), 392–405; Robert Dallek, "Three New Revelations about LBJ," *Atlantic*, April 1998, 42–44.

10. Reedy, *Lyndon B. Johnson*, 17–18, 22, 59–68; Jack Valenti, *A Very Human President* (New York: Norton, 1975), 271–72; Sidey, *Very Personal Presidency*, 83–84, 116, 157–61, 192–93; Mackenzie and Weisbrot, *Liberal Hour*, 327–32; Peter Lisagor, "They Don't Dig This Security Jazz," *Nation's Business*, August 1966, 19–20; Larry L. King, "An Epitaph for LBJ," *Harper's*, April 1968, 17–21.

11. George W. Ball, *The Past Has Another Pattern: Memoirs* (New York: Norton, 1982), 374–403; Herbert Y. Schandler, *The Unmaking of a President: Lyndon Johnson and Vietnam* (Princeton, N.J.: Princeton University Press, 1977), 320–50; Tom Wicker, "The Wrong Rubicon: LBJ and the War," *Atlantic Monthly*, May 1968, 65–84; David Halberstam, "Losing Big," *Esquire*, September 1972, 90–98, 170–80; David Halberstam, *The Best and the Brightest* (New York: Random House, 1969), 302–65; Dallek, *Flawed Giant*, 152–56, 244–45, 272–79, 291–92, 299–302, 358–90; Paul H. Nitze, *From Hiroshima to Glasnost: At the Center of Decision* (New York: Grove Weidenfeld, 1989), 258–62; Stanley Karnow, *Vietnam: A History*, 2nd ed. (New York: Penguin, 1997), 372–527; Robert Mann, *A Grand Delusion: America's Descent into Vietnam* (New York: Basic Books, 2001), 303–569.

12. "A Failure of Communication," *Time*, August 25, 1967, 13–14; "The Paradox of Power," *Time*, January 5, 1968, 13–22; Hugh Sidey, "Commander-in-Chief Who Leaves His Generals Alone," *Life*, December 1, 1967, 38; "An LBJ Cartoon Chronicle," *Time*, January 5, 1968, 15–18; Jules Feiffer, "LBJ in Caricature," *Harper's*, February 1968, 48–52; Max Frankel, "Why the Gap Between L.B.J. and the Nation," *New York Times Magazine*, January 7, 1968, 26–27, 37–43; Hugh Sidey, "A View from the Heartland," *Life*, August 25, 1967, 34B; Ferdinand Mount, "Nobody Loves the Poor Prez," *National Review*, January 18, 1968, 24–27; "Poll Finds Johnson Reverses His Popularity Loss," *New York Times*, December 5, 1967, 18; "How the New Year Looks to Johnson," *New York Times*, December 31, 1967, 91.

13. Steven V. Roberts, "The Pressures Mount on LBJ," *Commonweal*, October 20, 1967, 70–71; J. William Fulbright, *The Arrogance of Power* (New York: Random House, 1967), 178–200; "Dump LBJ?," *Newsweek*, October 9, 1967, 24–25; "Why Intellectuals Dislike LBJ," *Nation*, June 5, 1967, 709–10; Bryce Nelson, "Communication Gap: LBJ's Monologue with the Intellectuals," *Science*, July 14, 1967, 173–76; "How the President Feels about His Troubles," *U.S. News & World Report*, September 18, 1967, 50–51; George Christian, *The President Steps Down: A Personal Memoir of the Transfer of Power* (New York: Macmillan, 1970), 159–60; Lady Bird Johnson, *A White House Diary* (New York: Holt, Rinehart and Winston, 1970), 622–23; "Eartha Kitt Denounces War Policy to Mrs. Johnson," *New York Times*, January 19, 1968, 1.

14. Max Frankel, "President Honors Lincoln and Likens Their War Ordeals," *New York Times*, February 13, 1968, 1; James Reston, "Washington: Mr. Lincoln and Mr. Johnson," *New York Times*, February 14, 1968, 46; Hugh Sidey, "Seeking Solace amid the Shrill Dissent," *Life*, November 17, 1967, 38B; "Why Johnson Sticks to His Vietnam Guns," *U.S. News & World Report*, September 4, 1967, 12; "How the President Feels about His Troubles," *U.S. News & World Report*, September 18, 1967, 50–51; "Johnson Is Still Playing to Win," *Business Week*, December 23, 1967, 14–17; Max Frankel, "Johnson Appears Adamant on Raids," *New York Times*, January 11, 1968, 1; "Pacific Mission," *Time*, December 29, 1967, 9–10; "LBJ Goes All the Way," *Newsweek*, January 4, 1968, 10–11; Hugh Sidey, "Around the World with Lyndon B. Magellan," *Life*, January 5, 1968, 24C–24D; "Johnson Confers with Pope Paul on Vietnam War," *New York Times*, December 24, 1967, 1.

15. Reedy, *Lyndon B. Johnson*, 31–38; David Wyatt, *When America Turned: Reckoning with 1968* (Amherst: University of Massachusetts Press, 2014), 19–21; Robert D. Dean, *Imperial Brotherhood: Gender and the Making of Cold War Foreign Policy* (Amherst: University of Massachusetts Press, 2001), 49, 210–40; Doris Kearns, *Lyndon Johnson and the American Dream* (New York: Harper and Row, 1976), 251–53.

16. Dallek, *Flawed Giant*, 491.

17. Cabell Phillips, "Johnson Has the Kind of Troubles Truman Had," *New York Times Magazine*, October 22, 1967, 35, 110–16.

18. "The Big Show," *Newsweek*, January 8, 1968, 17–24; "A Democrat Appraises His Party's Chances," *U.S. News & World Report*, November 27, 1967, 44; "The Move to 'Dump' Johnson," *Newsweek*, November 27, 1967, 25–28; "The Price of Fiction," *Time*, March 15, 1968, 19; "Who Will Win the '68 Election?," *Nation's Business*, November 1967, 60–85; Jules Witcover, *Party of the People: A History of the Democrats* (New York: Random House, 2003), 359–569; Stewart Alsop, "Can Anyone Beat LBJ?," *Saturday Evening Post*, June 3, 1967, 29–31.

19. Alsop, "Can Anyone Beat LBJ?," 29–31.

20. "Delegate Survey Shows Johnson Has Wide Lead," *Washington Post, Times Herald*, December 21, 1967, A2; David R. Jones, "All the Way with L.B.J.," *New York Times*, February 25, 1968, E3; "Johnson Endorsed by House Democrats," *New York Times*, March 20, 1968, 31; Warren Weaver, "65% at Convention to Back Johnson, Survey Indicates," *New York Times*, March 24, 1968, 1; "Meet Candidate Lyndon Johnson," *Newsweek*, November 18, 1967, 31–32; Lawrence F. O'Brien, *No Final Victories: A Life in Politics—from John F. Kennedy to Watergate* (Garden City, N.Y.: Doubleday, 1974), 215; "Political Magic," *Newsweek*, January 15, 1968, 15–16; "Under the Way with LBJ," *Newsweek*, April 1, 1968, 21; "The Roots of Power," *Newsweek*, April 8, 1968, 37–38; "Five Ways for LBJ," *Time*, January 19, 1968, 13–14; "Fly Now, Tell Later," *Time*, March 8, 1968, 19–20; "Challenge and Swift Response," *Time*, March 29, 1968, 19–21; "A Test of Time," *Time*, April 5, 1968, 24; "Why It Will Be a Johnson-Humphrey Ticket Again in '68," *U.S. News & World Report*, February 13, 1967, 40–43; "'68 Election as LBJ Sees It," *U.S. News & World Report*, February 5, 1968, 36–37; "Stumping from the White House," *Business Week*, December 30, 1967, 18–20; Max Frankel, "On the Trail: Johnson Has Answers," *New York Times*, March 3, 1968, 1.

21. "Stanching the Flood," *Time*, January 12, 1968, 10–11; "Jobs for 500,000," *Time*, February 2, 1968, 19; "Where 'New Economics' Went Wrong," *U.S. News & World*

Report, January 15, 1968, 36–39; Walter LaFeber, *The Deadly Bet: LBJ, Vietnam, and the 1968 Election* (Lanham, Md.: Rowman & Littlefield, 2005), 55–56; "Advocate & Judge," *Time*, February 2, 1968, 19–20; "Wilbur the Willful," *Time*, February 9, 1968, 17–18; "Some Modest Proposals," *Newsweek*, February 19, 1968, 24–25; "Ev's Mutation," *Time*, March 8, 1968, 26.

22. "Signal in the Night," *Newsweek*, March 18, 1968, 15–16; Joseph Califano, *The Triumph and Tragedy of Lyndon Johnson: The White House Years* (College Station: Texas A&M Press, 2000), 260–62.

23. "The Impotence of Power," *Time*, February 2, 1968, 11–12; "A New Belligerence," *Time*, February 2, 1968, 22–25; "Prometheus Bound," *Newsweek*, February 5, 1968, 15–24; Walter Lippman, "A Crumbling Policy," *Newsweek*, February 12, 1968, 21; "Pueblo Crisis: An Impossible Choice?," *Newsweek*, February 12, 1968, 33–34; Christian, *President Steps Down*, 138–41; Richard H. Rovere, "Letter from Washington," *New Yorker*, February 3, 1968, 85–90.

24. Lingley, *LBJ's 1968*, 33–54; "Showdown at Khe Sanh," *Time*, February 2, 1968, 25–26; "How Goes the War?," *Newsweek*, January 1, 1968, 17–26; Hugh Sidey, "In Crisis: 'Feelin', Smellin', Knowin',"" *Life*, February 9, 1968, 32B; "If War Spreads Now in Asia . . . ," *U.S. News & World Report*, January 15, 1968, 29–31; "Now a Bigger War Threat in Asia?," *U.S. News & World Report*, February 5, 1968, 23–26; "If Reds Open Up a 'Second Front' in Korea," *U.S. News & World Report*, February 26, 1968, 31–32.

25. "The General's Gamble," *Time*, February 9, 1968, 22–32; "Picking Up the Pieces," *Time*, February 16, 1968, 32–38; "Bracing for More," *Time*, February 23, 1968, 31–33; "Hanoi Attacks," *Newsweek*, February 12, 1968, 23–32; "Man on the Spot," *Newsweek*, February 19, 1968, 33–43; "The Tet Offensive: How They Did It," *Newsweek*, March 11, 1968, 64–66; "As Climax Mounts in Vietnam," *U.S. News & World Report*, February 12, 1968, 23–24; "Big Setback for U.S. in Countryside," *U.S. News & World Report*, March 4, 1968, 25–26.

26. "More of the Same Won't Do," *Newsweek*, March 18, 1968, 25; "Critical Season," *Time*, March 1, 1968, 11–12; "Westmoreland's Strategy: Will It Pass the Acid Test?," *U.S. News & World Report*, February 12, 1968, 13; Walter Lippman, "Defeat," *Newsweek*, March 11, 1968, 25; Charles Kaiser, *1968 in America: Music, Politics, Chaos, Counterculture, and the Shaping of a Generation* (New York: Grove Press, 1988), 68–78; "'Living Room War'—Impact of TV," *U.S. News & World Report*, March 4, 1968, 28–29; "Walter Cronkite: The Most Trusted Man," *Columbia Journalism Review* 40, no. 4 (November/December 2001): 64; LaFeber, *Deadly Bet*, 27–31.

27. "Is There a Way Out of the War?," *U.S. News & World Report*, February 26, 1968, 33–34; Max Frankel, "Johnson Holds Reins," *New York Times*, February 10, 1968, 1; Hugh Sidey, "Shaken Assumptions about the War," *Life*, February 16, 1968, 32B; Hugh Sidey, "Searching for a Sense of the Battle," *Life*, March 1, 1968, 30B; "How the President Sees the War," *New York Times*, February 25, 1968, E1; "On the Move with Lyndon Johnson," *U.S. News & World Report*, March 4, 1968, 14–15; "Johnson Sons-in-Law to Join Military Units," *New York Times*, March 17, 1968, 3; "Thin Green Line," *Time*, February 23, 1968, 15–18; "From Duty, with Strength," *Time*, March 22, 1968, 21; "Watching and Waiting," *Newsweek*, February 26, 1968, 21–22.

28. William C. Westmoreland, *A Soldier Reports* (1976; reprint, New York: Da Capo Press, 1989), 310–62; Karnow, *Vietnam*, 562–65; "A Showdown in Vietnam?,"

U.S. News & World Report, February 19, 1968, 35–38; "General Westmoreland: Hero or Scapegoat in the War?," *U.S. News & World Report*, February 26, 1968, 19; "As the War's Toll Grows . . . New Pressure for More U.S. Troops," *U.S. News & World Report*, March 4, 1968, 6; "Million Americans Soon in Vietnam?," *U.S. News & World Report*, March 18, 1968, 35–38; "Hard Facts about the Vietnam War," *U.S. News & World Report*, March 25, 1968, 36–39; "The General's Biggest Battle," *Time*, February 16, 1968, 19–20.

29. "Rusk vs. Senators: The War Explained," *U.S. News & World Report*, March 25, 1968, 74–78; "Debate in a Vacuum," *Time*, March 15, 1968, 13–14; "Standoff," *Time*, March 22, 1968, 20–21; "In These Long Nights We Pray," *Newsweek*, February 12, 1968, 39–40; "The War: More Men, More Doubts," *Newsweek*, March 4, 1968, 19–20; "Time of Decisions," *Newsweek*, March 11, 1968, 32; "And from the White House—Silence," *Newsweek*, March 18, 1968, 45; "Growing Dissent," *Newsweek*, March 25, 1968, 33–36.

30. Robert S. McNamara, *In Retrospect: The Tragedy and Lessons of Vietnam* (New York: Times Books, 1995), 266–317; James Reston, "Washington: Back to the Alamo," *New York Times*, December 3, 1967, 266; Karnow, *Vietnam*, 523–25.

31. "Changing of the Guard," *Newsweek*, March 11, 1968, 35; "Calling the Handyman," *Time*, January 26, 1968, 14–15; Max Frankel, "Johnson Names Clark Clifford to Head Defense," *New York Times*, January 20, 1968, 1; Valenti, *Very Human President*, 229–30; "Clifford Takes Over," *Time*, March 8, 1968, 17–19; "Why LBJ Picked Clark Clifford to Run the Pentagon," *U.S. News & World Report*, January 29, 1968, 14; "Clark Clifford for the Defense," *Newsweek*, January 29, 1968, 15–16.

32. "The Clifford Era," *Newsweek*, July 22, 1968, 28–29; "When LBJ Had to Choose on Vietnam," *U.S. News & World Report*, April 15, 1968, 52; Charles Roberts, "Inside Story: LBJ's Switch on Vietnam," *Newsweek*, March 10, 1969, 32–33; Merle Miller, *Lyndon: An Oral Biography* (New York: G. P. Putnam's Sons, 1980), 502–3; Clark Clifford with Richard Holbrooke, *Counsel to the President: A Memoir* (New York: Random House, 1991), 473–83, 488–89, 496–97.

33. Walter Isaacson and Evan Thomas, *The Wise Men: Six Friends and the World They Made* (New York: Simon and Schuster, 1986), 676–703; Schandler, *Unmaking of a President*, 256–65; Johnson, *Vantage Point*, 416–24; Clifford with Holbrooke, *Counsel to the President*, 511–19.

34. Isaacson and Thomas, *Wise Men*, 695; Johnson, *White House Diary*, 638; Clifford with Holbrooke, *Counsel to the President*, 515–16.

35. Clifford with Holbrooke, *Counsel to the President*, 519–22; Dean Rusk, as told to Richard Rusk, *As I Saw It* (New York: Norton, 1990), 466, 477–83.

36. McPherson, *Political Education*, 437–38.

37. "Why He Did It—What Now," *Newsweek*, April 15, 1968, 42–43; "Why Johnson Withdrew," *U.S. News & World Report*, April 15, 1968, 39–41; "Why LBJ Is Quitting," *U.S. News & World Report*, July 22, 1968, 25–27; Reedy, *Lyndon B. Johnson*, 56; Valenti, *Very Human President*, 154–55; Miller, *Lyndon*, 496–97; Theodore H. White, *The Making of the President, 1968* (New York: Atheneum, 1969), 118–19; McPherson, *Political Education*, 427–48.

38. Max Frankel, "Johnson Pullout Conceived in '65," *New York Times*, April 2, 1968, 1; Johnson, *Vantage Point*, 427–31; Johnson, *White House Diary*, 573, 611–12; Charles Ashman, *Connally: The Adventures of Big Bad John* (New York: William

Morrow, 1974), 136–37; Tom Lambert, "Turning Point for Decision Came in Westmoreland Talk," *Los Angeles Times*, April 1, 1968, 1; Longley, *LBJ's 1968*, 18–22; Sidey,
"Surrender of Power," 32; Miller, *Lyndon*, 498–99.

39. "The Fight to Dump LBJ," *Newsweek*, March 25, 1968, 21–22; "'That Man' and
'That Boy,'" *Newsweek*, March 20, 1967, 25–26; Evan Thomas, *Robert Kennedy: His Life*
(New York: Touchstone, 2000), 98–99; Jeff Shesol, *Mutual Contempt: Lyndon Johnson,
Robert Kennedy, and the Feud That Defined a Decade* (New York: Norton, 1997), 66;
Kearns, *Lyndon Johnson and the American Dream*, 259, 343.

40. Kearns, *Lyndon Johnson and the American Dream*, 343–48.

41. Sidey, "Surrender of Power," 30–33; Pearson, "Ghosts That Haunted LBJ," 25–29;
Miller, *Lyndon*, 510–11; Warren Weaver, "Impact on McCarthy," *New York Times*,
April 1, 1968, 28.

42. "The Renunciation," *Time*, April 12, 1968, 22–26; "When Johnson Bowed Out—
Speech That Rocked the World," *U.S. News & World Report*, April 15, 1968, 98–102;
Sidey, "Surrender of Power," 33.

43. Tom Wicker, "Johnson Says He Won't Run," *New York Times*, April 1, 1968, 1;
Robert J. Donovan, "Withdrawal Announcement Captures Nation by Surprise," *Los
Angeles Times*, April 1, 1968, 1; Kenneth Crawford, "The Credibility Myth," *Newsweek*,
April 29, 1968, 32; Alan L. Otten, "How Irrevocable?," *Wall Street Journal*, April 17,
1968, 18; Dwight McDonald, "Politics," *Esquire*, July 1968, 8–12, 134; "The President's
Decision," *Los Angeles Times*, April 2, 1968, B4; Tom Wicker, "In the Nation: The First
and the Last," *New York Times*, April 2, 1968, 46; "The Presidency: A New Dimension,"
Life, April 12, 1968, 4.

44. "Johnson, Relaxed, Talks of Returning to Ranch," *New York Times*, April 3,
1968, 28; "The Liberated President," *New York Times*, April 7, 1968, E12; Max Frankel,
"The Liberation of Lyndon Johnson," *New York Times*, April 14, 1968, E1; Longley,
LBJ's 1968, 101–4; Mann, *Grand Delusion*, 603–5; "L.B.J., Revised Edition," *Time*,
April 12, 1968, 49; "Shadow and Substance," *Reporter*, April 18, 1968, 10–12; Richard
Rovere, "Letter from Washington," *New Yorker*, April 13, 1968, 145–49; "Most Happy
Fella," *New Republic*, April 23, 1968, 4.

CHAPTER TWO

1. Robert B. Semple, "Nixon's Campaign Is Stately, Dignified, Proud—and Slow,"
New York Times, February 18, 1968, 164; "What's New in Nixon?," *New Republic*,
March 9, 1968, 4; Loudon Wainwright, "One More Try for the Heights," *Life*, March 1,
1968, 60–68.

2. "Nixon Comes On Strong," *Business Week*, March 30, 1968, 31–33.

3. Jules Witcover, *The Resurrection of Richard Nixon* (New York: G. P. Putnam's
Sons, 1970), 249–50; Patrick K. Buchanan, "An Outline of Strategy," in *The Selling
of the President*, by Joe McGinniss (1969; reprint, New York: Penguin, 1988), 221–25;
"Nixon Pulls Crowds in New Hampshire," *Christian Science Monitor*, February 10,
1968, 12; Neal B. Freeman, "Armageddon in New Hampshire," *National Review*, February 13, 1968, 126–28; "Report from the Front," *Newsweek*, March 4, 1968, 22.

4. Jules Witcover, *The Year the Dream Died: Revisiting 1968 in America* (New York:
Warner Books, 1997), 86–87.

5. Theodore H. White, *The Making of the President, 1960* (1961; reprint, Franklin Center, Pa.: Franklin Library, 1987), 267, 283–94, 302–7, 316–17, 336–38; Witcover, *Resurrection of Richard Nixon*, 16–24; Lawrence O'Donnell, *Playing with Fire: The 1968 Election and the Transformation of American Politics* (New York: Penguin, 2017), 139–40.

6. Richard M. Nixon, *Six Crises* (Garden City, N.Y.: Doubleday, 1962); Anthony Summers with Robbyn Swan, *The Arrogance of Power: The Secret World of Richard Nixon* (New York: Viking, 2000), 92–93, 236; Tom Wicker, *One of Us: Richard Nixon and the American Dream* (New York: Random House, 1991), 22–31, 427, 651–54; Raymond Price, *With Nixon* (New York: Viking, 1977), 19, 29; Stewart Alsop, "Living with Two Nixons," *Newsweek*, August 19, 1968, 92; Isidore Silver, "True-Blue Dick," *Commonweal*, April 3, 1968, 65–68.

7. John A. Farrell, *Richard Nixon: The Life* (New York: Doubleday, 2017), 80–209; Evan Thomas, *Being Nixon: A Man Divided* (New York: Random House, 2015), 3–90; David Abrahamsen, *Nixon vs. Nixon: An Emotional Tragedy* (New York: Farrar, Straus and Giroux, 1977), 110–12, 164–65.

8. Farrell, *Richard Nixon*, 210–311; Rick Perlstein, *Nixonland: The Rise of a President and the Fracturing of America* (New York: Scribner, 2008), 44–50.

9. Tim Weiner, *One Man against the World: The Tragedy of Richard Nixon* (New York: Henry Holt, 2015), 14–15; Stephen E. Ambrose, *The Triumph of a Politician, 1962–1972*, vol. 2 of *Nixon* (New York: Simon and Schuster, 1989), 12–15, 39–50; Patrick J. Buchanan, *The Greatest Comeback: How Richard Nixon Rose from Defeat to Create the New Majority* (New York: Crown Forum, 2014), 21, 204; John Bird, "Will He or Won't He?," *Saturday Evening Post*, March 1, 1964, 21–23; Witcover, *Resurrection of Richard Nixon*, 68–95.

10. Mary C. Brennan, *Turning Right in the Sixties: The Conservative Capture of the GOP* (Chapel Hill: University of North Carolina Press, 1995), 60–103; Rick Perlstein, *Before the Storm: Barry Goldwater and the Unmaking of the American Consensus* (2001; reprint, New York: Nation Books, 2009), 371–516; Theodore H. White, *The Making of the President, 1964* (New York: Atheneum, 1965), 190–220, 380–86.

11. Witcover, *Resurrection of Richard Nixon*, 98–103; Perlstein, *Nixonland*, 17–18; Theodore H. White, *The Making of the President, 1968* (New York: Atheneum, 1969), 47–52; Garry Wills, *Nixon Agonistes: The Crisis of the Self-Made Man* (Boston: Houghton Mifflin, 1970), 4–5, 306–7; Richard Nixon, *RN: The Memoirs of Richard Nixon* (New York: Grosset & Dunlap, 1978), 267–68.

12. "Secrets of the Nixon Comeback: Years of Hard Work," *U.S. News & World Report*, August 19, 1968, 30–31; Ambrose, *Triumph of a Politician*, 86–90; Stephen C. Shadegg, *Winning's a Lot More Fun* (London: Macmillan, 1969), 64–69; Buchanan, *Greatest Comeback*, 48–80; "Old Pro in Action," *Newsweek*, September 5, 1966, 18–19; "Nixon: '66 Campaigner with '68 in Mind," *U.S. News & World Report*, September 5, 1966, 12; Tom Wicker, "The Unhappy Warriors," *Atlantic*, April 1966, 76–77.

13. Perlstein, *Nixonland*, 137–40, 160–62; "Mr. Nixon Advises Mr. Kennedy," *National Review*, November 15, 1966, 1146; "Mr. Nixon Comes to Town," *America*, September 17, 1966, 273; "Mr. Nixon Back in Business," *America*, November 19, 1966, 647; George Christian, *The President Steps Down: A Personal Memoir of the Transfer of Power* (New York: Macmillan, 1970), 154–56.

14. Warren Weaver, "Four Hearties of the Good Ship G.O.P.," *New York Times Magazine*, November 27, 1966; "LBJ Likes Nixon," *New Republic*, December 16, 1967, 4; William Safire, *Before the Fall: An Inside View of the Pre-Watergate White House* (Garden City, N.Y.: Doubleday, 1975), 37–41.

15. "Will It Be Nixon vs. LBJ in '68?," *U.S. News & World Report*, October 3, 1966, 54–58; Jules Witcover, "Nixon for President in '68?," *Saturday Evening Post*, February 25, 1967, 93–97; Meg Greenfield, "My Generation Is Missing," *Reporter*, May 4, 1967, 35–37; Stephen Hess and David S. Broder, "What Keeps Nixon Running," *Harper's*, August 1967, 56–67; James Jackson Kilpatrick, "Crisis Seven," *National Review*, November 14, 1967, 1263–74; Fletcher Knebel, "The Puzzling Case of Richard Nixon," *Look*, March 5, 1968, 67–76; Garry Wills, "What Makes the Newest Nixon Run?," *Esquire*, May 1968, 89–96, 196; Robert B. Semple, "It's Time Again for the Nixon Phenomenon," *New York Times Magazine*, January 21, 1968, 24, 77–84.

16. Ambrose, *Triumph of a Politician*, 102–17; Safire, *Before the Fall*, 42–51; Buchanan, *Greatest Comeback*, 162–94; Richard H. Rovere, "Letter from Washington," *New Yorker*, April 22, 1967, 153–60; "On the Rim," *Time*, March 24, 1967, 16; "The Morning Line," *Newsweek*, April 3. 1967, 33–34; "Around the World, a Block Away," *Time*, May 19, 1967, 29–30; Jules Witcover, "Nixon: The Reentry Problem," *New Republic*, June 17, 1967, 11–12.

17. "Forever Amber," *Newsweek*, March 27, 1967, 31–32; "Dick's Lucky Palm," *Time*, June 2, 1967, 15; Michael Nelson, *Resilient America: Electing Nixon in 1968, Channeling Dissent, and Dividing Government* (Lawrence: University Press of Kansas, 2014), 117–20; Leonard Garment, *Crazy Rhythm: My Journey from Brooklyn, Jazz, and Wall Street to Nixon's White House, Watergate, and Beyond* (New York: Times Books, 1997), 99–100, 118–19; Neal B. Freeman, "The Men around Nixon," *National Review*, October 17, 1967, 1118–19; Richard M. Nixon, "Asia after Viet Nam," *Foreign Affairs* 46 (October 1967): 111–25; Richard M. Nixon, "Asia after Vietnam," *Reader's Digest*, March 1968, 88–92; Richard M. Nixon, "What Has Happened to America," *Reader's Digest*, October 1967, 49–54.

18. "Nixon Tells How '68 Race Stands," *U.S. News & World Report*, November 20, 1967, 74–80; Hugh Sidey, "Philosophy of Office and the Ache of Ambition," *Life*, November 3, 1967, 30; "See Dick Run," *Newsweek*, December 25, 1967, 17–18; Goodman Ace, "A Dab of Powder, a Dab of Paint," *Saturday Review*, December 16, 1967, 6; A. James Reichley, "How Nixon Plans to Bring It Off," *Fortune*, December 1967, 124–27, 156–68; Gilbert A. Harrison, "Richard Nixon's Return Engagement," *New Republic*, November 4, 1967, 11–12; Stewart Alsop, "Richard Nixon and the Locked Door," *Saturday Evening Post*, December 2, 1967, 19.

19. Nixon, *RN*, 290–94; Summers with Swan, *Arrogance of Power*, 93, 118, 220–21, 233; Ambrose, *Triumph of a Politician*, 131–32; Mary C. Brennan, *Pat Nixon: Embattled First Lady* (Lawrence: University Press of Kansas, 2011), 94–96.

20. "Nixon Announces for Presidency," *New York Times*, February 2, 1968, 1.

21. "Nixon Maps Plans to Enter Primary Races in Five Other States," *Christian Science Monitor*, February 5, 1968, 7; Michael A. Cohen, *American Maelstrom: The 1968 Election and the Politics of Division* (New York: Oxford University Press, 2016), 116–17; Shadegg, *Winning's a Lot More Fun*, 74–77; "Nixon's Views in a Nutshell," *U.S. News &*

World Report, March 11, 1968, 43–44; Robert B. Semple, "A Familiar Face, but a New Script," *New York Times*, February 4, 1968, E5.

22. Witcover, *Resurrection of Richard Nixon*, 232–37; "Nixon's Dream," *Time*, February 9, 1968, 20–21; "Richard the Relentless," *Newsweek*, February 12, 1968, 40–41; "Stately Pace v. Aggressive Courtship," *Time*, March 1, 1968, 14–15.

23. Witcover, *Resurrection of Richard Nixon*, 236–40; Garment, *Crazy Rhythm*, 128–33.

24. White, *Making of the President, 1968*, 153–56; McGinniss, *Selling of the President*, 36–40.

25. Robert B. Semple Jr., "Nixon Forecasts Victory in Fall," *New York Times*, March 13, 1968, 1; "And Then There Was Nixon," *Newsweek*, March 11, 1968, 27–32; "Is Nixon Now Sure of Nomination?," *U.S. News & World Report*, March 11, 1968, 38–41; "Luxury of Choice," *Reporter*, March 21, 1968, 10–11; "Nixon's New Image, Rocky's New Clothes," *Time*, March 22, 1968, 19–20; "Nixon's Triumph," *Newsweek*, March 25, 1968, 32–33; "Granite Voices," *National Review*, March 26, 1968, 274; "We're Comfortable Now," *Newsweek*, April 8, 1968, 38–43; Robert B. Semple Jr., "Nixon Looks for Opponents," *New York Times*, April 7, 1968, E2.

26. Theodore C. Sorensen, "Of Course the War Will Be a Campaign Issue," *New York Times Magazine*, March 17, 1968, 30–31, 120–26; "Congress Hears from Home," *U.S. News & World Report*, March 4, 1968, 32–34.

27. "The Persistent Suitor," *New York Times*, February 4, 1968, E12; "The Crucial Test," *Time*, February 16, 1968, 21–22; "The Nixon Record," *U.S. News & World Report*, July 15, 1968, 48–52; Robert Mann, *A Grand Delusion: America's Descent into Vietnam* (New York: Basic Books, 2001), 606–7; Robert B. Semple, "Nixon Vows to End War with a 'New Leadership,'" *New York Times*, March 6, 1968, 11.

28. Robert B. Semple, "Nixon Withholds His Peace Ideas," *New York Times*, March 11, 1968, 1; Rowland Evans and Robert Novak, "Nixon's 'End the War' Pledge Seen as Ambiguous but Aimed at Doves," *Washington Post, Times Herald*, March 8, 1968, A21; Summers with Swan, *Arrogance of Power*, 294–95; "Mr. Nixon's Campaign," *Christian Science Monitor*, March 8, 1968, 1; "Nixon on the War," *New Republic*, March 16, 1968, 4; "The Nixon View," *Time*, April 5, 1968, 21–22; Richard J. Whalen, *Catch the Falling Flag: A Republican's Challenge to His Party* (Boston: Houghton Mifflin, 1972), 130–40.

29. Clayton Knowles, "Nixon Delays War Statement," *New York Times*, April 2, 1968, 1; Whalen, *Catch the Falling Flag*, 140–44.

30. Robert B. Semple, "Nixon's Strategy under Study," *New York Times*, April 4, 1968, 20; "Dick's Dilemma," *Newsweek*, April 15, 1968, 49–50; "As Nixon Sees the Race at This Point," *U.S. News & World Report*, May 13, 1968, 38–39.

31. "Violence & History," *Time*, April 19, 1968, 44–45; "Seven Days in April," *Newsweek*, April 15, 1968, 26; "Hot and Cool," *Newsweek*, April 22, 1968, 24–25; "An Hour of Need," *Time*, April 12, 1968, 17–21; "King Is the Man, Oh Lord," *Newsweek*, April 15, 1968, 34–38; Perlstein, *Nixonland*, 250–63.

32. Whalen, *Catch the Falling Flag*, 148–49; Garment, *Crazy Rhythm*, 124–25; "Leaders at Rites," *New York Times*, April 10, 1968, 1; "King's Last March," *Time*, April 19, 1968, 18.

33. Wicker, *One of Us*, 327; Whalen, *Catch the Falling Flag*, 168–69; Clay Risen, *A Nation on Fire: America in the Wake of the King Assassination* (New York: John Wiley & Sons, 2009), 54–58, 63–67, 105–7, 116–39; "Take Everything You Need, Baby," *Newsweek*, April 15, 1968, 31–33; "Mobs Run Wild in the Nation's Capital," *U.S. News & World Report*, April 15, 1968, 8–10; "More Violence and Race War?," *U.S. News & World Report*, April 15, 1968, 31–34; "Aftermath of Riots—What's Next?," *U.S. News & World Report*, April 22, 1968, 27–29; "The Second Sacking of Washington," *U.S. News & World Report*, April 22, 1968, 32–37; "Insurrection: Outlook in U.S.," *U.S. News & World Report*, April 29, 1968, 38–41; "Violence, Dissent, Rebellion—Warning by Top Prosecutor," *U.S. News & World Report*, April 29, 1968, 15; "How Riots Are Stirred Up," *U.S. News & World Report*, May 6, 1968, 68–71; David Lawrence, "How to Fight a Domestic War," *U.S. News & World Report*, May 6, 1968, 112; "A Threat of Anarchy in Nation's Capital," *U.S. News & World Report*, May 20, 1968, 47–49; "Tragedy of Nation's Capital: A Story of Crime and Fear," *U.S. News & World Report*, July 29, 1968, 46–49.

34. David Burnham, "Nixon Puts Rights Ahead of Vietnam," *New York Times*, December 9, 1967, 1; Robert B. Semple, "Nixon Scores Panel for 'Undue' Stress on White Racism," *New York Times*, March 7, 1968, 1; Robert B. Semple, "Nixon Decries 'Lawless Society' and Urges Limited Wiretapping," *New York Times*, May 9, 1968, 1; "Three Candidates Speak Out on Three Big Issues," *U.S. News & World Report*, May 20, 1968, 98–99; Robert L. Asher, "Nixon Labels D.C. a 'Crime Capital,' Blames Johnson," *Washington Post, Times Herald*, June 23, 1968, A1.

35. Michael W. Flamm, *Law and Order: Street Crime, Civil Unrest, and the Crisis of Liberalism in the 1960s* (New York: Columbia University Press, 2005), 1–11, 31–103.

36. Timothy N. Thurber, *Republicans and Race: The GOP's Frayed Relationship with African Americans, 1945–1974* (Lawrence: University Press of Kansas, 2013), 265–72; Joshua D. Farrington, *Black Republicans and the Transformation of the GOP* (Philadelphia: University of Pennsylvania Press, 2016), 170–78.

37. "Nixon on Racial Accommodation," *Time*, May 3, 1968, 21; Tom Wicker, "In the Nation: A Coalition for What?," *New York Times*, May 19, 1968, E12; "Mr. Nixon's New Alignment," *New York Times*, May 21, 1968, 46; "Nixon's 'New' Coalition," *Nation*, June 3, 1968, 715–16; "Campaigning: Nixon," *Atlantic*, July 1968, 4–8; "Nixon," *National Review*, June 4, 1968, 533–34.

38. "Siege on Morningside Heights," *Time*, May 3, 1968, 48–49; "Columbia at Bay," *Newsweek*, May 6, 1968, 40–53; "Crisis at Columbia's Campus," *U.S. News & World Report*, May 13, 1968, 8–10; "The End of a Siege—and an Era," *Newsweek*, May 13, 1968, 59–62; "Toward Reform at Columbia," *Time*, May 17, 1968, 58–59; Charles Kaiser, *1968 in America: Music, Politics, Chaos, Counterculture, and the Shaping of a Generation* (New York: Grove Press, 1988), 155–68; Mark Kurlansky, *1968: The Year That Rocked the World* (New York: Ballantine, 2004), 178–208.

39. "Nixon," *National Review*, June 4, 1968, 533–34; "Nixon Calls Uprising at Columbia Disgrace," *Washington Post, Times Herald*, May 5, 1968, A6; Flamm, *Law and Order*, 1–11.

40. Wills, *Nixon Agonistes*, 53–54; Perlstein, *Nixonland*, 212–13, 277–79.

41. Wicker, *One of Us*, 686–87.

CHAPTER THREE

1. "A Voice for Dissent," *Time*, December 8, 1967, 21–22; Gerald Moore, "They All Love Gene until He Takes the Stump," *Life*, January 19, 1968, 50B–54; Tom Wells, *The War Within: America's Battle over Vietnam* (Berkeley: University of California Press, 1994), 224–25; William Chafe, *Never Stop Running: Allard Lowenstein and the Struggle to Save American Liberalism* (Princeton, N.J.: Princeton University Press, 1998), 278–79; Roger Kahn, "The Revolt against LBJ," *Saturday Evening Post*, February 10, 1968, 17–21.

2. Moore, "They All Love Gene until He Takes the Stump," 50B–52; "McCarthy in Chicago," *New Republic*, December 16, 1967, 9–11.

3. Kahn, "Revolt against LBJ," 20; Arthur Herzog, *McCarthy for President* (New York: Viking, 1969), 76–77; Eugene J. McCarthy, *The Year of the People* (Garden City, N.Y.: Doubleday, 1969), 284–89; Andrew Kopkind, "The McCarthy Campaign," *Ramparts*, March 1968, 50–55; Moore, "They All Love Gene until He Takes the Stump," 52.

4. McCarthy, *Year of the People*, 58–59; Moore, "They All Love Gene until He Takes the Stump," 52.

5. David Murray, "New Support Is Pledged to McCarthy," *Washington Post, Times Herald*, December 4, 1967, A1, A14; Rowland Evans and Robert Novak, "Party's Dump-Johnson Branch Offers Little Aid to McCarthy," *Washington Post, Times Herald*, December 6, 1967, A29; "McCarthy in Chicago," 10–11; Moore, "They All Love Gene until He Takes the Stump," 52; David S. Broder, "McCarthy Rates Strong Contender in Several Primaries," *Washington Post, Times Herald*, December 2, 1967, 2; Godfrey Sperling Jr., "McCarthy Rallies War Critics," *Christian Science Monitor*, December 2, 1967, 1; Douglas Ireland, "Ready, Willing, and Able," *Commonweal*, December 22, 1967, 375–76.

6. "McCarthy in New York," *New Yorker*, March 2, 1968, 31–33; "The McCarthy Style," *New Republic*, December 23, 1967, 8–9; Michael C. Janeway, "Washington," *Atlantic*, January 1968, 4–12; David Halberstam, "McCarthy and the Divided Left," *Harper's*, March 1968, 33–44; William H. Honan, "A Would-Be Candidate for This Season," *New York Times Magazine*, December 10, 1967, 27, 36–37, 134–36; Shana Alexander, "McCarthy's Trojan Horse," *Life*, February 9, 1968, 21.

7. Dominic Sandbrook, *Eugene McCarthy: The Rise and Fall of American Liberalism* (New York: Knopf, 2004), 3–53.

8. Sandbrook, *Eugene McCarthy*, 53–93; Albert Eisele, *Almost to the Presidency: A Biography of Two American Politicians* (Blue Earth, Minn.: Piper Company, 1972), 109–34; John D. Morris, "The Other McCarthy," *New York Times Magazine*, August 8, 1954, SM16; Eugene J. McCarthy, "The State and Human Freedom," *Commonweal*, May 18, 1951, 135–37; Eugene J. McCarthy, "Morality in Government," *Commonweal*, December 14, 1951; Eugene J. McCarthy, "The Christian in Politics," *Commonweal*, August 1, 1954, 626–28; Eugene J. McCarthy, "An Inquiry into Political Morality," *New York Times Magazine*, July 1, 1962, 7, 22; Eugene J. McCarthy, "The Liberal: What He Is and Isn't," *New York Times Magazine*, September 1, 1963, 8, 16; Marshall Smelser, "Senator Eugene McCarthy," *Harper's*, June 1964, 76–78; Eugene J.

McCarthy, "My Hopes for the Democrats," *Saturday Review*, November 5, 1966, 21–23, 50; Eugene McCarthy, *Up 'til Now: A Memoir* (San Diego: Harcourt Brace Jovanovich, 1987), 53–56; Eugene J. McCarthy, *Frontiers in American Democracy* (Cleveland: World Publishing, 1960), 106.

9. Sandbrook, *Eugene McCarthy*, 99–116; Eisele, *Almost to the Presidency*, 217–21, 256–57; Lewis Chester, Geoffrey Hodgson, and Bruce Page, *An American Melodrama: The Presidential Campaign of 1968* (New York: Viking, 1969), 74–75; Michael Nelson, *Resilient America: Electing Nixon in 1968, Channeling Dissent, and Dividing Government* (Lawrence: University Press of Kansas, 2014), 25.

10. McCarthy, *Up 'til Now*, 170–84; McCarthy, *Year of the People*, 17–50; Eugene McCarthy, "The CIA Is Getting out of Hand," *Saturday Evening Post*, February 29, 1964, 6; Eugene McCarthy, "Arms and the Man Who Sells Them," *Atlantic Monthly*, October 1967, 82–86; Eugene J. McCarthy, *The Limits of Power: America's Role in the World* (New York: Holt, Rinehart and Winston, 1967).

11. Eugene J. McCarthy, "Why I'm Battling LBJ," *Look*, February 6, 1968, 22–29; Eugene J. McCarthy, "Why I Want the Job," *Look*, August 20, 1968, 33; "Interview with McCarthy," *America*, December 16, 1967, 734–39; "Pull Out or Stay in Vietnam," *U.S. News & World Report*, February 5, 1968, 28–31; Michael A. Cohen, *American Maelstrom: The 1968 Election and the Politics of Division* (New York: Oxford University Press, 2016), 55–60.

12. "Limited Candidate," *Time*, November 17, 1967, 30; "As LBJ's Political Troubles Mount," *U.S. News & World Report*, November 20, 1967, 8; Eugene McCarthy, "The Young People Revitalized America," *Look*, December 30, 1969, 32; Eugene McCarthy, "An Opinion," *Mademoiselle*, April 1968, 98; "Mrs. Eugene McCarthy Tells Why 'My Son Is a Conscientious Objector,'" *Good Housekeeping*, November 1969, 98–99, 208; Betty Rolin, "Mary McCarthy: The Senator's Spunky Daughter," *Look*, May 28, 1968, M21–M22; "Face to Face with a Girl Who Is Trying to Get Her Father Elected President," *Seventeen*, June 1968, 107; Abigail McCarthy, *Private Faces/Public Places* (Garden City, N.Y.: Doubleday, 1972), 286–87, 294; Haynes Johnson, "McCarthy," *Good Housekeeping*, August 1968, 67.

13. Herzog, *McCarthy for President*, 15–36; "The McCarthy Candidacy," *Commonweal*, November 17, 1967, 193–94; "Gene McCarthy," *New Republic*, November 18, 1967, 7–8; E. W. Kenworthy, "Eugene McCarthy Hits the Road," *New Republic*, November 25, 1967, 11–13; Walter Lippmann, "Eugene McCarthy's Mission," *Newsweek*, December 18, 1967, 25.

14. Rhodri Jeffreys-Jones, *Peace Now! American Society and the Ending of the Vietnam War* (New Haven: Yale University Press, 1999), 61–67; Wells, *War Within*, 9–121; James Miller, *"Democracy Is in the Streets": From Port Huron to the Siege of Chicago* (New York: Simon and Schuster, 1987), 218–59.

15. Wells, *War Within*, 115–222.

16. Arthur Schlesinger Jr., "Joe College Is Dead," *Saturday Evening Post*, September 23, 1968, 24–27, 66–73; "What's a Mother to Do?," *Newsweek*, September 23, 1968, 68–71; "Why Those Students Are Protesting," *Time*, May 3, 1968, 24–25; "Campus Rebels: Who, Why, What," *Newsweek*, September 30, 1968, 63–68; "The Dissenters," *Time*, April 5, 1968, 69; "How Good Is the Megaversity?," *Newsweek*, February 26,

1968, 78–82; "Why Students Revolt," *U.S. News & World Report*, June 10, 1968, 36–38; "The Failing University," *Newsweek*, January 22, 1968, 59; "The Cynical Idealists of '68," *Time*, June 7, 1968, 78–83.

17. Mark Kurlansky, *1968: The Year That Rocked the World* (New York: Ballantine, 2004); David Caute, *The Year of the Barricades: A Journey through 1968* (New York: Harper and Row, 1988); Kirkpatrick Sale, *SDS* (New York: Random House, 1973), 345–458; "'Hell No!' at Harvard," *Newsweek*, January 29, 1968, 26; "Student Callup," *Newsweek*, May 13, 1968, 33–34; "Who Are the SDS?," *Newsweek*, May 20, 1968, 62–63; "Sniffing the Devil's Presence," *Time*, June 2, 1968, 42.

18. Chafe, *Never Stop Running*, 262–69; Richard T. Stout, *People* (New York: Harper and Row, 1970), 76, 122–29; Bailey Laird, "A Political Fiction," *New Yorker*, September 16, 1967, 42–46; "Hitched to LBJ?," *New Republic*, September 30, 1967, 1, 5–11; Steven V. Roberts, "The Dump-Johnson Movement," *Commonweal*, October 27, 1967, 106–7; Max Ascoli, "That Man in the White House," *Reporter*, November 2, 1967, 12–13; Kahn, "Revolt against LBJ," 17–18.

19. "Now Is the Time," *New Republic*, December 9, 1967, 7–9; "Colleagues' Silence Irks McCarthy," *Washington Post, Times Herald*, January 6, 1968, A2; Rowland Evans and Robert Novak, "'Respectable Liberals' Shy from McCarthy Due to Peacenik Support," *Washington Post, Times Herald*, December 22, 1967, A15; "Schism on the Left," *Time*, February 23, 1968, 19; "ADAdvocacy," *Newsweek*, February 26, 1968, 25; Andrew Hacker, "The McCarthy Candidacy," *Commentary*, February 1968, 34–39; Kenneth Crawford, "The McCarthy Bomb," *Newsweek*, December 4, 1967, 32; Stewart Alsop, "Hedging, Waffling, and Straddling," *Saturday Evening Post*, January 27, 1968, 14; "McCarthy and the Campaign Problem," *New York Times*, January 14, 1968, E2; "McCarthy's Moral Imperative," *Wall Street Journal*, December 13, 1967, 18; Jack Newfield, "A Man for This Season?," *Commonweal*, December 29, 1967, 400–401.

20. Ward Just, "McCarthy Is Testing N.H. Support," *Washington Post*, December 15, 1967, A3; David Charles Hoeh, *1968, McCarthy, New Hampshire: I Hear America Singing* (Rochester, Minn.: Lone Oak Press, 1994), 45–132; "The Eagle & the Chickens," *Time*, February 23, 1968, 80–81; John H. Averill, "McCarthy Will Run in New Hampshire," *Los Angeles Times*, January 4, 1968, 1; Alan L. Otten, "Primary Time," *Wall Street Journal*, January 11, 1968, 10; Warren Weaver Jr., "As New Hampshire Goes," *New York Times*, February 4, 1968, E5; Eugene J. McCarthy, "How to Snow the Voters in New Hampshire," *New York Times*, December 30, 1979, SM4; "Long Hot Winter," *Time*, January 12, 1968, 13.

21. Nelson, *Resilient America*, 78; Herzog, *McCarthy for President*, 79–84; Hoeh, *1968, McCarthy, New Hampshire*, 182–87; Moore, "They All Love Gene until He Takes the Stump," 54; "'Don't Run Away,'" *Newsweek*, February 5, 1968, 27–28.

22. "Crusade of the Ballot Children," *Time*, March 22, 1968, 13; Stout, *People*, 162–65; Ben Stavis, *We Were the Campaign: New Hampshire to Chicago for McCarthy* (Boston: Beacon Press, 1969), 4–12.

23. Hoeh, *1968, McCarthy, New Hampshire*, 316–42; Eugene J. McCarthy, "Political Pioneers," *Seventeen*, September 1968, 143, 240, 371–73; Martha Tod Dudman, *Expecting to Fly: A Sixties Reckoning* (New York: Simon and Schuster, 2004), 58–59; Theodore H. White, *The Making of the President, 1968* (New York: Atheneum, 1969),

97–101; Paul R. Wieck, "McCarthy: Alive and Well in New Hampshire," *New Republic*, March 2, 1968, 15–17; "McCarthy Rides on 'Student Power,'" *New York Times*, March 10, 1968, E1.

24. Jeremy Larner, *Nobody Knows: Reflections on the McCarthy Campaign of 1968* (New York: Macmillan, 1970), 34–37; Charles Kaiser, *1968 in America: Music, Politics, Chaos, Counterculture, and the Shaping of a Generation* (New York: Grove Press, 1988), 81–86; Lawrence O'Donnell, *Playing with Fire: The 1968 Election and the Transformation of American Politics* (New York: Penguin, 2017), 129; Mary McGrory, "'We Do Our Thing' for Gene," *America*, April 20, 1968, 531; "The Making of Gene McCarthy," *Newsweek*, March 25, 1968, 22–24; Tom Wicker, "Report on the Phenomenon Named McCarthy," *New York Times Magazine*, August 25, 1968, 24–25, 78–80.

25. Richard Goodwin, *Remembering America: A Voice from the Sixties* (Boston: Little, Brown, 1988), 481–82, 488–90, 502–4; Hoeh, *1968, McCarthy, New Hampshire*, 382–84; Wicker, "Report on the Phenomenon Named McCarthy," 78–79.

26. Rowland Evans and Robert Novak, "Canvass in N.H. Town Indicates McCarthy May Rock White House," *Washington Post, Times Herald*, March 7, 1968, A21; E. W. Kenworthy, "A Johnson Drive May Aid McCarthy," *New York Times*, February 11, 1968, 35; Stout, *People*, 169–70.

27. "Be Clean for Gene," *Newsweek*, March 18, 1968, 51–52; Carl Bernstein, *A Woman in Charge: The Life of Hillary Rodham Clinton* (New York: Knopf, 2007), 54; Hoeh, *1968, McCarthy, New Hampshire*, 451–52.

28. "The Story New Hampshire Told," *U.S. News & World Report*, March 25, 1968, 40–41; "Poll Finds Vote for McCarthy Was Anti-Johnson, Not Antiwar," *New York Times*, March 18, 1968, 50; Walter Lippman, "War News and Politics," *Newsweek*, April 8, 1968, 31; "The Parties Respond," *New York Times*, March 17, 1968, E12; "Widening the '68 Contest," *Los Angeles Times*, March 15, 1968, A4.

29. Chester, Hodgson, and Page, *American Melodrama*, 376–79; Kenneth Crawford, "Old vs. New Politics," *Newsweek*, June 3, 1968, 38; Paul Woodring, "The Children's Crusade," *Saturday Review*, May 18, 1968, 80; "McCarthy's Victory," *Nation*, March 25, 1968, 394–95; Gerald W. Johnson, "Hurrah for the Children's Crusade," *New Republic*, April 20, 1968, 12; "How McCarthy Did It in New Hampshire," *New York Times*, March 17, 1968, E1; Paul R. Wieck, "Mr. Clean Makes It in New Hampshire," *New Republic*, March 23, 1968, 13–15.

30. Eisele, *Almost to the Presidency*, 299–300.

31. Eisele, *Almost to the Presidency*, 300; "McCarthy Favors Delay by Kennedy," *New York Times*, March 15, 1968, 1; "Unforeseen Eugene," *Time*, March 22, 1968, 13–18.

32. Goodwin, *Remembering America*, 509; Sandbrook, *Eugene McCarthy*, 191–92; "Is It Really McCarthy?," *Reporter*, December 14, 1967, 10; "Whose Stalking Horse?," *Newsweek*, December 18, 1967, 32–33; Rowland Evans and Robert Novak, "Kennedys Finagle in McCarthy Plans," *Washington Post, Times Herald*, December 10, 1967, B7.

33. Herzog, *McCarthy for President*, 106–10; Eisele, *Almost to the Presidency*, 300–302; McCarthy, *Private Faces/Public Places*, 366–75; Adam Clymer, *Edward M. Kennedy: A Biography* (New York: Perennial, 1999), 108–9.

34. Richard Harwood, "McCarthy Is Scornful of Rival," *Washington Post, Times Herald*, March 17, 1968, A1; E. W. Kenworthy, "McCarthy Bars Any Deal and Will

Continue Drive," *New York Times*, March 17, 1968, 1; "Tart, Tough & Telegenic," *Time*, March 22, 1968, 16.

35. Jules Witcover, *The Year the Dream Died: Revisiting 1968 in America* (New York: Warner Books, 1997), 130–31; "McCarthy Spurns Help by Kennedy," *New York Times*, March 18, 1968, 1; E. W. Kenworthy, "McCarthy Is Cool to Kennedy Move," *New York Times*, March 19, 1968, 1; "McCarthy Talks about Kennedy and the Issues," *U.S. News & World Report*, April 1, 1968, 36–38; Kenneth Crawford, "Political Grace," *Newsweek*, March 25, 1968, 38; Lawrence Van Gelder, "Survey Shows College Students Back McCarthy over Kennedy," *New York Times*, March 17, 1968, 1; Jo Ann Levine, "'Don't Run,'" *Christian Science Monitor*, March 16, 1968, 15; Paul R. Wieck, "Act II—Confrontation with Robert Kennedy," *New Republic*, April 20, 1968, 10–11; Steven V. Roberts, "McCarthy Campaign Enters New Phase," *Commonweal*, April 26, 1968, 165–67; Murray Kempton, "Why I'm for McCarthy," *New Republic*, May 25, 1968, 17–18.

36. Stout, *People*, 18–21; Patrick Anderson, "They Chant, 'We Want Gene!' (But Don't Forget Bobby)," *New York Times Magazine*, March 31, 1968, 26–27, 120–24.

37. Lucia Mouat, "McCarthy Students Win Political Spurs," *Christian Science Monitor*, April 4, 1968, 11; Herzog, *McCarthy for President*, 110–12; Goodwin, *Remembering America*, 521.

38. Paul R. Wieck, "Wisconsin's Response to an Honorable Man," *New Republic*, March 30, 1968, 16–19; Eugene J. McCarthy, "Topics: Thoughts on the Presidency," *New York Times*, March 30, 1968, 32; Tom Wicker, "In the Nation: McCarthy after Wisconsin," *New York Times*, April 4, 1968, 46; "McCarthy Defends Dissent on Vietnam," *New York Times*, February 22, 1968, 29; McCarthy, *Year of the People*, 96–100; Herzog, *McCarthy for President*, 114; Shana Alexander, "McCarthy: A Poet's Voice Stirs the Land," *Life*, April 12, 1968, 36–37.

39. "How McCarthy Scored," *Business Week*, April 6, 1968, 26; Lucia Mouat, "Oshkosh Catches Glimpse of Rival Campaigners," *Christian Science Monitor*, April 1, 1968, 3; Larner, *Nobody Knows*, 31–32; Herzog, *McCarthy for President*, 112–14; Stout, *People*, 195.

40. Audrey Weaver, "Blacks Sidestepped McCarthy," *Chicago Daily Defender*, April 13, 1968, 11; Rowland Evans and Robert Novak, "McCarthy Swamped by Johnson in Blue-Collar Milwaukee Areas," *Washington Post, Times Herald*, April 4, 1968, A21; "The McCarthy Phenomenon," *Nation*, April 8, 1968, 460; David Riesman, "McCarthy and Kennedy," *New Republic*, April 13, 1968, 21–23.

41. "Getting the Fever," *Newsweek*, April 8, 1968, 37; Witcover, *Year the Dream Died*, 137–38; "McCarthy Assails Johnson on Cities," *New York Times*, March 23, 1968, 12; E. W. Kenworthy, "McCarthy Shifts to the Issue of Race," *New York Times*, April 14, 1968, E3; "Calif. Minorities Are McCarthy Target," *Washington Post*, April 5, 1968, A2; Carl Greenberg, "McCarthy Cancels Rest of State Drive out of Respect to King," *Los Angeles Times*, April 6, 1968, B1; Eugene J. McCarthy, "Why Blacks Need Jobs in the Suburbs, Too," *Current*, August 1968, 44; Stout, *People*, 198–200, 212–18.

42. Larner, *Nobody Knows*, 28–41; Stavis, *We Were the Campaign*, 51–53, 132–34; Witcover, *Year the Dream Died*, 148–49.

43. Herzog, *McCarthy for President*, 119–20.

44. McCarthy, *Private Faces/Public Places*, 256–58; White, *Making of the President, 1968*, 143–45.

45. "First Vote with LBJ Not Running," *U.S. News & World Report*, April 15, 1968, 42; Paul Goodman, "In Praise of Populism," *Commentary*, June 1968, 25–30; Elmo Roper, "The Mood of America," *Saturday Review*, June 8, 1968, 30–31; Robert Lowell, "Why I'm for McCarthy," *New Republic*, April 13, 1968, 22.

CHAPTER FOUR

1. "'A Realistic Appraisal,'" *Newsweek*, April 1, 1968, 20–21; R. W. Apple Jr., "Friends Say Rockefeller Has Decided to Make Bid," *New York Times*, March 13, 1968, 1; Richard Reeves, "Governor to Run; He Will Disclose Plans Thursday," *New York Times*, May 19, 1968, 1; R. W. Apple Jr., "Morton Will Accept Role in Leadership of Rockefeller Race," *New York Times*, March 20, 1968, 1; Godfrey Sperling Jr., "GOP Doves Coo as Rockefeller Readies Race," *Christian Science Monitor*, March 21, 1968, 1; R. W. Apple Jr., "Rockefeller Not to Run, but Would Accept Draft," *New York Times*, March 22, 1968, 1; David Nevin, "Rockefeller: 'The Old Avidity Is Gone,'" *Life*, March 29, 1968, 33.

2. "Rockefeller Says He'd Accept Draft," *New York Times*, February 25, 1968, 1; "Rockefeller Drive Is Pushed," *Washington Post, Times Herald*, February 28, 1968, B2; "Romney Suddenly Quits; Rockefeller Reaffirms Availability to a Draft," *New York Times*, February 29, 1968, 1; James F. Clarity, "Rockefeller Could Open Campaign in 2 Weeks," *New York Times*, February 29, 1968, 1; "'Ready, Willing,' Rockefeller Says," *Los Angeles Times*, March 2, 1968, 1; "Rockefeller Says That He Will Run if Asked by G.O.P.," *New York Times*, March 2, 1968, 1; Joseph Alsop, "Rockefeller 'Semi-Candidacy' Is Gamble to Avoid Party Row," *Washington Post, Times Herald*, March 4, 1968, A13; Lewis Chester, Geoffrey Hodgson, and Bruce Page, *An American Melodrama: The Presidential Campaign of 1968* (New York: Viking, 1969), 209–10, 216–21; "Rockefeller Open to Oregon Race," *New York Times*, March 8, 1968, 1; "The New Rules of Play," *Time*, March 8, 1968, 20–24; "Rocky Is Urged to Run," *Washington Post, Times Herald*, March 11, 1968, A1; David S. Broder, "Nebraska Conservative Tells Why He Backed Rockefeller," *Washington Post, Times Herald*, March 12, 1968, A17; Rowland Evans and Robert Novak, "Dramatic Meeting of GOP Moderates Pushed Rockefeller into Oregon Race," *Washington Post, Times Herald*, March 13, 1968, A21; "Nelson Gets a Rainy-Day Message: Run, Rocky, Run," *Life*, March 22, 1968, 58.

3. Joseph Kraft, "Rockefeller's Natural Caution Is Handicap for Candidacy," *Washington Post, Times Herald*, March 21, 1968, A21; Warren Weaver Jr., "Rockefeller Bloc Loses Early Bid in G.O.P. Canvass," *New York Times*, March 1, 1968, 1; Godfrey Sperling Jr., "Time Short for Bid by Rockefeller," *Christian Science Monitor*, March 7, 1968, 1; David S. Broder, "Goldwater: Won't Support Rockefeller if He's Nominated," *Los Angeles Times*, March 5, 1968, 1; "Rockefeller's Parade," *Time*, March 15, 1968, 18; Emmett John Hughes, "A Rockefeller Questionnaire," *Newsweek*, March 18, 1968, 21.

4. Nevin, "Rockefeller: 'The Old Avidity Is Gone,'" 33–35; David S. Broder, "Why Rockefeller Bowed Out," *Washington Post, Times Herald*, March 22, 1968, A1; "Draftsmanship," *Newsweek*, March 18, 1968, 50–51; "'Draft Rockefeller'—Will It Work?," *U.S. News & World Report*, March 18, 1968, 49–50.

5. "Rocky: Majority of Party's Leaders Want . . . Nixon," *Washington Post, Times*

Herald, March 22, 1968, A10; Apple, "Rockefeller Not to Run, but Would Accept Draft," 1.

6. "Blockbuster," *Nation*, April 1, 1968, 428; "Mr. Rockefeller's Decision," *New York Times*, March 22, 1968, 46; "Rocky's Withdrawal," *Christian Science Monitor*, March 23, 1968, 22; "The Unpredictable Race," *New York Times*, March 25, 1968, 40; Apple, "Rockefeller Not to Run, but Would Accept Draft," 1; "'Realistic Appraisal,'" 20; "The Lost Leader," *Time*, March 25, 1968, 23–24; Jules Witcover, *The Year the Dream Died: Revisiting 1968 in America* (New York: Warner Books, 1997), 119–23.

7. Hugh Sidey, "How T.R.'s Giraffes Got Rocky Thinking About the Big Job," *Life*, January 12, 1968, 32B; Albin Krebs, "And Still Governor," *New York Times*, November 4, 1970, 19.

8. "The Rockefeller Record," *U.S. News & World Report*, July 29, 1968, 22–26; William Manchester, "Nelson Rockefeller's Moral Heritage," *Harper's*, May 1959, 25–31; Richard Norton Smith, *On His Own Terms: A Life of Nelson Rockefeller* (New York: Random House, 2014), 3–261.

9. Smith, *On His Own Terms*, xvi–xviii, xxvii, xxxiv, 265–309.

10. "Of All the Rockefeller Sons . . . Nelson Is the One to Watch in Public Life," *Newsweek*, April 28, 1958, 24–28; Richard L. Wilson, "Can Rockefeller Knock Off Nixon?," *Look*, April 28, 1959, 21–25; "The 'Great Society'—Rockefeller Style," *U.S. News & World Report*, January 18, 1965, 20; "Rockefeller Record," 23–24; Warren Weaver, "Political Evolution of Nelson Rockefeller," *New York Times Magazine*, February 16, 1964, 11, 72–73, 84; Joseph H. Boyd and Charles R. Holcomb, *Oreos and Dubonnet: Remembering Governor Nelson A. Rockefeller* (Albany: State University of New York Press, 2012).

11. Dennis H. Wrong, "Rockefeller as Liberal Hero," *Commentary*, September 1960, 201–5; Thomas B. Morgan, "Nelson Rockefeller: The Pitfalls of Party Politics," *Esquire*, October 1961, 81–83, 155–58; Theodore H. White, *The Making of the President, 1960* (1961; reprint, Franklin Center, Pa.: Franklin Library, 1987), 191–203; Geoffrey Kabaservice, *Rule and Ruin: The Downfall of Moderation and the Destruction of the Republican Party* (New York: Oxford University Press, 2012), 26–31; Donald T. Critchlow, *The Conservative Ascendancy: How the GOP Right Made Political History* (Cambridge, Mass.: Harvard University Press, 2007), 42–52.

12. Smith, *On His Own Terms*, 324–29, 405–9, 446–47; Theodore H. White, *The Making of the President, 1964* (New York: Atheneum, 1965), 74–80; David Farber, *The Rise and Fall of Modern American Conservatism: A Short History* (Princeton, N.J.: Princeton University Press, 2010), 96–97; Murray Kempton, "Rockefeller: He Has It if He Wants It, and He Does," *New Republic*, March 2, 1963, 11–14; Michael Nelson, *Resilient America: Electing Nixon in 1968, Channeling Dissent, and Dividing Government* (Lawrence: University Press of Kansas, 2014), 36; Stewart Alsop, "Is Nelson Rockefeller Dead?," *Saturday Evening Post*, October 12, 1963, 18.

13. Smith, *On His Own Terms*, xxviii–xxxii; White, *Making of the President, 1964*, 200–202.

14. Smith, *On His Own Terms*, 480–94; Emmet John Hughes, "The Return of Rockefeller," *Newsweek*, October 17, 1966, 23; "Happy Warrior," *Newsweek*, October 31, 1966, 36–41; Richard Reeves, "Rocky (Is, Is Not, May Be) Running," *New York Times*

Magazine, 29–31, 142–56; Larry L. King, "The Cool World of Nelson Rockefeller," *Harper's*, February 1968, 31–40.

15. "Rocky on the Rise," *Newsweek*, August 28, 1967, 20; "The Rocky Riddle," *Wall Street Journal*, December 13, 1967, 18; James Gannon, "Rocky: He Who Runs Least Runs Best," *Newsweek*, December 18, 1967, 34–35; Joseph Alsop, "Rockefeller's Chances Grow as He Continues to Sit Tight," *Washington Post, Times Herald*, December 22, 1967, A15; Martin Nolan, "Rockefeller's Waiting Game," *Reporter*, January 25, 1968, 32–33; Warren Weaver Jr., "G.O.P. Leaders Say Only Rockefeller Can Beat Johnson," *New York Times*, January 1, 1968, 1; Michael Kramer and Sam Roberts, *"I Never Wanted to Be Vice-President of Anything!": An Investigative Biography of Nelson Rockefeller* (New York: Basic Books, 1976), 322–23; Gerald Astor, "Rocky's Roughest Round," *Look*, October 18, 1966, 52–62.

16. Lewis L. Gould, *Grand Old Party: A History of the Republicans* (New York: Random House, 2003), 264–348; Heather Cox Richardson, *To Make Men Free: A History of the Republican Party* (New York: Basic Books, 2014), 221–38; Steven Wagner, *Eisenhower Republicanism: Pursuing the Middle Way* (DeKalb: Northern Illinois University Press, 2006).

17. Kabaservice, *Rule and Ruin*, 1–31.

18. Kabaservice, *Rule and Ruin*, 161–93; Leah Wright Rigueur, *The Loneliness of the Black Republican: Pragmatic Politics and the Pursuit of Power* (Princeton, N.J.: Princeton University Press, 2015), 95–135; Warren Weaver, "Four Hearties of the Good Ship G.O.P.," *New York Times Magazine*, November 27, 1966, 50–55; "Key Republicans with New Stature," *U.S. News & World Report*, November 21, 1966, 26–27; "Republicans Need Rocky in the Race," *Life*, February 16, 1968, 4; Martha Cleveland, *Charles Percy: Strong New Voice from Illinois* (Jacksonville, Ill.: Harris-Wolfe, 1968); Stephen Hess and David S. Broder, *The Republican Establishment: The Present and Future of the G.O.P.* (New York: Harper & Row, 1967), 1–11.

19. Gabe Freeman, "The Rockefeller-Lindsay Feud," *Nation*, December 4, 1967, 591–93; "More Trouble for New York—a Reform Mayor at Crossroads," *U.S. News & World Report*, February 12, 1968, 44–47; Geoffrey Kabaservice, "On Principle: A Progressive Republican," in *Summer in the City: John Lindsay, New York, and the American Dream*, ed. Joseph P. Viteriti (Baltimore: Johns Hopkins University Press, 2014), 27–60; "John Lindsay's Ten Plagues," *Time*, November 1, 1968, 20–29; Vincent J. Cannato, *The Ungovernable City: John Lindsay and His Struggle to Save New York* (New York: Basic Books, 2001), 194–204; Smith, *On His Own Terms*, 471–79, 506–11; "Lindsay and Rockefeller at Odds," *Newsweek*, February 26, 1968, 16; Emmet John Hughes, "A Fable from Fun City," *Newsweek*, March 4, 1968, 17; William V. Shannon, "Setback for Rockefeller," *New York Times*, February 18, 1968, 163; "Rockefeller's 'Garbage War' Role—a Blow to His Presidential Chances?," *U.S. News & World Report*, February 26, 1968, 20.

20. Benjamin Wallace-Wells, "George Romney for President, 1968," *New York*, May 20, 2012; "Romney—Republican Hope for '68?," *U.S. News & World Report*, September 5, 1966, 54–61; George Romney, "People Lack Confidence in Washington," *U.S. News & World Report*, November 21, 1966, 59–60; "A Romney-Javits Ticket for Republicans?," *U.S. News & World Report*, June 6, 1966, 20; "Boost for Romney—Scranton Bows Out," *U.S. News & World Report*, June 13, 1966, 22; "Lonesome

George," *Newsweek*, July 4, 1966, 20–21; "Romney's Chances to Head Ticket in '68," *U.S. News & World Report*, December 5, 1966, 29–31; "Consensus by Any Other Name," *Time*, December 2, 1966, 21–22; "The Dorado Summit," *Newsweek*, December 5, 1966, 30–31; "Let George Do It," *Time*, May 19, 1967, 29; "Nixon vs. Rockefeller—Choice Shaping Up," *U.S. News & World Report*, January 1, 1968, 38–40.

21. "See How He Runs," *Time*, December 16, 1966, 32; "The GOP: It's Spring," *Newsweek*, April 17, 1967, 31–32; "Lukewarm at the Lake," *Time*, July 14, 1967, 16–17; Hess and Broder, *Republican Establishment*, 95–101; "Mormons and the Negro," *Newsweek*, March 6, 1967, 80; Jules Witcover, "George Romney's Road-Show Hamlet," *Reporter*, March 23, 1967, 36–37; "Inside Romney," *Newsweek*, December 25, 1967, 18–23.

22. George Romney, *The Concerns of a Citizen* (New York: G. P. Putnam's Sons, 1968); Ernest Havemann, "The George Romney Family: All Aboard for the White House!," *Ladies' Home Journal*, October 1966, 176–83; T. George Harris, "What Makes Romney Run?," *Look*, December 12, 1967, 92–105; William V. Shannon, "George Romney: Holy and Hopeful," *Harper's*, February 1967, 55–62; "Romney Rubs Noses with Voters," *Life*, November 3, 1967, 70–72; Warren Weaver Jr., "Romney Sounds an Uncertain Trumpet," *New York Times Magazine*, November 19, 1967, 46–47, 135–39; Jules Witcover, "George Romney: Battered but Unbowed," *Saturday Evening Post*, December 2, 1967, 38–42.

23. Wallace-Wells, "George Romney for President, 1968"; Kabaservice, *Rule and Ruin*, 214–17; "The Romney-LBJ Feud: Who Played Politics in the Rioting?," *U.S. News & World Report*, August 14, 1967, 14; "See America First," *Time*, September 8, 1967, 16; "Slumming It," *Newsweek*, September 11, 1967, 22; "The Bell Tolls for a Galloping Ghost," *Newsweek*, September 25, 1967, 27–28; James Jones, "Romney: Still Blooper-Prone, but Very Much Alive," *Newsweek*, October 9, 1967, 26.

24. "In Transition," *Time*, August 25, 1967, 15–16; George Romney, "The Fourth Largest War: Peace with Amnesty," *Vital Speeches of the Day*, May 15, 1967, 462–65; "The Brainwashed Candidate," *Time*, September 15, 1967, 22; Theodore H. White, *The Making of the President, 1968* (New York: Atheneum, 1969), 66–69; "The 'Brainwashing' Furor Romney Set Off," *U.S. News & World Report*, September 18, 1967, 22; "The GOP: The Man Whom . . . ?," *Newsweek*, September 18, 1967, 30–31; "Romney: Trouble Abroad—and at Home," *U.S. News & World Report*, January 8, 1968, 12; "Back to the Laundry," *Time*, December 15, 1967, 25; "World Rambler," *Newsweek*, December 18, 1967, 35; "Romney Goes to the War," *Time*, January 5, 1968, 25.

25. "The Word," *Time*, November 24, 1967, 25; James Jackson Kilpatrick, "Romney: Salesman on the Move," *National Review*, December 12, 1967, 1372–1400; Anthony Ripley, "Romney Opens Bid in New Hampshire; Challenges Nixon," *New York Times*, January 13, 1968, 1; "Romney Redivivus," *Time*, January 26, 1968, 15–16; "Mining the Mother Lode," *Time*, February 2, 1968, 20–21; David English and the Staff of the London *Daily Express*, *Divided They Stand* (Englewood Cliffs, N.J.: Prentice-Hall, 1969), 76; "I'm an Underdog," *Newsweek*, January 22, 1968, 20–21.

26. Anthony Ripley, "Romney Offers Peace Plan for Neutralizing Vietnam," *New York Times*, January 16, 1968, 1; George Romney, "Our Nation's Vietnam Policy," *Vital Speeches of the* Day, February 15, 1968, 263–66; Tom Wicker, "Beyond the Eleventh Commandment," *New York Times*, February 18, 1968, 171; Richard L. Strout,

"Underdog Romney Rips War Trend," *Christian Science Monitor*, February 27, 1968, 1; Stephen C. Shadegg, *Winning's a Lot More Fun* (London: Macmillan, 1969), 132–34.

27. Witcover, *Year the Dream Died*, 56.

28. Joseph E. Persico, *The Imperial Rockefeller: A Biography of Nelson Rockefeller* (New York: Simon and Schuster, 1982), 64–65; William V. Shannon, "Rockefeller on 'Tightrope,'" *New York Times*, February 4, 1968, E5; Charles McCarry, "Win with Rockefeller," *Saturday Evening Post*, February 24, 1968, 80–83; "Now Is the Time," *Nation*, January 22, 1968, 98–99; James Desmond, "Waiting for Rocky: Trials of a Non-Candidate," *Nation*, February 19, 1968, 234–35; "Waiting for Rocky," *Time*, January 19, 1968, 12–13; "Rocky's Dilemma," *Time*, February 9, 1968, 20–21; Nelson A. Rockefeller, "Policy and the People," *Foreign Affairs* 46, no. 2 (January 1968): 231–41; "A Full, Not an Empty Life," *Christian Science Monitor*, December 27, 1967, 16; "Nelson the Silent," *New York Times*, January 29, 1968, 30; Patrick J. Buchanan, *The Greatest Comeback: How Richard Nixon Rose from Defeat to Create the New Majority* (New York: Crown Forum, 2014), 222–27; Smith, *On His Own Terms*, 512–19.

29. Richard Dougherty, "Rocky Set to Run," *Los Angeles Times*, April 29, 1968, 1; George Lardner Jr., "Rockefeller Stresses That He Is Still Available," *Washington Post, Times Herald*, April 11, 1968, A2; Chester, Hodgson, and Page, *American Melodrama*, 379–81; Richard Witkin, "Rockefeller Hints That He'll Enter Race," *New York Times*, April 12, 1968, 1; "A Rockefeller Campaigns," *Christian Science Monitor*, April 12, 1968, 16; "Rockefeller Fans That 'Draft,'" *New York Times*, April 14, 1968, E3.

30. Godfrey Sperling Jr., "Rockefeller Musters a Will to Win," *Christian Science Monitor*, April 20, 1968, 1; "Rocky's Return," *Time*, April 19, 1968, 22–23; "The Draft Gets Hotter," *Business Week*, April 27, 1968, 38–39; "The Rocky Road," *Newsweek*, April 29, 1968, 34; Gerald Astor, "Where He Stands," *Look*, May 14, 1968, 71–78; Nelson A. Rockefeller, *Unity, Freedom, and Peace: A Blueprint for Tomorrow* (New York: Random House, 1968), 33–50.

31. Rick Perlstein, *Nixonland: The Rise of a President and the Fracturing of America* (New York: Scribner, 2008), 268; Boyd and Holcomb, *Oreos and Dubonnet*, 79–80; Smith, *On His Own Terms*, 528–29.

32. R. W. Apple, "'Choice' Offered by Rockefeller as He Joins Race," *New York Times*, May 1, 1968, 1; Richard Dougherty, "Fight to Last Vote: Rocky's Pledge," *Los Angeles Times*, May 1, 1968, 1; "The Rockefeller Decision," *New York Times*, May 1, 1968, 46; "Rocky and Humphrey: Late but Welcome," *Life*, May 10, 1968, 4; Edgar M. Mills, "Races Tighten," *Christian Science Monitor*, May 2, 1968, 1; "Act III," *Time*, May 10, 1968, 26–27.

33. Robert P. Hey, "Rockefeller Hopes to Warm Up Dixie during Series of Visits," *Christian Science Monitor*, May 20, 1968, 5; R. W. Apple Jr., "Rockefeller: Now It's for Real—and All Uphill," *New York Times*, May 5, 1968, E2; "Off and Running—Where?," *Newsweek*, May 13, 1968, 26–29; "In Search of Enthusiasm," *Time*, May 17, 1968, 23; "The Road to Nebraska," *Newsweek*, May 20, 1968, 40; R. W. Apple Jr., "Rockefeller Sees Reagan in South," *New York Times*, May 21, 1968, 1.

34. Richard J. Whalen, *Catch the Falling Flag: A Republican's Challenge to His Party* (Boston: Houghton Mifflin, 1972), 127; Shadegg, *Winning's a Lot More Fun*, 181–82; Robert B. Semple, "Survey Shows 725 Are Leaning or Committed to Ex-Vice-President," *New York Times*, May 5, 1968, 1; "A Noted Republican's Serene

Certainty," *Life*, June 7, 1968, 42–43; "A Hard Man to Stop," *Newsweek*, June 10, 1968, 26–27; Robert B. Semple, "The Republican Race: The Front-Runner Looks over His Shoulder," *New York Times*, May 5, 1968, E2; Warren Weaver Jr., "Nixon Shuns Fight with Rockefeller," *New York Times*, June 15, 1968, 1; "The Negative Campaigners," *New York Times*, June 19, 1968, 46; Robert B. Semple Jr., "Nixon: Keeping Cool," *New York Times*, June 30, 1968, E3; Robert B. Semple Jr., "Nixon Tries to Stay on That Peak," *New York Times*, July 28, 1968, 133; David Butwin, "Nixon in Rebozoland," *Saturday Review*, March 8, 1969, 40–41, 108–11.

35. R. W. Apple Jr., "Rockefeller: Gloves Off," *New York Times*, June 23, 1968, E1; "Rocky Assails Nixon 'Evasion,'" *Washington Post, Times Herald*, June 20, 1968, A2; Persico, *Imperial Rockefeller*, 71–73; "Knocks by the Rock," *Newsweek*, July 1, 1968, 18–19; Nelson A. Rockefeller, "The Building of a Just World Order," *Vital Speeches of the Day*, June 1, 1968, 488–91; R. W. Apple Jr., "Rockefeller Says U.S. Policy Lags," *New York Times*, May 2, 1968, 1; Carl Greenberg, "Rockefeller Pledges He Would Call Atlantic Summit Meeting," *Los Angeles Times*, June 13, 1968, 1; Richard Dougherty, "Rockefeller Offers Four-Point Peace Plan for Vietnam," *Los Angeles Times*, July 14, 1968, 1; "Nixon Advised to Lay Off Wallace in Southern Tour," *Christian Science Monitor*, June 3, 1968, 23; Buchanan, *Greatest Comeback*, 296–98; R. W. Apple Jr., "Rockefeller Calls Wallace a 'Racist' and Taunts Nixon," *New York Times*, June 23, 1968, 1; R. W. Apple Jr., "Rockefeller Sees Wallace 'Inroads,'" *New York Times*, July 11, 1968, 24; "Rocky Politicks on Steamboat," *Washington Post, Times Herald*, July 11, 1968, A2.

36. "In Search of Political Miracles," *Time*, July 26, 1968, 18–22; "Rockefeller Talks on the Issues," *U.S. News & World Report*, June 24, 1968, 44–53; Walter Lippmann, "The Nation Needs a Broader Choice in Time of Crisis," *Washington Post, Times Herald*, July 7, 1968, B2; Thruston B. Morton, "Why I'm for Rockefeller," *New Republic*, June 15, 1968, 20–23; Roscoe Drummond, "Rocky's Only Chance," *Christian Science Monitor*, June 29, 1968, 14; Lewis H. Lapham, "Rocky's Last Hurrah," *Saturday Evening Post*, August 10, 1968, 32–33, 84–86.

37. "Tough Talk," *Time*, June 28, 1968, 15; David S. Broder, "Rocky Sees Campaign Getting 'Critical' Now," *Washington Post, Times Herald*, June 14, 1968, A2; R. W. Apple Jr., "Kirk Endorses Rockefeller—for the Time Being," *New York Times*, July 13, 1968; Norman C. Miller, "GOP Governors See Nixon as Party Nominee Despite Shafer's Support of Rockefeller," *Wall Street Journal*, June 17, 1968, 6; "Rocky Pushes On," *Time*, July 19, 1968, 12.

38. John Osborne, "What Are Nixon and Rockefeller Saying?," *New Republic*, June 29, 1968, 15–17; Dennis Wainstock, *Election Year 1968: The Turning Point* (New York: Enigma Books, 2012), 99; R. W. Apple Jr., "Rockefeller Says 'Tide Has Turned,'" *New York Times*, June 4, 1968, 1; Alan L. Otten, "Sold Like Soap?," *Wall Street Journal*, June 5, 1968, 14; James F. Clarity, "Rockefeller: Can Dollars Do It?," *New York Times*, July 21, 1968, E4; Chester, Hodgson, and Page, *American Melodrama*, 379–93; Lawrence O'Donnell, *Playing with Fire: The 1968 Election and the Transformation of American Politics* (New York: Penguin, 2017), 256.

39. "The Polls and the Pols and the Public," *Newsweek*, July 8, 1968, 23–27; Leroy F. Aarons, "Poll Use Debated by Rocky's Aides," *Washington Post, Times Herald*, July 13, 1968, A12; R. W. Apple Jr., "Rockefeller: His Only Hope Is the Polls," *New York Times*,

July 14, 1968, E4; James Reston, "The Northern Vote: Nelson Rockefeller's Main Argument," *New York Times*, July 17, 1968, 42; "The Republicans, 1968," *Newsweek*, July 22, 1968, 20–21; Chester, Hodgson, and Page, *American Melodrama*, 391–92; "Can Nixon Win in November? (and Could Rocky Do Better?)," *Time*, July 12, 1968, 16–17.

40. "Rockefeller Optimistic," *Christian Science Monitor*, June 22, 1968, 5; "Nelson's Hundred Days," *Time*, July 5, 1968, 18–19; "To the Bitter End," *Newsweek*, July 15, 1968, 24–26; Donald Jackson, "Rocky Stalks His Dream," *Life*, July 16, 1968, 18B; "In Search of Political Miracles," 18–20; James M. Naughton, "Nelson (Zap) Rockefeller and Richard (Cool) Nixon," *New York Times Magazine*, July 28, 1968, 6–7, 44–58.

41. R. W. Apple Jr., "Rockefeller Tries to Close the Gap," *New York Times*, July 28, 1968, 133; Vermont Royster, "The Rocky Road," *Wall Street Journal*, July 9, 1968, 18; Shadegg, *Winning's a Lot More Fun*, 192; Lewis H. Lapham, "Rocky's Last Hurrah," *Saturday Evening Post*, August 10, 1968, 32–33, 80–86; R. W. Apple Jr., "Rockefeller: Was the Fight Good Enough?," *New York Times*, August 4, 1968, E1.

42. Leroy F. Aarons, "Rockefeller Seeks Kennedy Mantle," *Washington Post, Times Herald*, June 12, 1968, A1; R. W. Apple Jr., "Rockefeller Links His Goals to Those of Kennedy," *New York Times*, June 12, 1968, 22; James Reston, "New York: Rockefeller Comes out of His Trance," *New York Times*, June 12, 1968, 46; R. W. Apple Jr., "Students Mob Rockefeller," *New York Times*, June 12, 1968, 1; R. W. Apple Jr., "Rockefeller Aims at Kennedy Vote," *New York Times*, June 26, 1968, 27; Nelson Rockefeller, "Why I Want the Job," *Look*, August 20, 1968, 34; "Rocky: Out of the Trance," *Time*, June 21, 1968, 20–21; White, *Making of the President, 1968*, 272–73.

CHAPTER FIVE

1. Thurston Clarke, *The Last Campaign: Robert F. Kennedy and 82 Days That Inspired America* (New York: Henry Holt, 2008), 85–90; Jean Stein and George Plimpton, *American Journey: The Times of Robert Kennedy* (New York: Harcourt Brace Jovanovich, 1970), 255.

2. Clarke, *Last Campaign*, 91–98; John Lewis with Michael D'Orso, *Walking with the Wind: A Memoir of the Movement* (New York: Simon and Schuster, 1998), 385–88; "With Kennedy," *New Republic*, April 20, 1968, 6.

3. Clay Risen, *A Nation on Fire: America in the Wake of the King Assassination* (New York: John Wiley & Sons, 2009), 39–155; Stein and Plimpton, *American Journey*, 256; Clarke, *Last Campaign*, 102–11; Jack Newfield, *Robert Kennedy: A Memoir* (New York: Dutton, 1969), 248–51.

4. Clarke, *Last Campaign*, 112–36; Risen, *Nation on Fire*, 183–86, 208–12; Homer Bigart, "Leaders at Rites," *New York Times*, April 10, 1968, 1; "King's Last March: 'We Lost Somebody,'" *Newsweek*, April 22, 1968, 26, 31; Stein and Plimpton, *American Journey*, 258–61.

5. "Robert F. Kennedy and the Negro," *Ebony*, July 1968, 29–46.

6. Newfield, *Robert Kennedy*, 29–30; David Frost, *The Presidential Debate, 1968* (New York: Stein and Day, 1968), 118; William V. Shannon, "Said Robert Kennedy, 'Maybe We're All Doomed Anyway,'" *New York Times Magazine*, June 16, 1968, 7, 42–47; David Talbot, *Brothers: The Hidden History of the Kennedy Years* (New York: Free

Press, 2007), 3–4, 12, 277; John R. Bohrer, *The Revolution of Robert Kennedy: From Power to Protest after JFK* (New York: Bloomsbury, 2017), 9–27.

7. Evan Thomas, *Robert Kennedy: His Life* (New York: Touchstone, 2000), 26–46; Larry Tye, *Bobby Kennedy: The Making of a Liberal Icon* (New York: Random House, 2016), xi, 5–18.

8. Thomas, *Robert Kennedy*, 47–108; Tye, *Bobby Kennedy*, 50–131; Arthur M. Schlesinger Jr., *Robert Kennedy and His Times* (Boston: Houghton Mifflin, 1978), 99–169.

9. Hugh Sidey, "The Questioner for Two Presidents," *Life*, June 21, 1968, 36; Pat Anderson, "Robert's Character," *Esquire*, April 1965, 65, 140–46; Thomas, *Robert Kennedy*, 109–275; Edwin Guthman, *We Band of Brothers* (New York: Harper & Row, 1971), 86–223; Tye, *Bobby Kennedy*, 184–93; Schlesinger, *Robert Kennedy and His Times*, 222–583.

10. "What Americans Expect from Robert Kennedy," *Ladies' Home Journal*, October 1965, 71–73, 166; Bohrer, *Revolution of Robert Kennedy*, 28–67; Rick Perlstein, *Before the Storm: Barry Goldwater and the Unmaking of the American Consensus* (2001; reprint, New York: Nation Books, 2009), 454.

11. Peter Lisagor, "Portrait of a Man Emerging from Shadows," *New York Times Magazine*, July 19, 1964, 15, 28–29; Shannon, "Said Robert Kennedy, 'Maybe We're All Doomed Anyway,'" 45–46; Oriana Fallaci, "Robert Kennedy Answers Some Blunt Questions," *Look*, March 9, 1965, 60–63; Terry Smith, "Bobby's Image," *Esquire*, April 1965, 62–65, 140; Warren Weaver Jr., "Will the Real Robert Kennedy Stand Up?," *New York Times Magazine*, June 20, 1965, 9–10, 40–43; Stewart Alsop, "Robert Kennedy and the Liberals," *Saturday Evening Post*, August 28, 1965, 18; William V. Shannon, "Bob Kennedy's Future," *Commonweal*, March 18, 1966, 686–87; Penn Kimball, "He Builds His Own Kennedy Identity and the Power Flows Freely to Him," *Life*, November 18, 1966, 43, 129–39; Gail Cameron, "What It Takes to Be a Kennedy," *Ladies' Home Journal*, February 1967, 76–77, 142–46; Robert S. Bird, "At Home with the Heir Apparent," *Saturday Evening Post*, August 26, 1967, 28–35.

12. Frank Mankiewicz with Joel L. Swerdlow, *So as I Was Saying . . . : My Somewhat Eventful Life* (New York: Thomas Dunne Books, 2016), 190–92; Schlesinger, *Robert Kennedy and His Times*, 617–20, 801–4, 811–14.

13. Edward R. Schmitt, *President of the Other America: Robert Kennedy and the Politics of Poverty* (Amherst: University of Massachusetts Press, 2010), 119–94; Tye, *Bobby Kennedy*, 348–96; Robert F. Kennedy, "Suppose God Is Black," *Look*, August 23, 1966, 44–48; "The Favorite American," *Newsweek*, June 27, 1966, 53–54; "A Redbook Dialogue: Robert Kennedy and Oscar Lewis," *Redbook*, September 1967, 74–75, 104–6; "Crest of the Wave," *Newsweek*, July 17, 1967, 24–25.

14. Andrew Kopkind, "He's a Happening," *New Republic*, April 2, 1966, 18–22; "Another Kennedy Seeks the Presidency," *U.S. News & World Report*, June 27, 1966, 56–61; Stewart Alsop, "The Kennedy Hurricane," *Saturday Evening Post*, August 27, 1966, 14; "Making of the President, 1972?," *Newsweek*, September 5, 1966, 17–18; "The Bobby Phenomenon," *Newsweek*, October 24, 1966, 30–38; Helen Hill Miller, "Kennedy in '68?," *New Republic*, October 25, 1966, 11–13; William V. Shannon, "The Making of President Robert Kennedy," *Harper's*, October 1966, 62–68; Douglas Kiker, "Robert Kennedy and the What If Game," *Atlantic*, October 1966, 66–70; Jack Newfield, "The Bobby Phenomenon," *Nation*, November 14, 1966, 505–7.

15. Sam Houston Johnson, *My Brother Lyndon* (New York: Cowles Book Co., 1970), 252; Jeff Shesol, *Mutual Contempt: Lyndon Johnson, Robert Kennedy, and the Feud That Defined a Decade* (New York: Norton, 1997), 10–232; Stewart Alsop, "LBJ and RFK," *Saturday Evening Post*, February 29, 1964, 10; "'Bobby' Kennedy on LBJ's '64 Ticket?," *U.S. News & World Report*, March 23, 1964, 42–44; "Is It to Be the Kennedy Brothers vs. LBJ?," *U.S. News & World Report*, July 12, 1965, 50–52; Hugh Sidey, "He Makes a Truce with a Man He Almost Came to Hate—L.B.J.," *Life*, November 18, 1966.

16. Shesol, *Mutual Contempt*, 3–9, 305–27; David Halberstam, *The Unfinished Odyssey of Robert Kennedy* (New York: Random House, 1968), 34; Richard Goodwin, *Remembering America: A Voice from the Sixties* (Boston: Little, Brown, 1988), 295; "Two Men—So Alike yet So Different," *New York Times*, March 17, 1968, E1; "LBJ vs. RFK?," *Newsweek*, June 13, 1966, 35.

17. Thomas, *Robert Kennedy*, 268–73, 311–16, 332–33; "The Kennedy Caper," *Newsweek*, March 7, 1966, 24–25; "'A Fox in a Chicken Coop,'" *Time*, March 4, 1966, 26–27; "Senator Robert Kennedy Explains His Position," *U.S. News & World Report*, March 14, 1966, 68–70; "'That Man' and 'That Boy,'" *Newsweek*, March 20, 1967, 25–26.

18. "RFK's Moves to Stand Apart from LBJ," *U.S. News & World Report*, February 20, 1967, 21; Shesol, *Mutual Contempt*, 363–83; "The Other War," *Newsweek*, February 20, 1967, 31–32; Hugh Sidey, "Needed: Peace Feeler in a Capital War," *Life*, March 17, 1967, 40B; Tye, *Bobby Kennedy*, 368–70; "Toughened Mood," *Time*, March 10, 1967, 21; "Men at War: RFK vs. LBJ," *Newsweek*, March 13, 1967, 33–34; "The 'Embarrassing' Mr. Kennedy," *America*, March 18, 1967, 366–67; Emmet John Hughes, "The Careful Kennedy Hurry," *Newsweek*, March 20, 1967, 23; Kenneth Crawford, "Henry A. Kennedy?," *Newsweek*, March 20, 1967, 36; "Bobby Kennedy: New Thoughts about Tackling LBJ in '68?," *U.S. News & World Report*, September 11, 1967, 20; "Is Robert Kennedy Trying to Upset LBJ in '68?," *U.S. News & World Report*, October 2, 1967, 39–40; "Will Kennedy Challenge LBJ?," *U.S. News & World Report*, February 12, 1968, 42–43.

19. Penn Kimball, *Bobby Kennedy and the New Politics* (Englewood Cliffs, N.J.: Prentice-Hall, 1968), 1–31; Kenneth Crawford, "Kennedy on TV," *Newsweek*, December 11, 1967, 39; Robert F. Kennedy, "What Can the Young Believe?," *New Republic*, March 11, 1967, 11–12; Robert F. Kennedy, "What Our Young People Are Really Saying," *Ladies' Home Journal*, January 1968, 35–38; Robert F. Kennedy, "What We Can Do to End the Agony of Vietnam," *Look*, November 28, 1967, 34–46; Robert F. Kennedy, *To Seek a Newer World* (Garden City, N.Y.: Doubleday, 1967).

20. Jules Witcover, *85 Days: The Last Campaign of Robert Kennedy* (New York: G. P. Putnam's Sons, 1969), 30–31; Stein and Plimpton, *American Journey*, 221–22, 228–29; Edward M. Kennedy, *True Compass: A Memoir* (New York: Twelve, 2009), 251–53.

21. "The Senator's Dilemma," *Nation*, December 11, 1967, 612; Richard Witkin, "Kennedy Refuses to Back McCarthy," *New York Times*, January 9, 1968, 25; "Kennedy and the McCarthy Problem," *New York Times*, January 14, 1968, E2; David S. Broder, "Unruh's Turnabout on Liberals Reflects His New Look at RFK," *Washington Post, Times Herald*, January 16, 1968, A15; Newfield, *Robert Kennedy*, 196–202; Goodwin, *Remembering America*, 474–80; Halberstam, *Unfinished Odyssey of Robert Kennedy*, 56–67; Harris Wofford, *Of Kennedys and Kings: Making Sense of the Sixties* (1980; reprint, Pittsburgh: University of Pittsburgh Press, 1992), 422–24; Richard Witkin,

"Pressure on Kennedy," *New York Times*, January 22, 1968, 28; "Kennedy's Quandary," *New Republic*, January 27, 1968, 7; "Bobby: To Be or Not to Be," *Newsweek*, January 29, 1968, 18–19; William V. Shannon, "Kennedy's Problem Is How Not to Run," *New York Times*, January 28, 1968, E6.

22. E. W. Kenworthy, "Kennedy Repeats: No Johnson Fight," *New York Times*, January 31, 1968, 19; Thomas, *Robert Kennedy*, 356–59.

23. "A Broadside by Bobby," *Newsweek*, February 19, 1968, 24; "Misery at Vortex," *Time*, February 23, 1968, 20; Witcover, *85 Days*, 45–54; Newfield, *Robert Kennedy*, 203–11.

24. Witcover, *85 Days*, 62–80; "'We Want Camelot Again,'" *Newsweek*, March 25, 1968, 22–31; "Bobby Tells 'Keep Out' Offer," *Los Angeles Times*, March 18, 1968, 1; "The Inside Story of the Latest Bobby-LBJ Break," *U.S. News & World Report*, April 1, 1968, 30–32; Thomas J. Foley, "Bobby May Issue LBJ Challenge," *Los Angeles Times*, March 14, 1968, 1; Robert J. Donovan, "Kennedy News Chills McCarthy's Followers," *Los Angeles Times*, March 14, 1968, 1; "Enter Robert Kennedy," *New York Times*, March 15, 1968, 38; Rowland Evans and Robert Novak, "Kennedy Has What McCarthy Does Not Have: Political Power," *Washington Post, Times Herald*, March 18, 1968, A17; William S. White, "Kennedy's Dilemma Is Unique in American Political History," *Washington Post, Times Herald*, March 20, 1968, A19.

25. Warren Rogers, "Bobby's Decision," *Look*, April 16, 1968, 73–80; Tom Wicker, "Kennedy Refuses to Back Johnson for Renomination," *New York Times*, March 15, 1968, 1; "Hughes Strongly Opposed to Kennedy Candidacy," *New York Times*, March 15, 1968, 26; James Reston, "Boston: Robert Kennedy's Great Gamble," *New York Times*, March 15, 1968, 38; "Has Bobby Missed the Boat?," *Christian Science Monitor*, March 16, 1968, 18; Jack Newfield, "Kennedy Lays Out a 'Gut' Campaign," *Life*, March 29, 1968, 28–29; John Herbers, "Scene Is the Same, but 8 Years Later," *New York Times*, March 17, 1968, 68; "Kennedy Takes On President Johnson," *New York Times*, March 17, 1968, E1.

26. Mankiewicz with Swerdlow, *So as I Was Saying . . .* , 173–76; John Herbers, "'Sock It to 'Em' Kennedy Slogan," *New York Times*, March 29, 1968, 26; "Bobby on the Run," *Newsweek*, April 1, 1968, 24–30; Phil Kerby, "Kennedy in Disneyland," *Nation*, April 8, 1968, 464–65; Clarke, *Last Campaign*, 39–67.

27. John Herbers, "Kennedy Message Reaches Millions," *New York Times*, March 31, 1968, 60; John Herbers, "Kennedy Uses Humor to Relax Crowds and Disarm the Hostile," *New York Times*, March 27, 1968, 31; John Herbers, "Kennedy Charges Johnson Is Divisive," *New York Times*, March 22, 1968, 1; Lewis Chester, Geoffrey Hodgson, and Bruce Page, *An American Melodrama: The Presidential Campaign of 1968* (New York: Viking, 1969), 129–32; "Bobby's Groove," *Time*, March 29, 1968, 22–23; "Socking It to 'Em," *Time*, April 5, 1968.

28. David Wise, "How Bobby Plans to Win It," *Saturday Evening Post*, June 1, 1968, 23–27, 70; Homer Bigart, "Kennedy, Told News on Plane, Sits in Silence amid the Hubbub," *New York Times*, April 1, 1968, 27; Richard L. Strout, "Kennedy Offers to Talk with Johnson," *Christian Science Monitor*, April 2, 1968, 3; Lyndon Baines Johnson, *The Vantage Point: Perspectives of the Presidency, 1963–1969* (New York: Holt, Rinehart and Winston, 1971), 538–43; "Kennedy Fails to 'Blitz' Governors," *U.S. News & World Report*, April 29, 1968, 31–33; Alan L. Otten, "Front-Runner," *Wall Street*

Journal, April 3, 1968, 18; Jack Newfield, "Kennedy's Search for a New Target," *Life*, April 12, 1968, 35.

29. Frost, *Presidential Debate, 1968*, 114.

30. Tye, *Bobby Kennedy*, 408–9; Stewart Alsop, "Good Bobby and Bad Bobby," *Saturday Evening Post*, June 15, 1968, 18; Arthur Schlesinger Jr., "Why I Am for Kennedy," *New Republic*, May 4, 1968, 19–23; Milton Viorst, "The Skeptics," *Esquire*, November 1968, 123–29; Ben A. Franklin, "Southern Democratic Leaders Belittle McCarthy and Kennedy," *New York Times*, March 17, 1968, 63; A. James Reichley, "He's Running Himself out of the Race," *Fortune*, March 1968, 112–14, 166; Lawrence E. Davies, "Rising Anti-Kennedy Sentiment in California Becoming a Factor in Primary," *New York Times*, April 18, 1968, 26; "Can Kennedy Outrun His Image?," *Business Week*, May 25, 1968, 40–41; Edwin L. Dale, "Kennedy Favors Basic Tax on Rich," *New York Times*, May 12, 1968, 1; Kenneth Crawford, "Kennedy on Campus," *Newsweek*, April 8, 1968, 46; "Reaction to Bobby," *Time*, April 5, 1968, 53; "Bobby Freaks Out," *National Review*, April 9, 1968, 331; Theodore H. White, *The Making of the President, 1968* (New York: Atheneum, 1969), 194–95.

31. Charlotte Curtis, "White House Candidates Let the Women Down," *New York Times*, May 7, 1968, 40; Ruth Rosen, *The World Split Open: How the Modern Women's Movement Changed America* (New York: Penguin, 2006), 74–88.

32. Witcover, *85 Days*, 145–52; Clarke, *Last Campaign*, 139–65.

33. E. W. Kenworthy, "Test in Indiana," *New York Times*, May 5, 1968, E2; Robert J. Donovan, "Indiana Primary to Put Kennedy on Hottest Spot," *Los Angeles Times*, May 5, 1968, 1; John Bird, "Can These People Tell the Future?," *Saturday Evening Post*, March 30, 1968, 27–31, 82–84; Hal Higdon, "Indiana: A Test for Bobby Kennedy," *New York Times Magazine*, May 5, 1968, 32–33, 72–79.

34. Loudon Wainwright, "Down the Stretch on the Road West," *Life*, May 17, 1968, 72–79; "Acedia & Cannonball," *Time*, May 3, 1968, 20; "This One Counts," Newsweek, May 6, 1968, 27–29A; Rowland Evans and Robert Novak, "Sen. McCarthy and His Revolution Encountering Troubles in Indiana," *Washington Post, Times Herald*, May 6, 1968; Eugene J. McCarthy, *The Year of the People* (Garden City, N.Y.: Doubleday, 1969), 118–24; Jeremy Larner, *Nobody Knows: Reflections on the McCarthy Campaign of 1968* (New York: Macmillan, 1970), 68–81; Ben Stavis, *We Were the Campaign: New Hampshire to Chicago for McCarthy* (Boston: Beacon Press, 1969), 51–84; Richard T. Stout, *People* (New York: Harper and Row, 1970), 222–48.

35. Ray E. Boomhower, *Robert Kennedy and the 1968 Indiana Primary* (Bloomington: Indiana University Press, 2008), 31–36, 48–49, 54; "Indiana: First Big Test for RFK," *U.S. News & World Report*, May 6, 1968, 59–60; Godfrey Sperling Jr., "Branigin Style," *Christian Science Monitor*, April 27, 1968, 1; Warren Weaver Jr., "Branigin's Appeal in Indiana Is Strong on Surface," *New York Times*, April 22, 1968, 22; Witcover, *85 Days*, 139, 166, 171–72.

36. Richard Reeves, "The Making of a Candidate, 1968," *New York Times Magazine*, March 31, 1968, 25–27, 128–33; Goodwin, *Remembering America*, 527–30; Lawrence F. O'Brien, *No Final Victories: A Life in Politics—from John F. Kennedy to Watergate* (Garden City, N.Y.: Doubleday, 1974), 233–39; Tye, *Bobby Kennedy*, 416; William vanden Heuvel and Milton Gwirtzman, *On His Own: Robert F. Kennedy, 1964–1968*

(Garden City, N.Y.: Doubleday, 1970), 343; Boomhower, *Robert Kennedy and the 1968 Indiana Primary*, 104.

37. Victor S. Navasky, "The Haunting of Robert Kennedy," *New York Times Magazine*, June 2, 1968, 26–27, 78–83; David Halberstam, "Bobby's Last Campaign," *New York*, April 19, 1993, 106–9; Witcover, *85 Days*, 160–63.

38. Thomas B. Congdon Jr., "Kennedy among the People," *Saturday Evening Post*, July 13, 1968, 64; Hays Gorey, "Memories of a Historic Ride," *Time*, May 9, 1988, 42–43; Witcover, *85 Days*, 165–66.

39. John Herbers, "Indiana Seeing a New Kennedy with Shorter Hair, Calm Manner and Pleas for Local Rule," *New York Times*, May 3, 1968, 28; "'It Is Much Better to Win,'" *Newsweek*, May 20, 1968, 31–39; Boomhower, *Robert Kennedy and the 1968 Indiana Primary*, 77–79; Michael W. Flamm, *Law and Order: Street Crime, Civil Unrest, and the Crisis of Liberalism in the 1960s* (New York: Columbia University Press, 2005), 148–49; White, *Making of the President, 1968*, 204–6; Stein and Plimpton, *American Journey*, 246–48.

40. Clarke, *Last Campaign*, 214–18; Witcover, *85 Days*, 173–77.

41. "Tarot Cards, Hoosier Style," *Time*, May 17, 1968, 21–22; Thomas J. Foley, "Kennedy Views Indiana Results as Sign of Hope for Racial Peace," *Los Angeles Times*, May 9, 1968, 1; Karl O'Lessker, "From Indiana . . . ," *Nation*, May 27, 1968, 686–87; Tom Wicker, "The Impact of Indiana," *New York Times*, May 8, 1968, 26; John Herbers, "Kennedy Assays McCarthy's Role," *New York Times*, May 9, 1968, 32; Witcover, *85 Days*, 180–81; Boomhower, *Robert Kennedy and the 1968 Indiana Primary*, 115–16; vanden Heuvel and Gwirtzman, *On His Own*, 348–49; Michael A. Cohen, *American Maelstrom: The 1968 Election and the Politics of Division* (New York: Oxford University Press, 2016), 129–30.

42. Clarke, *Last Campaign*, 193–205; Witcover, *85 Days*, 183–99; Tye, *Bobby Kennedy*, 424–25; "A Domino Falls for RFK," *Newsweek*, May 27, 1968, 32–33; "Tails You Lose," *Time*, May 10, 1968, 28; "Four to Go," *New Republic*, May 25, 1968, 8; John Herbers, "Kennedy Solicits McCarthy as Ally," *New York Times*, May 15, 1968, 32; "The Politics of Restoration," *Time*, May 24, 1968, 22–26.

43. Anthony Netboy, ". . . To Oregon," *Nation*, May 27, 1968, 687–90; Richard Harwood, "McCarthy and Kennedy: Philosopher vs. Evangelist," *Washington Post, Times Herald*, May 26, 1968, A1; Stout, *People*, 249–92; Arthur Herzog, *McCarthy for President* (New York: Viking, 1969), 160–73; McCarthy, *Year of the People*, 146–50; "Getting Snappish," *Time*, May 31, 1968, 11; Shana Alexander, "'He Tried to Beat Me with a Dog and an Astronaut,'" *Life*, June 17, 1968, 36–39; E. W. Kenworthy, "McCarthy Calls Rivals Ill-Equipped to Avoid Future Vietnams," *New York Times*, May 24, 1968, 22; E. W. Kenworthy, "McCarthy and Kennedy within 15 Yards of Meeting in Oregon," *New York Times*, May 27, 1968, 27.

44. Witcover, *85 Days*, 200–202, 208–21; Fred P. Graham, "Drew Pearson Says Robert Kennedy Ordered Wiretap on Phone of Dr. King," *New York Times*, May 25, 1968, 17; Halberstam, *Unfinished Odyssey of Robert Kennedy*, 173–83; O'Brien, *No Final Victories*, 241–42; Lewis with D'Orso, *Walking with the Wind*, 393; "In the 'New' Politics," *Time*, June 7, 1968, 23–25.

45. Warren Weaver Jr., "McCarthy Beats Kennedy in Oregon Primary Upset," *New*

York Times, May 29, 1968, 1; "The Horse Platitudes," *Newsweek*, June 3, 1968, 28–30; Paul R. Wieck, "Eugene McCarthy Hits His Stride," *New Republic*, June 8, 1968, 14–15; "Perils of the Primaries," *Newsweek*, June 10, 1968, 25–26; Rowland Evans and Robert Novak, "Kennedy's Oregon Defeat Gives Party Fence-Riders to Humphrey," *Washington Post, Times Herald*, May 30, 1968, A17; "Uncertain Juggernaut at the End of the Winning Streak," *Life*, June 17, 1968, 40–41.

46. Lawrence E. Davies, "California Democrats Confused over Trends in 3-Way Race," *New York Times*, April 28, 1968, 70; "Do Re Mi," *Newsweek*, May 6, 1968, 29A; Charlotte Curtis, "California Primary: A Political Test of 'Newness,'" *New York Times*, June 2, 1968, 1; Warren Weaver Jr., "For Kennedy, It's California or Bust," *New York Times*, June 2, 1968, E3; "Robert Kennedy's Chances: What a Survey Shows," *U.S. News & World Report*, June 3, 1968, 48–50; Jonathan Bell, *California Crucible: The Forging of Modern American Liberalism* (Philadelphia: University of Pennsylvania Press, 2012); Halberstam, *Unfinished Odyssey of Robert Kennedy*, 188–89.

47. Daryl E. Lembke, "Kennedy Hints at Withdrawal if He Loses in California Test," *Los Angeles Times*, May 30, 1968, 1; John Herbers, "Kennedy Assails McCarthy Tactics," *New York Times*, June 1, 1968, 25; Joseph Alsop, "Kennedy at the Turning Point, Must Reassess His Campaign," *Washington Post, Times Herald*, June 3, 1968, A17; John McLaughlin, "Political Debates," *America*, June 15, 1968, 778–80; David English and the Staff of the London *Daily Express*, *Divided They Stand* (Englewood Cliffs, N.J.: Prentice-Hall, 1969), 235–38.

48. Rowland Evans and Robert Novak, "Flood of Kennedy Money May Sway California Primary in Blitz," *Washington Post, Times Herald*, May 22, 1968, A21; "The Star-Spangled Look of the '68 Campaign," *Life*, May 10, 1968, 64A–69; Clarke, *Last Campaign*, 249–63; Stein and Plimpton, *American Journey*, 299.

49. Evan Thomas, "RFK's Last Campaign," *Newsweek*, June 8, 1968, 46–47; John Herbers, "Kennedy Hopes for Alliance with McCarthy to Stop Humphrey," *New York Times*, June 3, 1968, 39; William V. Shannon, "Divided They Conquer," *New York Times*, June 3, 1968, 44.

50. Richard Bergholz, "Kennedy Wins Race; Rafferty Apparent Victor over Kuchel," *Los Angeles Times*, June 5, 1968, 1; Jules Witcover, "Another 'What If?,'" *Washingtonian*, July 2008, 35–36; Goodwin, *Remembering America*, 536–38.

51. Clarke, *Last Campaign*, 272–75; Dan E. Moldea, *The Killing of Robert F. Kennedy: An Investigation of Motive, Means, and Opportunity* (New York: Norton, 1995); Rafer Johnson with Philip Goldberg, *The Best That I Can Be: An Autobiography* (New York: Doubleday, 1998), 199–200; "For Perspective & Determination," *Time*, June 14, 1968, 15–22; "Bobby's Last, Longest Day," *Newsweek*, June 17, 1968, 22–35; Schlesinger, *Robert Kennedy and His Times*, 901–2, 912–13; Goodwin, *Remembering America*, 538.

52. Gladwin Hill, "Kennedy Is Dead, Victim of Assassin," *New York Times*, June 6, 1968, 1; Robert Lowell, "R.F.K.," *New Republic*, June 22, 1968, 27; James Reston, "Washington: The Qualities of Robert Kennedy," *New York Times*, June 7, 1968, 38; Richard Harwood, "The Old and New Kennedy Illusions," *Washington Post, Times Herald*, June 8, 1968, A12; Theodore H. White, "The Wearing Last Weeks and a Precious Last Day," *Life*, June 14, 1968, 39–41; "A Flame Burned Fiercely," *Newsweek*, June 17, 1968, 37–41; Theodore C. Sorensen, "RFK: A Personal Memoir," *Saturday Review*, June 22, 1968, 19; Warren Rogers and Stanley Tretick, "The Bob Kennedy We Knew," *Look*,

July 9, 1968, 31–32; "Notes and Comment," *New Yorker*, March 13, 1969, 29; Stein and Plimpton, *American Journey*, 5–30; "Notes and Comment," *New Yorker*, June 15, 1968, 21–23; "Impressions at St. Patrick's," *Saturday Review*, June 22, 1968, 21; Anthony Howard, "Logistics of the Funeral," *Esquire*, November 1968, 119–21; Pete Hamill, "Why, God, Why?," *Good Housekeeping*, September 1968, 80–81, 187.

53. Stein and Plimpton, *American Journey*, 31–34, 46–48, 60–64, 76–77, 88–89, 106–7, 126–27, 140–45, 157–59, 176–77, 190–91, 201–2, 220–21, 234–35, 250–51, 262–65, 288–91, 296–98, 315–16, 330–31; Loudon Wainwright, "A Constituency of Sorrow along 225 Miles of Track," *Life*, June 21, 1968, 22–23; Clarke, *Last Campaign*, 2–6.

54. "Second Thoughts on Bobby," *Time*, June 21, 1968, 48; Charles Frankel, "The Meaning of Political Murder," *Saturday Review*, June 22, 1968, 17–18; Arthur Miller, "Topics: On the Shooting of Robert Kennedy," *New York Times*, June 8, 1968, 30; "Once Again . . . Once Again," *Newsweek*, June 17, 1968, 20–21; Marquis Childs, "The Political Void Left by Kennedy," *Washington Post, Times Herald*, June 10, 1968, A20; Alan L. Otten, "Dear Democrats," *Wall Street Journal*, June 13, 1968, 18; James Reston, "Washington: The Final Irony of Death," *New York Times*, June 9, 1968, E14.

CHAPTER SIX

1. Gladwin Hill, "Reagan and His Backers Huddle with a Half-Dozen Delegations," *New York Times*, August 5, 1968, 24.

2. David English and the Staff of the London *Daily Express*, *Divided They Stand* (Englewood Cliffs, N.J.: Prentice-Hall, 1969), 284–85; Harry S. Dent, *The Prodigal South Returns to Power* (New York: John Wiley & Sons, 1978), 91–92.

3. Lyn Nofziger, *Nofziger* (Washington, D.C.: Regnery Gateway, 1992), 73; Gladwin Hill, "Reagan Officially in Race; Acts to Bar Nixon Sweep," *New York Times*, August 6, 1968, 1; Carl Greenberg, "Reagan's Switch," *Los Angeles Times*, August 6, 1968, 1.

4. Lewis Chester, Geoffrey Hodgson, and Bruce Page, *An American Melodrama: The Presidential Campaign of 1968* (New York: Viking, 1969), 457; Chalmers Roberts, "Reagan Declares Candidacy, Nixon Is Endorsed by Agnew," *Washington Post, Times Herald*, August 6, 1968, A1; F. Clifton White and William J. Gill, *Why Reagan Won: A Narrative History of the Conservative Movement, 1964–1981* (Chicago: Regnery Gateway, 1981), 117–18.

5. Leroy F. Aarons, "Rocky Greets Bid by Reagan as Boost," *Washington Post, Times Herald*, August 6, 1968, A4; Robert J. Donovan, "Nixon's Still in Front by Wide Margin," *Los Angeles Times*, August 6, 1968, 1.

6. H. W. Brands, *Reagan: The Life* (New York: Anchor Books, 2015), 7–128; Lou Cannon, *Governor Reagan: His Rise to Power* (New York: PublicAffairs, 2003), 3–114.

7. Stewart Alsop, "The Good Guy," *Saturday Evening Post*, November 20, 1965, 18; Brands, *Reagan*, 1–6; Cannon, *Governor Reagan*, 122–26; Ronald Reagan, "A Moment of Truth: Our Rendezvous with Destiny," *Vital Speeches of the Day*, September 1, 1965, 681–86.

8. Matthew Dallek, *The Right Moment: Ronald Reagan's First Victory and the Decisive Turning Point in American Politics* (New York: Free Press, 2000); "Ronald for Real," *Time*, October 7, 1966, 31–35; Carey McWilliams, "How to Succeed with the Backlash," *Nation*, October 31, 1966, 438–42.

9. A. James Reichley, "Ronald Reagan Faces Life," *Fortune*, July 1967, 98–103, 152–57; Rowland Evans and Robert Novak, "Now That Reagan Is Governor, How's He Doing?," *Saturday Evening Post*, July 1, 1967, 40–46; "Fast Start," *Time*, August 11, 1967, 17.

10. Michael Miles, "Reagan and the Respectable Right," *New Republic*, April 20, 1968, 25–28; Frank S. Meyer, "Why I Am for Reagan," *New Republic*, May 11, 1968, 17–18; Julius Duscha, "Not Great, Not Brilliant, but a Good Show," *New York Times Magazine*, December 10, 1967, 28–29, 122–27; "Reagan's Road Show," *Time*, October 13, 1967, 28–29; "Ronald Reagan: Rising Star in the West?," *Newsweek*, May 22, 1967, 27–36; Joan Didion, "Pretty Nancy," *Saturday Evening Post*, June 1, 1968, 20; "California's Leading Lady," *Look*, October 31, 1967, 37–43.

11. Herbert Gold, "Notes from the Land of Political Pop," *New York Times Magazine*, December 11, 1966, 48–49, 140–44; Henry Brandon, "Reagan on the Rise?," *Saturday Review*, August 26, 1967, 12; Leo E. Litwak, "The Ronald Reagan Story; or, Tom Sawyer Enters Politics," *New York Times Magazine*, November 14, 1965, 46–47, 174–86; Horace Sutton, "Politics in the Palmlands," *Saturday Review*, September 23, 1967, 22–24; "Reagan in the Wilderness," *Newsweek*, March 28, 1966, 30–33; Andrew Kopkind, "Reagan, Ex-Radical," *New Republic*, July 15, 1967, 17–21; Phil Kerby, "Revolt against the Poor," *Nation*, September 25, 1967, 262–67; Jim Murray, "Ronald Reagan to the Rescue!," *Esquire*, February 1966, 76–78, 117–18.

12. Lisa McGirr, *Suburban Warriors: The Origins of the New American Right* (Princeton, N.J.: Princeton University Press, 2001), 3–216; Darren Dochuk, *From Bible Belt to Sunbelt: Plain-Folk Religion, Grassroots Politics, and the Rise of Evangelical Conservatism* (New York: Norton, 2011), xi–222; Rick Perlstein, *Before the Storm: Barry Goldwater and the Unmaking of the American Consensus* (2001; reprint, New York: Nation Books, 2009), 120–40.

13. David Farber, *The Rise and Fall of Modern American Conservatism: A Short History* (Princeton, N.J.: Princeton University Press, 2010), 9–76; Jonathan M. Schoenwald, *A Time for Choosing: The Rise of Modern American Conservatism* (New York: Oxford University Press, 2001), 3–99; Mary C. Brennan, *Turning Right in the Sixties: The Conservative Capture of the GOP* (Chapel Hill: University of North Carolina Press, 1995), 1–38.

14. Brennan, *Turning Right in the Sixties*, 39–59; Gregory L. Schneider, *Cadres for Conservatism: Young Americans for Freedom and the Rise of the Contemporary Right* (New York: New York University Press, 1999), 31–71; Catherine Rymph, *Republican Women: Feminism and Conservatism from Suffrage through the Rise of the New Right* (Chapel Hill: University of North Carolina Press, 2006), 131–74; Nicole Hemmer, *Messengers of the Right: Conservative Media and the Transformation of American Politics* (Philadelphia: University of Pennsylvania Press, 2016), ix–xvi; F. Clifton White with William J. Gill, *Suite 3505: The Story of the Draft Goldwater Movement* (New Rochelle, N.Y.: Arlington House, 1967), 30–112.

15. Donald T. Critchlow, *Phyllis Schlafly and Grassroots Conservatism: A Woman's Crusade* (Princeton, N.J.: Princeton University Press, 2005), 12–136; Marjorie J. Spruill, *Divided We Stand: The Battle over Women's Rights and Family Values That Polarized American Politics* (New York: Bloomsbury, 2017), 76–79; Farber, *Rise and Fall*, 120–34.

16. Farber, *Rise and Fall*, 77–118; White with Gill, *Suite 3505*, 113–423; Perlstein, *Before the Storm*, 248–516.

17. Joshua D. Farrington, *Black Republicans and the Transformation of the GOP* (Philadelphia: University of Pennsylvania Press, 2016), 129–40; McGirr, *Suburban Warriors*, 11–15; Kevin M. Kruse, *White Flight: Atlanta and the Making of Modern Conservatism* (Princeton, N.J.: Princeton University Press, 2005), 3–15, 259–66; Matthew D. Lassiter, *The Silent Majority: Suburban Politics in the Sunbelt South* (Princeton, N.J.: Princeton University Press, 2006), 1–19; Julian E. Zelizer, *Governing America: The Revival of Political History* (Princeton, N.J.: Princeton University Press, 2012), 68–72.

18. Nofziger, *Nofziger*, 65–66; White and Gill, *Why Reagan Won*, 66–92; William A. Rusher, "The Blunder of 1968," *American Spectator*, April 2006, 16–19; "The Making of a Candidate: A Look at the Reagan Boom," *U.S. News & World Report*, July 24, 1967, 53–55; "On the Run," *Newsweek*, March 20, 1967, 28–29.

19. Nofziger, *Nofziger*, 66; "Nancy Nixes Presidency," *Washington Post, Times Herald*, December 11, 1967, B2; F. Clifton White, *Politics as a Noble Calling: The Memoirs of F. Clifton White* (Ottawa, Ill.: Jameson Books, 1994), 171, 174; William A. Rusher, *The Rise of the Right* (New York: William Morrow, 1984), 202–6; "Reagan Takes a Look Ahead . . . and Explains Some '67 Decisions," *U.S. News & World Report*, January 8, 1968, 11; "Reagan Won't Campaign," *Washington Post, Times Herald*, January 11, 1968, A2; Chester, Hodgson, and Page, *American Melodrama*, 197.

20. "George, Dick, Ronnie," *Newsweek*, November 6, 1967, 27–28; "Now Reagan Tries a Cross-Country Tour," *U.S. News & World Report*, October 9, 1967, 20; Nofziger, *Nofziger*, 70; "The Most Happy Fellow," *Newsweek*, December 18, 1967, 35–36; Douglas W. Rae and Peter A. Lupsha, "The Politics of Theatre: Reagan at Yale," *New Republic*, February 3, 1968, 11–12; Chester, Hodgson, and Page, *American Melodrama*, 205–8.

21. Karl Fleming, "Reagan for President?," *Newsweek*, February 26, 1968, 24; "Conservatives to Back Nominee, Reagan Says," *Washington Post, Times Herald*, January 18, 1968, A2; James Reston, "Reagan View: Fresh Leader Wanted," *New York Times*, March 4, 1968, 1; Godfrey Sperling Jr., "Reagan Urges Unity Candidate," *Christian Science Monitor*, February 7, 1968, 1; "Now Reagan Is Moving on the National Scene," *U.S. News & World Report*, January 22, 1968, 44–45; David Holmstrom, "Reagan Urges Care on Vietnam Negotiations," *Christian Science Monitor*, January 20, 1968, 11; "Pueblo Incident Shameful—Reagan," *Washington Post*, January 31, 1968, A14; "Reagan Hits Riots Report," *Christian Science Monitor*, March 8, 1968, 17; "Reagan Talks of His Issues and His Plans," *U.S. News & World Report*, March 25, 1968, 54–62.

22. White, *Politics as a Noble Calling*, 176–77; "Reagan Still Shies from Nixon Stand," *Washington Post, Times Herald*, April 3, 1968, A2; "Reagan Hints Reassessment of His '68 Plans," *Washington Post, Times Herald*, April 17, 1968, A4; Tom Wicker, "In the Nation: Reagan on the Move," *New York Times*, April 28, 1968, E19; "Sounding the South," *Time*, May 31, 1968, 12–13; White and Gill, *Why Reagan Won*, 109.

23. "Reagan Chides LBJ for Promising More Than Could Be Delivered," *Washington Post, Times Herald*, May 19, 1968, A2; "California's 'Sick Campuses,'" *Nation*, July 8, 1968, 6; Philip Fradkin, "Reagan Compares Humphrey's Hecklers to Nazi

'Monsters,'" *Washington Post, Times Herald*, July 29, 1968, 1; "Reagan Calls Tyranny of Mob Threat to America," *New York Times*, July 5, 1968, 14; Ronald Goetz, "Reagan and the Poor," *Christian Century*, June 12, 1968, 776–77; Tom Wicker, "Reagan Questions Motive for Warren's Retirement," *New York Times*, June 24, 1968, 1.

24. John C. Waugh, "Reagan Looks Like a Hopeful but Sounds Like a Doubtful," *Christian Science Monitor*, June 5, 1968, 1; "Rival Road Shows," *Newsweek*, June 3, 1968, 30; "The G.O.P.'s Missing Men," *New York Times*, May 26, 1968, E18; Carl Greenberg, "Reagan Says GOP Nominees Should Have Similar Views," *Los Angeles Times*, July 22, 1968, 1; Leroy F. Aarons, "Governors Visited by Reagan," *Washington Post, Times Herald*, July 22, 1968, 55; John C. Waugh, "Reagan Learns Brinkmanship," *Christian Science Monitor*, July 15, 1968, 1; Gladwin Hill, "Reagan Says Aim Is to Help Party," *New York Times*, July 10, 1968, 20; "Reagan in South to Aid G.O.P. Fund," *New York Times*, July 25, 1968; White and Gill, *Why Reagan Won*, 114; "Nixon and the Veepstakes," *Newsweek*, August 5, 1968, 18–19; Nofziger, *Nofziger*, 72.

25. "A Place in the Sun," *Newsweek*, July 29, 1968, 21–22; "Pleasure Domes and Pastrami," *Newsweek*, August 12, 1968, 20–25; "The Scene on the Strip," *Time*, August 9, 1968, 13–14; Theodore H. White, *The Making of the President, 1968* (New York: Atheneum, 1969), 276–77.

26. "Those Much-Wooed Delegates," *Time*, August 2, 1968, 14–15; Stewart Alsop, "I Intend to Be Wooed," *Saturday Evening Post*, June 29, 1968, 16; Paul O'Neil, "A Correspondent's Observations on the Grand Old Proceedings," *Life*, August 16, 1968, 26–27; Norman Mailer, *Miami and the Siege of Chicago* (1968; reprint, New York: New York Review Books, 2008), 35–36; Marquis Childs, "Steady and Silent, Nixon Is on Top," *Washington Post, Times Herald*, July 22, 1968, A16; William A. Rusher, "What Happened at Miami Beach," *National Review*, December 3, 1968, 1206–9, 1231.

27. Ward Just, "Eisenhower Endorses Nixon," *Washington Post, Times Herald*, July 19, 1968, A1; Robert B. Semple Jr., "Nixon Hideout Is Oasis of Calm," *New York Times*, August 4, 1968, 53; Patrick J. Buchanan, *The Greatest Comeback: How Richard Nixon Rose from Defeat to Create the New Majority* (New York: Crown Forum, 2014), 302–3; John Herbers, "Nixon Aides Confident of Nomination," *New York Times*, August 4, 1968, 53; "The Convention Countdown," *Newsweek*, August 12, 1968, 16–20; Ward Just, "Nixon Serene, Genial," *Washington Post*, August 7, 1968, A1.

28. "Rocky Tops Harris Survey," *Washington Post, Times Herald*, August 1, 1968, A1; Mailer, *Miami and the Siege of Chicago*, 19–27; James Reston, "Nixon or Rockefeller: Does It Really Matter?," *New York Times*, August 4, 1968, E14; "Nixon or Rockefeller: Domestic Issues," *Wall Street Journal*, August 1, 1968, 6; "Nixon or Rockefeller: Foreign Issues," *Wall Street Journal*, August 2, 1968, 12; "Is This the Man?," *Newsweek*, July 29, 1968, 22–23; "Polls: Confusing and Exaggerated," *Time*, August 9, 1968, 19; Leroy F. Aarons, "Rocky Says Nixon, Reagan Would Lose," *Washington Post, Times Herald*, July 24, 1968, A4.

29. "Chienlit (or Is It Chic-en Lit?)," *National Review*, June 18, 1968, 594–95; R. W. Apple Jr., "Rockefeller Clings to Hope of Winning Nomination," *New York Times*, August 6, 1968, 21; Gerald Astor, "Nelson Rockefeller Talks about the Gap between the People," *Look*, September 17, 1968, 58–59; Richard Norton Smith, *On His Own Terms: A Life of Nelson Rockefeller* (New York: Random House, 2014), 536–37; Chester,

Hodgson, and Page, *American Melodrama*, 453–55; English et al., *Divided They Stand*, 271–75, 283–84.

30. "Rocky-Reagan 'Hot Line' Set Up at Miami," *Washington Post, Times Herald*, August 5, 1968, A4; "Reagan Steps Up Convention Drive," *Washington Post, Times Herald*, August 1, 1968, A6; Dent, *Prodigal South Returns to Power*, 84–85; "Nixon Slips to 591," *Newsweek*, August 5, 1968, 22–23; "15 to 20 Nixon Votes in South Shift to Reagan, Survey Finds," *New York Times*, August 1, 1968, 20; "A Nibbling Process," *Time*, August 2, 1968, 13; Gladwin Hill, "A Gain by Reagan Is Reported," *New York Times*, August 7, 1968, 1.

31. William Chapman, "Masters of Crowdsmanship Primed for Big Test in Miami," *Washington Post, Times Herald*, August 3, 1968, A8; Mailer, *Miami and the Siege of Chicago*, 71–72; English et al., *Divided They Stand*, 276.

32. Hill, "Gain by Reagan Is Reported," 1; Ivy Baker Priest Stevens, "Ronald Reagan," *New York Times*, August 8, 1968, 24; White and Gill, *Why Reagan Won*, 123; Rusher, *Rise of the Right*, 214–16; William Chapman, "Reagan Pitch for Delegates Never Let Up," *Washington Post, Times Herald*, August 8, 1968, A6.

33. White, *Politics as a Noble Calling*, 178–79; Rusher, *Rise of the Right*, 214–16; Chester, Hodgson, and Page, *American Melodrama*, 457; White, *Making of the President, 1968*, 279–80.

34. "Eyeball to Eyeball with Strom," *Newsweek*, August 19, 1968, 26–27; Joseph Crespino, *Strom Thurmond's America* (New York: Hill and Wang, 2012), 3–11, 61–184; Jack Bass and Marilyn W. Thompson, *Strom: The Complicated Personal and Political Life of Strom Thurmond* (New York: PublicAffairs, 2005), 102–27.

35. "Coy, with Clout," *Time*, August 23, 1968, 16; Margaret O'Mara, *Pivotal Tuesdays: Four Elections That Shaped the Twentieth Century* (Philadelphia: University of Pennsylvania Press, 2015), 130–33; Dennis Wainstock, *Election Year 1968: The Turning Point* (New York: Enigma Books, 2012), 37–38; Crespino, *Strom Thurmond's America*, 185–206.

36. Jules Witcover, *The Resurrection of Richard Nixon* (New York: G. P. Putnam's Sons, 1970), 146–47, 309–213; Richard Nixon, *RN: The Memoirs of Richard Nixon* (New York: Grosset & Dunlap, 1978), 304–5; Nadine Cohodas, *Strom Thurmond and the Politics of Southern Change* (Atlanta: Mercer University Press, 1993), 396–98; Dent, *Prodigal South Returns to Power*, 81–84; Chester, Hodgson, and Page, *American Melodrama*, 446–48.

37. Robert B. Semple Jr., "The Nixon Strategy: Unity and Caution," *New York Times*, August 11, 1968, 1; "GOP Votes for Unity," *Business Week*, August 10, 1968, 21–24.

38. Dent, *Prodigal South Returns to Power*, 96–98; Richard H. Rovere, "Letter from Miami Beach," *New Yorker*, August 17, 1968, 93–100; Tom Wicker, "Rockefeller and Reagan Struggle to Deny Nixon Victory on First Ballot," *New York Times*, August 7, 1968, 1; William Chapman, "How Nixon Held Southern Delegations," *Washington Post, Times Herald*, August 9, 1968, A10; Witcover, *Resurrection of Richard Nixon*, 342–44; John A. Farrell, *Richard Nixon: The Life* (New York: Doubleday, 2017), 331–34.

39. Cohodas, *Strom Thurmond and the Politics of Southern Change*, 398–99; Jack Nelson, "Thurmond Stops Reagan, Holds South for Nixon," *Los Angeles Times*, August 7, 1968, 1.

40. Crespino, *Strom Thurmond's America*, 219; "Eyeball to Eyeball with Strom,"

26–27; Joseph Alsop, "Southern Strategy of Nixon Is Seen as Likely to Succeed," *Washington Post, Times Herald*, August 12, 1968, A21; Garry Wills, *Nixon Agonistes: The Crisis of the Self-Made Man* (Boston: Houghton Mifflin, 1970), 263–65.

41. Hollie I. West, "Negro Protests Aired at Miami," *Washington Post, Times Herald*, August 6, 1968, A4; John Dillin, "Can Party Regain Black Vote?," *Christian Science Monitor*, August 6, 1968, 1; Leah Wright Rigueur, *The Loneliness of the Black Republican: Pragmatic Politics and the Pursuit of Power* (Princeton, N.J.: Princeton University Press, 2015), 130–35; Timothy N. Thurber, *Republicans and Race: The GOP's Frayed Relationship with African Americans, 1945–1974* (Lawrence: University Press of Kansas, 2013), 272–75; Mailer, *Miami and the Siege of Chicago*, 50–56.

42. Thomas A. Johnson, "Racial Violence Erupts in Miami," *New York Times*, August 8, 1968, 17; John Dillin, "Black Riot Scarcely Ruffles Convention," *Christian Science Monitor*, August 9, 1968, 7; "3 Negroes Killed in New Miami Riot," *New York Times*, August 9, 1968, 1.

43. White, *Making of the President, 1968*, 283–85; "Medium over Tedium," *Time*, August 16, 1968, 36–37; "Safe, Sane, and Soporific," *Life*, August 16, 1968, 36; "TV and Conventions," *Life*, August 23, 1968, 26B; Richard L. Tobin, "Nixon's Second Chance," *Saturday Review*, August 24, 1968, 19–22; Tom Wicker, "In the Nation: One for All and All for What?," *New York Times*, August 8, 1968, 32.

44. Tom Wicker, "Nixon Is Nominated on the First Ballot," *New York Times*, August 8, 1968, 1; Richard L. Strout, "The Unsinkable Molly Brown of Politics," *Christian Science Monitor*, August 9, 1968, 1; John Osborne, "So the Republicans Took Richard Nixon," *New Republic*, August 17, 1968, 13–14.

45. "The Unlikely No. 2," *Time*, August 16, 1968, 19–20; Jules Witcover, *White Knight: The Rise of Spiro Agnew* (New York: Random House, 1972), 230–31.

46. Kenneth T. Jackson, *Crabgrass Frontier: The Suburbanization of the United States* (New York: Oxford University Press, 1985), 3–11, 231–71; "Suburbs and the '68 Election," *U.S. News & World Report*, August 12, 1968, 32–34; Gerald W. Johnson, "Who's Spiro T. Agnew?," *New Republic*, August 24, 1968, 11; Richard O'Mara, "Discovering Spiro Agnew," *Nation*, September 2, 1968, 175–77; Joseph Albright, *What Makes Spiro Run: The Life and Times of Spiro Agnew* (New York: Dodd, Mead, 1972), 1–167; Theo Lippman Jr., *Spiro Agnew's America* (New York: Norton, 1972), 13–95.

47. Witcover, *White Knight*, 10–29; "Where Governor Agnew Stands on Civil Rights," *Reader's Digest*, November 1968, 119–21; Albright, *What Makes Spiro Run*, 168–92; "Agnew Transition Traced to GOP," *Christian Science Monitor*, August 10, 1968, 6; Clay Risen, *A Nation on Fire: America in the Wake of the King Assassination* (New York: John Wiley & Sons, 2009), 174–76.

48. Witcover, *White Knight*, 180–225; Lawrence O'Donnell, *Playing with Fire: The 1968 Election and the Transformation of American Politics* (New York: Penguin, 2017), 291–95; Richard Homan, "Agnew Cools on Rocky, Lauds Nixon," *Washington Post, Times Herald*, May 4, 1968, A1; "Agnew Raps Rocky on 'Lack of Views,'" *Washington Post, Times Herald*, A1; Richard Homan, "'Snub' by Rockefeller Influenced Agnew's Shift," *Washington Post, Times Herald*, August 7, 1968, A8.

49. Robert B. Semple Jr., "Nixon Considering Moderate on Ticket," *New York Times*, June 30, 1968, 1; Warren Weaver Jr., "Nixon Said to Want Rockefeller, Lindsay, or Percy for 2d Place," *New York Times*, August 5, 1968, 1; "Nixon Said to Bar

Southerners' Bid," *New York Times*, August 7, 1968, 30; "Nixon Nominated on the First Ballot; Hatfield Seen Leading for No. 2 Spot," *Wall Street Journal*, August 8, 1968, 2; Dent, *Prodigal South Returns to Power*, 100–101.

50. "How Agnew Was Chosen to Be No. 2 on Ticket," *U.S. News & World Report*, August 19, 1968, 32; "The Name Is Agnew," *Newsweek*, August 9, 1968, 30–33; Dent, *Prodigal South Returns to Power*, 102–3; Albright, *What Makes Spiro Run*, 215–18.

51. "Flare-Up over Agnew—Its Meaning," *U.S. News & World Report*, August 19, 1968, 6; "Nixon's Running Mate Answers His Critics," *U.S. News & World Report*, August 26, 1968, 27–29; Nixon, *RN*, 312–14; Richard J. Whalen, *Catch the Falling Flag: A Republican's Challenge to His Party* (Boston: Houghton Mifflin, 1972), 202–3; Leroy F. Aarons, "Rocky Camp Is Rankled over Agnew," *New York Times*, August 9, 1968, A1; "Nixon Naming of Agnew Dismays Liberals, but Their Last-Ditch Romney Push Fails," *Wall Street Journal*, August 9, 1968, 2; Robert J. Donovan, "Nixon's Selection of Agnew for No. 2 Spot Astounds Politicians," *Los Angeles Times*, August 9, 1968, 1; Norman C. Miller, "Striking Out the Liberal Moderates," *Wall Street Journal*, August 9, 1968, 6; "Once and Future Candidates," *Time*, August 16, 1968, 21; Donald Jackson, "Rockefeller: 'See You in Albany,'" *Life*, August 16, 1968, 21.

52. Nofziger, *Nofziger*, 74; "Reagan Cheerful Despite Setback," *New York Times*, August 9, 1968, 18; Joseph Alsop, "The Nation's Mood Swings to Right," *Washington Post, Times Herald*, August 7, 1968, A21; "Portents and Pitfalls," *Wall Street Journal*, August 9, 1968, 6; Robert Mason, *Richard Nixon and the Quest for a New Majority* (Chapel Hill: University of North Carolina Press, 2004), 29.

53. Ronald Reagan, *An American Life* (New York: Simon and Schuster, 1990), 176–78.

54. "A Chance to Lead," *Time*, August 16, 1968, 10–11; "Right down the Middle," *Newsweek*, August 19, 1968, 18; Vermont Royster, "Thinking Things Over about Durability," *Wall Street Journal*, August 9, 1968, 6; "Durable Leader of the Republicans," *New York Times*, August 8, 1968, 22; "Nixon the Nominee," *New York Times*, August 8, 1968, 32; Michael A. Cohen, *American Maelstrom: The 1968 Election and the Politics of Division* (New York: Oxford University Press, 2016), 246.

55. "Nixon: 'The Long Dark Night for America Is About to End,'" *U.S. News & World Report*, August 19, 1968, 54–56, 78–79; "A Chance to Lead," 10.

56. Wills, *Nixon Agonistes*, 308–16.

CHAPTER SEVEN

1. Susanna McBee, "Victory—but the Fumes of Battle Fill the Air," *Life*, September 6, 1968, 23–24; Daniel Walker, *Rights in Conflict: Chicago's 7 Brutal Days* (New York: Grosset & Dunlap, 1968), 154–65.

2. Carl Solberg, *Hubert Humphrey: A Biography* (1984; reprint, Minneapolis: Borealis Books, 2003), 364–65.

3. Norman Mailer, *Miami and the Siege of Chicago* (1968; reprint, New York: New York Review Books, 2008), 169; Shana Alexander, "Eyewitness," in *Law and Disorder: The Chicago Convention and Its Aftermath*, ed. Donald Myrus (Chicago, 1968), 22–24; Walker, *Rights in Conflict*, 165–75; Jean Strouse, "A Taste of Fascism," *Commonweal*, September 20, 1968, 616–18; "Lots of Law, Little Order," *Newsweek*, September 9, 1968, 38–42.

4. "Mule Teams at Work," *Newsweek*, September 9, 1968, 68–69; Kenneth Crawford, "In Living Color," *Newsweek*, September 16, 1968, 36; Rick Perlstein, *Nixonland: The Rise of a President and the Fracturing of America* (New York: Scribner, 2008), 315–27.

5. Solberg, *Hubert Humphrey*, 364–65; Albert Eisele, *Almost to the Presidency: A Biography of Two American Politicians* (Blue Earth, Minn.: Piper Company, 1972), 358; Theodore H. White, *The Making of the President, 1968* (New York: Atheneum, 1969), 342–54.

6. "The Winner: How—and What—He Won," *Newsweek*, September 9, 1968, 30–36; "The Man Who Would Recapture Youth," *Time*, September 6, 1968, 15–20; Solberg, *Hubert Humphrey*, 365–66.

7. Stewart Alsop, "Hubert Horatio Humphrey," *Saturday Evening Post*, August 24, 1968, 21–25; Richard Wilson, "This Is Humphrey," *Look*, July 9, 1968, 41–46; Edgar Berman, *Hubert: The Triumph and Tragedy of the Humphrey I Knew* (New York: G. P. Putnam's Sons, 1979), 152–53; Solberg, *Hubert Humphrey*, 321–23.

8. Hubert H. Humphrey, *Education of a Public Man: My Life and Politics* (Garden City, N.Y.: Doubleday, 1976), 22–165; Eisele, *Almost to the Presidency*, 11–70; Solberg, *Hubert Humphrey*, 34–129; Dale Kramer, "Young Man in a Hurry," *New Republic*, June 16, 1947, 14–16.

9. "Education of a Senator," *Time*, January 17, 1949, 13–16; Rufus Jarman, "The Senate's Gabbiest Freshman," *Saturday Evening Post*, October 1, 1949, 30, 120–22; Solberg, *Hubert Humphrey*, 133–227; "Cracking the Whip for Civil Rights," *Newsweek*, April 13, 1964, 26–32; Timothy N. Thurber, *The Politics of Equality: Hubert H. Humphrey and the African American Freedom Struggle* (New York: Columbia University Press, 1999), 127–48; Clay Risen, *The Bill of the Century: The Epic Battle for the Civil Rights Act* (New York: Bloomsbury, 2014), 173–237.

10. Fletcher Knebel, "Advance Man for the Great Society," *Look*, April 6, 1965, 80–88; "'I Enjoy It,'" *Newsweek*, March 15, 1965, 28–29; "The Bright Spirit," *Time*, April 1, 1966, 21–23; James Deakin, "Humphrey," *New Republic*, May 29, 1965, 10–12; Peter Lisagor, "Ask Not 'What Became of Hubert Humphrey?,'" *New York Times Magazine*, July 25, 1965, 6–7, 42–47; Hugh Sidey, "LBJ's Ombudsman for the Cities," *Life*, October 6, 1967, 36; William Bowen, "What's New about Hubert Humphrey," *Fortune*, August 1965, 142–44; "Hubert Unbound," *Time*, January 7, 1966, 22; "Humphrey's African Safari," *Ebony*, March 1968, 50–54; "Making the Rounds with HHH," *Newsweek*, April 17, 1967, 56–57; "Veep on the Wing," *Time*, January 12, 1968, 12–13; "Hubert Humphrey Takes Time Off," *Look*, April 19, 1966, 47–52; "Muriel: Humphrey's Staunch and Gentle Half," *Look*, October 29, 1968, 92–94; Hubert H. Humphrey, "The Joy of Being 'Boppa,'" *McCall's*, June 1967, 74–75, 113; Robert Sherrill and Harry W. Ernst, *The Drugstore Liberal* (New York: Grossman, 1968), 1–16; William V. Shannon, "Why Humphrey Gets Taken for Granted," *New Republic*, July 4, 1964, 10–12.

11. "Head of Steam," *Newsweek*, February 8, 1965, 22–23; Richard B. Stolley, "The Backup Man Winds Up Congress and Has a Few Tense Hours," *Life*, October 22, 1965, 39, 42–42A; Hugh Sidey, "A Diligent Student Who Is Nothing but May Be Everything," *Life*, September 19, 1966, 50; Douglas Kiker, "Washington," *Atlantic*, January 1967, 6–10; "Kennedy vs. Humphrey—Who Has Gained in '65," *U.S. News & World*

Report, November 8, 1965, 52–53; Warren Weaver Jr., "One of Them Will Probably Be Next in the White House," *New York Times Magazine*, May 22, 1966, 26–27, 89–104; "Memo to HHH," *Newsweek*, January 3, 1966, 14–15; Jack Richardson, "Who Is Hubert, What Is He?," *Esquire*, November 1966, 106–8, 205–9; Eisele, *Almost to the Presidency*, 236–38; Solberg, *Hubert Humphrey*, 240, 265–66, 302–3; Robert G. Sherrill, "Hubert Humphrey Speaking in Tongues," *Nation*, April 29, 1968, 564–69.

12. Humphrey, *Education of a Public Man*, 318–28; Solberg, *Hubert Humphrey*, 270–78.

13. "Life of a Salesman," *Newsweek*, March 7, 1966, 25–26; "Still Talking," *Time*, March 18, 1966, 27A–27B; Hubert H. Humphrey, "Vietnam: Why We Stay," *Reader's Digest*, July 1966, 47–49; "Stumping in Saigon," *Newsweek*, November 13, 1967, 32–33; "Dissenting from the Dissenters," *Newsweek*, November 6, 1967, 25–26; Walter LaFeber, *The Deadly Bet: LBJ, Vietnam, and the 1968 Election* (Lanham, Md.: Rowman & Littlefield, 2005), 121; "Right Track," *Newsweek*, May 8, 1967, 39; Michael Novak, "Humphrey at Stanford," *Commonweal*, March 24, 1967, 7–8; Don Robinson, "Humphrey, at AU, Derides Protestors," *Washington Post, Times Herald*, February 25, 1968, A1.

14. Solberg, *Hubert Humphrey*, 324; Godfrey Sperling Jr., "An Untold Humphrey Story," *Christian Science Monitor*, March 28, 1968, 1; Rowland Evans and Robert Novak, "Humphrey Gets a Belated Start in Trying to Buck Bobby Blitz," *Washington Post, Times Herald*, April 3, 1968, A17; "Can Humphrey Block Kennedy?," *U.S. News & World Report*, April 29, 1968, 14; Humphrey, *Education of a Public Man*, 360–62; Richard Wilson, "This Is Humphrey," *Look*, July 9, 1968, 41–46; Meg Greenfield, "Hubert Humphrey in 1968," *Reporter*, June 13, 1968, 19–24; Kenneth Crawford, "Last Man In," *Newsweek*, April 15, 1968, 53.

15. "The Democrats' New Ball Game," *Newsweek*, April 15, 1968, 44–48B; John Osborne, "The Dogged Loyalty That Dogs HHH," *New Republic*, May 4, 1968, 11–13; Humphrey, *Education of a Public Man*, 362–68.

16. "Hubert the Happy," *Newsweek*, April 22, 1968, 34–38A; "Can Hubert Humphrey Stop RFK?," *Newsweek*, April 29, 1968, 23–30; "Hubert's Nonsecret," *Time*, April 26, 1968, 22–23; "Unions' New Favorite for '68: Now It's Hubert H. Humphrey," *U.S. News & World Report*, April 15, 1968, 84; Rowland Evans and Robert Novak, "Businessmen to Raise $4 Million War Chest for HHH Candidacy," *Washington Post, Times Herald*, April 24, 1968, A21; Thurber, *Politics of Equality*, 261; Roy Reed, "Humphrey Found Decision Difficult," *New York Times*, April 28, 1968, 66; Warren Weaver Jr., "Humphrey Joins Presidential Race; Calls for Unity," *New York Times*, April 28, 1968, 1.

17. Humphrey, *Education of a Public Man*, 369–72; Fred Harris, *Potomac Fever* (New York: Norton, 1977), 161–63; Lewis Chester, Geoffrey Hodgson, and Bruce Page, *An American Melodrama: The Presidential Campaign of 1968* (New York: Viking, 1969), 151–52; Berman, *Hubert*, 160–69.

18. "Humphrey Favored by Party Leaders," *Christian Science Monitor*, June 4, 1968, 3; Chester, Hodgson, and Page, *American Melodrama*, 153–54; "Humphrey's Bandwagon," *Newsweek*, June 10, 1968, 27–28; Roy Reed, "Humphrey Sews Up the Delegates," *New York Times*, June 2, 1968, E3.

19. Meg Greenfield, "Hubert Humphrey—the Making of a Candidate, 1968,"

Washington Post, Times Herald, November 11, 1968, A24; "Humphrey Steps Out on His Own," *Business Week*, April 20, 1968, 40–41; "Humphrey's Optimism," *New York Times*, July 31, 1968, 23; "The Once and Future Humphrey," *Time*, May 3, 1968, 15–19; "HHH—Hop, Hum, Heal," *Newsweek*, May 13, 1968, 31–32; "Playing Favorites," *Newsweek*, August 12, 1968, 25–26; Victor S. Navasky, "Report on the Candidate Named Humphrey," *New York Times Magazine*, August 25, 1968, 22–23, 73–77; David English and the Staff of the London *Daily Express*, *Divided They Stand* (Englewood Cliffs, N.J.: Prentice-Hall, 1969), 216–17.

20. William S. White, "Humphrey Campaign Intended to Reflect Dignity, Restraint," *Washington Post, Times Herald*, May 1, 1968, A25; Susanne McBee, "How He Plans to Get the Boss's Job," *Life*, May 3, 1968, 32B; Marquis Childs, "The 'New' Hubert: A Contrast in Style," *Washington Post, Times Herald*, May 27, 1968, A18; "Humphrey Campaign Glides Along," *Christian Science Monitor*, May 17, 1968, 17; Roy Reed, "Humphrey Hovers on the Threshold," *New York Times*, April 14, 1968, E3; "Humphrey Leads Rivals in Survey," *New York Times*, May 15, 1968, 31.

21. Marquis Childs, "Humphrey Image Doesn't Tell All," *Washington Post, Times Herald*, June 19, 1968, A20; Michael A. Cohen, *American Maelstrom: The 1968 Election and the Politics of Division* (New York: Oxford University Press, 2016), 150; Humphrey, *Education of a Public Man*, 372–75; Alan L. Otten, "Politics and People," *Wall Street Journal*, June 13, 1968, 18.

22. "Man in the Middle," *Newsweek*, July 29, 1968, 23–24; "Politics without Joy," *U.S. News & World Report*, August 12, 1968, 30–31; Warren Weaver Jr., "Humphrey's Campaign," *New York Times*, July 4, 1968, 10; "Waiting for an Alternative," *Time*, July 12, 1968, 14–15; Carl Greenberg, "Heckling Can't Halt Me," *Los Angeles Times*, July 29, 1968, 1; "Looking toward Chicago," *Time*, August 9, 1968, 20–21; Jules Witcover, *The Year the Dream Died: Revisiting 1968 in America* (New York: Warner Books, 1997), 284.

23. James Reston, "Problem for Humphrey," *New York Times*, June 17, 1968, 33; James Reston, "Washington: Hubert's Ahead, but Which Hubert?," *New York Times*, May 31, 1968, 28; Robert J. Donovan, "Quit and Run on Own, Gov. Hoff Asks Humphrey," *Los Angeles Times*, July 22, 1968, 1; Hugh Sidey, "A Gentleman's Understanding with Hubert Humphrey," *Life*, June 28, 1968, 32B; William S. White, "Humphrey Confuses Voters with His Zigzags on Vietnam," *Washington Post, Times Herald*, August 19, 1968, A17.

24. Paul Hofmann, "Moyers Says Humphrey Will Stress Own Policies," *New York Times*, June 17, 1968, 1; Roy Reed, "Humphrey Vows He'll Be Own Man if He Is Elected," *New York Times*, June 21, 1968, 1; Max Frankel, "Humphrey: A Need to Be His Own Man," *New York Times*, June 23, 1968, E1; Stewart Alsop, "Hubert Humphrey and the Presidential Smell," *Saturday Evening Post*, May 18, 1968, 18; John Reddy, "Can Humphrey Hold His Party Together?," *Reader's Digest*, July 1968, 105–10; Victor S. Navasky, "Report on the Candidate Named Humphrey," *New York Times Magazine*, August 25, 1968, 22–23, 73–77; Philip D. Carter, "Campaigning: Humphrey," *Atlantic*, July 1968, 9–16.

25. Tom Wicker, "Report on the Phenomenon Named McCarthy," *New York Times Magazine*, August 25, 1968, 24–25, 78–80; "A Fourth Party?," *Newsweek*, July 15, 1968, 23–24; Homer Bigart, "McCarthy Talks at Garden," *New York Times*, August 16, 1968, 1;

"The Dream vs. Reality," *Newsweek*, August 26, 1968, 19–21; Eugene J. McCarthy, *The Year of the People* (Garden City, N.Y.: Doubleday, 1969), 191–93; Paul R. Wieck, "An Open Democratic Convention," *New Republic*, July 6, 1968, 15–17; John J. Quirk, "McCarthy Fights for an Open Convention," *Commonweal*, August 9,1968, 516–18.

26. Shana Alexander, "Gene McCarthy Goes Back to Work," *Life*, June 28, 1968, 21; Rowland Evans and Robert Novak, "McCarthy's Agony," *Washington Post, Times Herald*, June 9, 1968, B7; "Gene: Back to the Faithful," *Time*, June 21, 1968, 21; "McCarthy: Confident, Pessimistic," *Washington Post, Times Herald*, August 14, 1968, A1; Sol Stern, "And Then There Was Gene," *Ramparts*, August 10, 1968, 58–63; Gloria Steinem, "Trying to Love Eugene," *New York*, August 1968, 14–19, 60–61; Dominic Sandbrook, *Eugene McCarthy: The Rise and Fall of American Liberalism* (New York: Knopf, 2004), 205–9; Jeremy Larner, *Nobody Knows: Reflections on the McCarthy Campaign of 1968* (New York: Macmillan, 1970), 122–40.

27. Peter Grose, "A 'Dove' Who Flew Bombers," *New York Times*, August 11, 1968, 62; George McGovern, "We Can Solve the Vietnam Dilemma," *Saturday Review*, October 16, 1965, 37–38; "The Democrats, 1968," *Newsweek*, July 22, 1968, 21–22; "Rallying the Kennedy Vote," *Time*, August 16, 1968, 22; "An Old Friend of Bobby's Jumps into the Race," *Life*, August 23, 1968, 24–25; "McGovern," *New Yorker*, August 24, 1968, 23–25; "McGovern," *New Republic*, August 24, 1968, 3–5; "Why George Did It," *Newsweek*, August 26, 1968, 22; George McGovern, *Grassroots: The Autobiography of George McGovern* (New York: Random House, 1977), 108–23; Thomas J. Knock, *The Rise of a Prairie Statesman: The Life and Times of George McGovern* (Princeton, N.J.: Princeton University Press, 2016), 379–402.

28. Dennis Wainstock, *Election Year 1968: The Turning Point* (New York: Enigma Books, 2012), 127–28; Witcover, *Year the Dream Died*, 313–15; Walter Rugaber, "A Bitter Maddox, Assailing 'Socialist' Politicians, Drops Campaign for Presidency," *New York Times*, August 29, 1968, 26.

29. Clark Clifford with Richard Holbrooke, *Counsel to the President: A Memoir* (New York: Random House, 1991), 562–64; James Reston, "Washington: From Miami Beach to Chicago," *New York Times*, August 11, 1968, E10; Robert J. Donovan, "Bombing Statement Intensifies Democratic Rift over Vietnam," *Los Angeles Times*, August 16, 1968, 1; Richard Bergholz, "Humphrey's Dilemma: How to Soothe Both Hawks and Doves," *Los Angeles Times*, August 24, 1968, 1.

30. Solberg, *Hubert Humphrey*, 347–51; Lewis L. Gould, *1968: The Election That Changed America*, 2nd ed. (Chicago: Ivan R. Dee, 1993), 86–87; Sam Houston Johnson, *My Brother Lyndon* (New York: Cowles Book Co., 1970), 260–61.

31. Doris Kearns, *Lyndon Johnson and the American Dream* (New York: Harper and Row, 1976), 350–51; Hugh Sidey, "It's Only a Fantasy Now But . . . ," *Life*, July 26, 1968, 4; Merle Miller, *Lyndon: An Oral Biography* (New York: G. P. Putnam's Sons, 1980), 523; George Christian, *The President Steps Down: A Personal Memoir of the Transfer of Power* (New York: Macmillan, 1970), 148–50.

32. White, *Making of the President, 1968*, 325; "The Politics of War," *Time*, August 23, 1968, 10–11; "No Bombing Halt, President Vows," *Los Angeles Times*, August 20, 1968, 1; Ken Hughes, *Chasing Shadows: The Nixon Tapes, the Chennault Affair, and the Origins of Watergate* (Charlottesville: University of Virginia Press, 2014), 17–18; Hugh Sidey, "It Was Nixon's Day at the LBJ," *Life*, August 23, 1968, 2.

33. Mark Kurlansky, *1968: The Year That Rocked the World* (New York: Ballantine, 2004), 287–305; Kyle Longley, *LBJ's 1968: Power, Politics, and the Presidency in America's Year of Upheaval* (New York: Cambridge University Press, 2018), 185–204; "The Vietnam Plank," *Newsweek*, September 2, 1968, 24–25; Eisele, *Almost to the Presidency*, 344–45; White, *Making of the President, 1968*, 326.

34. Solberg, *Hubert Humphrey*, 351–54

35. Berman, *Hubert*, 181; Humphrey, *Education of a Public Man*, 389–90.

36. Garry Wills, *Nixon Agonistes: The Crisis of the Self-Made Man* (Boston: Houghton Mifflin, 1970), 323–73.

37. David Farber, *Chicago '68* (1988; reprint, Chicago: University of Chicago Press, 1994), 3–79; Tom Hayden, *Reunion: A Memoir* (New York: Random House, 1988), 254–64, 293–94; Todd Gitlin, *The Sixties: Years of Hope, Days of Rage* (New York: Bantam, 1987), 232–38, 286–89; Kurlansky, *1968*, 93–94, 97–99; "The Politics of Yip," *Time*, April 3, 1968, 61.

38. Walker, *Rights in Conflict*, 19–49.

39. "Inside and Out," *Newsweek*, January 22, 1968, 21–22; "Stalag '68," *Time*, August 23, 1968, 12–13; "Daley City under Siege," *Time*, August 30, 1968, 18–19; "Chicago: 'An Armed Camp' for Democratic Convention," *U.S. News & World Report*, August 26, 1968, 24–25; "Safe for Democracy?," *Newsweek*, August 5, 1968, 18; "Down to the Barbed Wire," *Newsweek*, August 26, 1968, 17–19.

40. Mike Royko, *Boss: Richard J. Daley of Chicago* (New York: Dutton, 1971), 62–69; Adam Cohen and Elizabeth Taylor, *American Pharaoh: Mayor Richard J. Daley—His Battle for Chicago and the Nation* (Boston: Little, Brown, 2000), 48–325; David Halberstam, "Daley of Chicago," *Harper's*, August 1968, 25–36; D. J. R. Bruckner, "Daley May Wait until August to Name Preference," *Los Angeles Times*, April 3, 1968, 1.

41. John Kearney, "Mayor Daley: Decision-Maker in Chicago," *Commonweal*, August 9, 1968, 518–19; "A City Run by a Machine," *U.S. News & World Report*, February 12, 1968, 47; "Reading the Riot Act," *Newsweek*, April 29, 1968, 22; Clay Risen, *A Nation on Fire: America in the Wake of the King Assassination* (New York: John Wiley & Sons, 2009), 146–81; Cohen and Taylor, *American Pharaoh*, 326–458.

42. Milton Viorst, "Can the Ringmaster Keep His Show Going?," *Saturday Evening Post*, August 24, 1968, 26, 70–74; Keith Wheeler, "This Is Daley's Chicago—He Doesn't Dig Anything Else," *Life*, September 6, 1968, 28–29; Mailer, *Miami and the Siege of Chicago*, 103–4; "Switch in Time?," *Newsweek*, July 29, 1968, 23; "Dementia in the Second City," *Time*, September 6, 1968, 21–24; "Boss Daley's Fatherly Fist," *Newsweek*, September 9, 1968, 40–41.

43. Terry Southern, "Grooving in Chi," *Esquire*, November 1968, 83–86; Farber, *Chicago '68*, 167–68, 178–88; Walker, *Rights in Conflict*, viii–ix, 83–100.

44. John Schultz, *No One Was Killed: Documentation and Meditation: Convention Week, Chicago, August 1968* (Chicago: Big Table, 1969), 94–124; Walker, *Rights in Conflict*, 103–13.

45. Mark Lane, *Chicago Eyewitness* (New York: Astor-Honor, 1968), 16–45; Walker, *Rights in Conflict*, 114–50; Schultz, *No One Was Killed*, 124–61.

46. John Sack, "In a Pig's Eye," *Esquire*, November 1968, 91–94; "Beat the Press," *Newsweek*, September 9, 1968, 70–71; Stewart Alsop, "Virus X and the Body Politic,"

Newsweek, September 16, 1968, 108; "The Police Need Help," *Time*, October 4, 1968, 26–27; Farber, *Chicago '68*, 128–31, 141–46, 250–51; Gitlin, *The Sixties*, 319.

47. Alan L. Otten, "Humphrey's Handicaps," *Wall Street Journal*, August 23, 1968, 8; "And Now Chicago," *Newsweek*, September 2, 1968, 22–23; White, *Making of the President, 1968*, 316–17; Mailer, *Miami and the Siege of Chicago*, 108–13; "Convention of the Lemmings," *Time*, August 30, 1968, 15–16; Vermont Royster, "Old Politics, New Times," *Wall Street Journal*, August 27, 1968, 12.

48. Solberg, *Hubert Humphrey*, 357–59; Eisele, *Almost to the Presidency*, 348–49; Victor S. Navasky, "The Nomination, as Seen and Directed by the Best Politician in the Country," *New York Times Magazine*, 32, 134–38; Lawrence F. O'Brien, *No Final Victories: A Life in Politics—from John F. Kennedy to Watergate* (Garden City, N.Y.: Doubleday, 1974), 250–51; Roy Reed, "Nomination of Humphrey: Details of a 5-Month Drive," *New York Times*, September 1, 1968, 1; Larner, *Nobody Knows*, 171.

49. Larner, *Nobody Knows*, 167–71; English et al., *Divided They Stand*, 308–9; Rowland Evans and Robert Novak, "McCarthy-Connally Ploy," *Washington Post, Times Herald*, September 1, 1968, B7; Richard Harwood, "Humphrey Advisers Back McCarthy for Second Spot on Ticket," *Washington Post, Times Herald*, August 28, 1968, A7; Richard T. Stout, *People* (New York: Harper and Row, 1970), 351–54.

50. Thomas B. Morgan, "Teddy," *Esquire*, April 1962, 60, 145–52; Joseph Roddy, "Coming Up Strong in the Senate," *Look*, July 13, 1965, 29–32; "Two Senators Named Kennedy," *Newsweek*, January 17, 1966, 17–25; Robert B. Semple, "The Future of Edward Kennedy," *New York Times*, June 7, 1968, 21; Robert J. Donovan, "Political Attention Focusing on Last Surviving Brother," *Los Angeles Times*, June 8, 1968, 1; "A Memorial of Action," *Nation*, June 17, 1968, 779; "He's Not the Same Old Ted," *Newsweek*, June 24, 1968, 28–30; Edward M. Kennedy, *True Compass: A Memoir* (New York: Twelve, 2009), 274–75.

51. "Will Edward Kennedy Now Move Up?," *U.S. News & World Report*, June 24, 1968, 40–41; "Teddy Kennedy's Decision," *Newsweek*, August 5, 1968, 13–18; Loudon Wainwright, "A Good Time to Take a Man at His Word," *Life*, August 9, 1968, 13; "Who for No. 2?," *Time*, August 2, 1968, 16; Richard Dougherty, "Kennedy Decries Viet War," *Los Angeles Times*, August 22, 1968, 1; Kennedy, *True Compass*, 272–73.

52. "The Way the Democrats Made Their Big Decision," *U.S. News & World Report*, September 9, 1968, 40–41; William H. Honan, "Is Teddy, as They Say, Ready?," *New York Times*, February 23, 1969, 27–29, 54–69; Warren Rogers, "Ted Kennedy Talks About His Past, and His Future," *Look*, March 4, 1969, 41–46; Cohen and Taylor, *American Pharaoh*, 469–71; Chester, Hodgson, and Page, *American Melodrama*, 568–70.

53. Adam Clymer, *Edward M. Kennedy: A Biography* (New York: Perennial, 1999), 124–25; Tom Wicker, "In the Nation: The Man Who Isn't Here," *New York Times*, August 27, 1968, 40; Richard Goodwin, "The Night McCarthy Turned to Kennedy," *Look*, October 15, 1968, 102; English et al., *Divided They Stand*, 309–14; Lawrence O'Donnell, *Playing with Fire: The 1968 Election and the Transformation of American Politics* (New York: Penguin, 2017), 354–56; Chester, Hodgson, and Page, *American Melodrama*, 572–76.

54. Mailer, *Miami and the Siege of Chicago*, 118–27.

55. Longley, *LBJ's 1968*, 218–24; Solberg, *Hubert Humphrey*, 360–61; English et al., *Divided They Stand*, 316–17.

56. Mailer, *Miami and the Siege of Chicago*, 165–78; Chester, Hodgson, and Page, *American Melodrama*, 576–83; Arthur Miller, "Eyewitness," in Myrus, *Law and Disorder*, 16–18; Murray Kempton, "The Decline and Fall of the Democratic Party," *Saturday Evening Post*, November 2, 1968, 66–79; Shana Alexander, "McCarthy—Almost Pulled His Name from Nomination," *Life*, September 6, 1968, 4; "The Government in Exile," *Time*, September 6, 1968, 25–27.

57. "The Mess We Made: An Oral History of the '68 Convention," *GQ*, August 2008, 196; Walker, *Rights in Conflict*, 221–26.

58. Richard Norton Smith, *On His Own Terms: A Life of Nelson Rockefeller* (New York: Random House, 2014), 539–40; Scott Stossel, "Knifed," *Atlantic*, May 2004, 106–12; White, *Making of the President, 1968*, 355; Solberg, *Hubert Humphrey*, 366–67; Humphrey, *Education of a Public Man*, 390–93.

59. Harris Wofford, *Of Kennedys and Kings: Making Sense of the Sixties* (1980; reprint, Pittsburgh: University of Pittsburgh Press, 1992), 427–45; Lane, *Chicago Eyewitness*, 106–45; Walker, *Rights in Conflict*, 227–33.

60. "Humphrey: 'The End of an Era—the Beginning of a New Day,'" *U.S. News & World Report*, September 9, 1968, 85–88; John Barber, "The Making of Hubertism," *Commonweal*, November 7, 1968, 145–49; "The Winner: How—and What—He Won," 36–37; "The Battle of Chicago," *Newsweek*, September 9, 1968, 24–29; "The Man Who Would Recapture Youth," 16; Mailer, *Miami and the Siege of Chicago*, 208–12.

61. Loudon Wainwright, "Alarming Assault on the Young," *Life*, September 13, 1968, 33; Humphrey, *Education of a Public Man*, 384–86; Walker, *Rights in Conflict*; "Verdict on the Violence," *Newsweek*, December 9, 1968, 29–31; "Daley on the Defensive," *Newsweek*, December 16, 1968, 33; "Chicago Examined: Anatomy of a 'Police Riot,'" *Time*, December 6, 1968, 24–25; "The Blue Curtain," *Time*, December 13, 1968, 21.

62. "Humphrey Wins Battered Prize," *Business Week*, August 31, 1968, 11–12; Peter Schrag, "From Chicago to November," *Saturday Review*, September 21, 1968, 19–22, 54; Michael Novak, "Building a New Party," *Commonweal*, September 20, 1968, 618–20; Steven V. Roberts, "Young McCarthy Aides Will Not Go Away," *New York Times*, August 30, 1968, 20; Vermont Royster, "Peering under the Democratic Debris," *Wall Street Journal*, August 30, 1968, 6; "Can Humphrey Be Put Together Again?," *Washington Post*, August 30, 1968; Richard H. Rovere, "Letter from Chicago," *New Yorker*, September 7, 1968, 116–27.

63. Farber, *Chicago '68*, 206–7; James Miller, *"Democracy Is in the Streets": From Port Huron to the Siege of Chicago* (New York: Simon and Schuster, 1987), 304–5; Strouse, "Taste of Fascism," 618.

64. Warren Weaver Jr., "Democratic Split Buoys GOP," *New York Times*, August 30, 1968, 13; "Nixon Says HHH Hurt by Convention," *Washington Post, Times Herald*, August 29, 1968, A7; William Safire, *Before the Fall: An Inside View of the Pre-Watergate White House* (Garden City, N.Y.: Doubleday, 1975), 60–62; *Crisis in Chicago: 1968* (New York: Bee-Line Books, 1968); "Chicago: The Reassessment," *Time*, September 13, 1968, 20–21; "The King Richard Version," *Newsweek*, September 23, 1968, 35; "Daley's

Defense," *Time*, September 20, 1968, 27–28; Cohen and Taylor, *American Pharaoh*, 3–6, 482–85; "The Other Side of the Chicago Police Story," *U.S. News & World Report*, September 16, 1968, 60–67; *The Official Report of the Chicago Riots (Complete)* (Wheaton, Ill.: Church League of America, 1968); "Costume Party," *Time*, October 11, 1968, 26; "Yo-Yo Power," *Newsweek*, October 14, 1968, 31; Perlstein, *Nixonland*, 413–17, 447–58; Tom Hayden, *Trial* (New York: Holt, Rinehart and Winston, 1970).

65. Perlstein, *Nixonland*, 334–37.

CHAPTER EIGHT

1. Philip Crass, *The Wallace Factor* (New York: Mason/Charter, 1976), 14–15; T.R.B., "Wallace," *New Republic*, November 9, 1968, 4; Kenneth Lamott, "'It Isn't a Mirage They're Seeing,' Says George Wallace," *New York Times Magazine*, September 22, 1968, 32–33, 69–78; Robert P. Hey, "Wallace Accuses Media of 'Conspiracy,'" *Christian Science Monitor*, October 26, 1968, 1.

2. Homer Bigart, "3,000 Police Ring Garden as Wallace Stages a Rally," *New York Times*, October 25, 1968, 1; Crass, *Wallace Factor*, 3–6.

3. Hey, "Wallace Accuses Media of 'Conspiracy,'" 17; Nicholas C. Chriss, "15,000 Cheer Wallace during New York Rally," *Los Angeles Times*, October 25, 1968, 6; Dan T. Carter, *The Politics of Rage: George Wallace, the Origins of the New Conservatism, and the Transformation of American Politics* (Baton Rouge: Louisiana State University Press, 1995), 366–67.

4. Crass, *Wallace Factor*, 2–12; Bigart, "3,000 Police Ring Garden as Wallace Stages a Rally," 32; Sydney H. Schanberg, "Wallace Suit Seeks Use of Shea Stadium," *New York Times*, September 28, 1968, 1; Seth S. King, "Lindsay Says Shea Stadium Ban on Wallace Rally Was Mistake," *New York Times*, October 12, 1968, 25; Hey, "Wallace Accuses Media of 'Conspiracy.'"

5. Michael Kazin, *The Populist Persuasion: An American History* (New York: BasicBooks, 1995), 1–5; T.R.B., "Wallace," 4.

6. Carter, *Politics of Rage*, 17–96; Marshall Frady, *Wallace* (New York: World Publishing, 1968), 1–106; Stephan Lesher, *George Wallace: American Populist* (Reading, Mass.: Addison-Wesley, 1994), 22–127.

7. Carter, *Politics of Rage*, 96–263; Lesher, *George Wallace*, 155–351; Frady, *Wallace*, 137–77.

8. Carter, *Politics of Rage*, 196–215; Lloyd Rohler, *George Wallace: Conservative Populist* (Westport, Conn.: Praeger, 2004), 32–39, 125–44; "Wallace's Wisconsin—264,100 Votes," *Newsweek*, April 20, 1964, 33–34; Harold H. Martin, "George Wallace Shakes Up the Political Scene," *Saturday Evening Post*, May 9, 1964, 85–89; "What Wallace Vote Proved in North," *U.S. News & World Report*, June 1, 1964, 29–32, 61–63; "Winning without Winning," *Newsweek*, June 1, 1964, 17–18.

9. Rick Perlstein, *Before the Storm: Barry Goldwater and the Unmaking of the American Consensus* (2001; reprint, New York: Nation Books, 2009), 431–32; "What Price Wallace?," *Newsweek*, August 3, 1964, 23–24; "Why Wallace Withdrew—in the Governor's Own Words," *U.S. News & World Report*, August 3, 1964, 56–58; Wayne Greenhaw, *Watch Out for George Wallace* (Englewood Cliffs, N.J.: Prentice Hall, 1976), 27; Jeff

Frederick, *Stand Up for Alabama: Governor George Wallace* (Tuscaloosa: University of Alabama Press, 2007), 134; "Wallace for President," *Time*, October 8, 1965, 35.

10. "Wallace's Pottage," *Time*, October 22, 1965, 25A–25B; "George's Better Half," *Time*, March 4, 1966, 28; "In the Governor's Race, Lurleen Sweeps toward a Wallace Dynasty," May 13, 1966, 42–43; Jack Richardson, "The Best Man's Wife," *Esquire*, July 1966, 68–71, 114–15; Ray Jenkins, "Mr. & Mrs. Wallace Run for Governor of Alabama," *New York Times Magazine*, April 24, 1966, 29, 74–94; Frederick, *Stand Up for Alabama*, 162–79; Marshall Frady, "Governor and Mister Wallace," *Atlantic*, August 1967, 35–40.

11. Carter, *Politics of Rage*, 295–96; Crass, *Wallace Factor*, 90–91; Thaddeus L. Knap, "George Wallace Maps His Way to the White House," *New Republic*, April 29, 1967, 7–9; Jules Witcover, "A Preview of Wallace's Appeal to the North," *New Republic*, May 27, 1967, 9–10; Raymond Moley, "The Wallace Threat," *Newsweek*, April 3, 1967, 100; "The Spoiler," *Newsweek*, May 8, 1967, 39–40; "Northern Hospitality," *Newsweek*, May 15, 1967, 36; Kenneth Crawford, "What George Is Doing," *Newsweek*, May 22, 1967, 45; Stewart Alsop, "George Wallace for President?," *Saturday Evening Post*, March 25, 1967, 18; "A Third Party in '68?: The George Wallace Story," *U.S. News & World Report*, March 20, 1967, 54–60; James Jackson Kilpatrick, "What Makes Wallace Run?," *National Review*, April 18, 1967, 400–409; Tom Wicker, "George Wallace: A Gross and Simple Heart," *Harper's*, April 1967, 41–49.

12. Lesher, *George Wallace*, 396–400; Ben A. Franklin, "Alabamians Go West to Help Wallace," *New York Times*, December 3, 1967, 70; "Wallace in the West," *Time*, December 8, 1967, 27; Howard Seelye, "Voters Explain Switch to Wallace," *Los Angeles Times*, December 10, 1967, 3; Tom Wicker, "In the Nation: Wallace's Powerful Medicine," *New York Times*, December 12, 1967, 46; Laurence Leamer, "Out West with Candidate Wallace," *New Republic*, December 16, 1967, 11–13; Mary Reinholz, "On the Hustings with Wallace in California," *Los Angeles Times*, B11; "California Countdown," *Newsweek*, January 1, 1968, 13.

13. Arnold Sawislak, "Wallace Expected to Get on Ballots in Most States," *Washington Post, Times Herald*, March 3, 1968, F7; "Third-Party 'Scare'—What It Means," *U.S. News & World Report*, June 17, 1968, 56; Crass, *Wallace Factor*, 106; Ralph McGill, "George Wallace: Tradition of Demagoguery," *Los Angeles Times*, December 17, 1967, B10, 17–23.

14. Ben A. Franklin, "Wallace in Race; Will 'Run to Win,'" *New York Times*, February 9, 1968, 1; William Chapman, "Wallace: 'I Will Run to Win,'" *Washington Post, Times Herald*, February 9, 1968, A1; "Irrevocably In," *Time*, February 16, 1968, 22; "Candidate Wallace," *Newsweek*, February 19, 1968, 27–28.

15. David S. Broder, "Wallace Nightmare Haunting Political Bedfellows in Capital," *Washington Post, Times Herald*, February 13, 1968, A13; Rowland Evans and Robert Novak, "Wallace Is Roughening the Road for the GOP," *Los Angeles Times*, February 23, 1968, A5; Ben A. Franklin, "Tour by Wallace Suddenly Curbed," *New York Times*, February 21, 1968, 28; "Support from the Guts," *Time*, March 1, 1968, 15; Ray Jenkins, "George Wallace Figures to Win Even if He Loses," *New York Times Magazine*, April 7, 1968, 25–26, 66–86; Neil Maxwell, "Observers See Wallace Possibly Benefiting from Johnson Move," *Wall Street Journal*, April 2, 1968, 10; Harold H.

Martin, "George Wallace, the Angry Man's Candidate," *Saturday Evening Post*, June 15, 1968, 23–24.

16. Ray Jenkins, "The Queen of Alabama and the Prince Consort," *New York Times Magazine*, May 21, 1967, 26–27, 56–63; "Political Complications," *Newsweek*, July 17, 1967, 26–27; Lesher, *George Wallace*, 356–57, 382–84; "Double Loss for Wallace," *New York Times*, May 12, 1968, E3; "The Pains of Loyalty," *Time*, May 17, 1968, 35.

17. Frederick, *Stand Up for Alabama*, 231–32; Crass, *Wallace Factor*, 151–52; Walter Rugaber, "Wallace Assets Placed at $77,000," *New York Times*, September 29, 1968, 75; Marshall Frady, "George Wallace: The Angry Man's Candidate," *Saturday Evening Post*, June 29, 1968, 34–48; Walter Pincus, "The Public and the Private George Wallace," *Washington Post, Times Herald*, August 10, 1968, A10.

18. "The Wallace Clout," *Life*, August 2, 1968, 17–22; Walter Rugaber, "Wallace Seeking Funds in 8 States," *New York Times*, June 12, 1968, 31; Lesher, *George Wallace*, 410; "That Old-Time Religion," *Newsweek*, July 1, 1968, 32; Rowland Evans and Robert Novak, "Support for Wallace in the East May Be Dangerously Underrated," *Washington Post, Times Herald*, July 31, 1968, A21; Walter Rugaber, "Survey Finds Political Chiefs Fear Wallace Gains," *New York Times*, July 21, 1968, 46; "George Less Risible," *Time*, July 19, 1968, 12–13; Max Frankel, "Wallace in the North: Friends and 'Anarchist' Critics Cheer and Scream," *New York Times*, July 27, 1968, 1; "Police Break Up Fights at Wallace Gathering," *Los Angeles Times*, July 4, 1968, 27; "LBJ Hits Attack on Wallace," *Washington Post, Times Herald*, July 5, 1968, A1; Greenhaw, *Watch Out for George Wallace*, 34–35.

19. "Wallace on the Rise," *Newsweek*, July 22, 1968, 22; Godfrey Sperling Jr., "Wallace Inroads Grow," *Christian Science Monitor*, July 12, 1968, 1; "Watch Out for Wallace," *Saturday Evening Post*, August 24, 1968, 4; Robert B. Semple Jr., "President Gives Briefings to Nixon and Wallace," *New York Times*, July 27, 1968, 10; Walter Rugaber, "13 of 16 Southern Governors Decline to Back Wallace Drive," *New York Times*, June 17, 1968, 31; R. W. Apple Jr., "Rockefeller Sees Wallace 'Inroads,'" *New York Times*, July 11, 1968, 11; John C. Waugh, "Republicans Eye Wallace 'Siphon,'" *Christian Science Monitor*, July 26, 1968, 5; Ben A. Franklin, "Wallace Says He Influenced G.O.P. on Agnew," *New York Times*, August 10, 1968, 11.

20. Robert G. Sherrill, "George Wallace: 'Running for God,'" *Nation*, May 8, 1967, 589–96; Nicholas C. Chriss, "Texan, Wallace Differ on Planes in Campaign," *Los Angeles Times*, December 29, 1967, 14; "Wallace's New Math," *Newsweek*, January 15, 1968, 18; Greenhaw, *Watch Out for George Wallace*, 148–49, 157–58; Val Adams, "A.B.C. Charges Wallace Aide Seized Film of Shelton Greeting," *New York Times*, June 28, 1968, 83; Roy Reed, "Wallace Studies No. 2 Prospects," *New York Times*, September 17, 1968, 38; Jack Nelson and Nicholas C. Chriss, "Radical Rightists Play Key Roles in Wallace Drive," *Los Angeles Times*, September 17, 1968, 1; Carter, *Politics of Rage*, 336; Martin Waldron, "Birchers in Texas Head Wallace Bid," *New York Times*, September 22, 1968, 56; Wallace Turner, "Rightists Strong in Wallace Drive," *New York Times*, September 29, 1968, 75; Martin Waldron, "Citrus Growers Backing Wallace," *New York Times*, October 6, 1968, 74.

21. Herbert Alexander, *Financing the 1968 Election* (Lexington, Mass.: Heath Lexington Books, 1971), 158–62; Ben A. Franklin, "Wallace Showered with Donations,"

New York Times, February 27, 1968, 28; Eileen Shanahan, "Wallace Backed by Small Donors," *New York Times*, October 30, 1968, 30; "Win or Lose: What's Ahead for Wallace's Party," *U.S. News & World Report*, October 14, 1968, 40–41; Ben A. Franklin, "Wallace 'Phenomenon' Drive Gains Momentum," *New York Times*, August 19, 1968, 33; Walter Rugaber, "Wallace Is Hailed in the South but Fund Sources Stay Closed," *New York Times*, June 16, 1968, 23; Jo Ann Levine, "A Wallace Team Long on Variety," *Christian Science Monitor*, September 26, 1968, 14.

22. David English and the Staff of the London *Daily Express*, *Divided They Stand* (Englewood Cliffs, N.J.: Prentice-Hall, 1969), 348–49; George Wallace Jr., *Governor George Wallace: The Man You Never Knew* (n.p.: Wallace Productions, LLC, 2011), 108–9, 200–201.

23. English et al., *Divided They Stand*, 349–51; Rohler, *George Wallace*, 151–53; Walter Pincus, "The Wallace Campaign: Not Just Whistling Dixie," *Washington Post*, August 4, 1968, A1; Nicholas C. Chriss, "Overtones of Racism Dog Wallace Campaign," *Los Angeles Times*, June 21, 1968, 16; *George Wallace: A Rebel and His Cause* (New York: Universal Publishing and Distribution, 1968), 14–20; Harold H. Martin, "Race of a Thousand Clowns," *Saturday Evening Post*, May 7, 1966, 25–29; William Bradford Huie, "Alabamians against Wallace," *Look*, April 30, 1968, 50–55.

24. Peter A. Jay, "Wallace Hits Riots, Dubs D.C. a Jungle," *Washington Post, Times Herald*, June 28, 1968, A1; George F. Kennan, "A 'Liberal' Looks at Violence in U.S. and Where It's Heading," *U.S. News & World Report*, June 17, 1968, 66–69; Arthur M. Schlesinger Jr., "America 1968: The Politics of Violence," *Harper's*, August 1968, 19–24; John V. Lindsey, "Law & Order," *Life*, September 27, 1968, 32–33; Nicholas deB. Katzenbach, "Law and Order: Has the Supreme Court Gone Too Far?," October 29, 1968, 27–29; "Rising Voice of the Right," *Time*, September 13, 1968, 16–17; "The Fear Campaign," *Time*, October 4, 1968, 21–25; Milton Friedman, "Politics and Violence," *Newsweek*, June 24, 1968, 90; "Disorder in U.S. at a Climax," *U.S. News & World Report*, June 17, 1968, 31–34; "Wallace Blames High Officials for Unrest," *Los Angeles Times*, June 12, 1968, 7; Ben A. Franklin, "Wallace Defends Chicago Police," *New York Times*, August 30, 1968, 15; Lawrence Stern, "Wallace Is Appealing to Viscera, Not Brain," *Washington Post, Times Herald*, October 20, 1968, B1; Ben A. Franklin, "Wallace Says Law Stand Deters Reprisal by Right," *New York Times*, September 26, 1968, 1.

25. Richard Hofstadter, "The Paranoid Style in American Politics," *Harper's*, November 1964, 77–86; Carter, *Politics of Rage*, 344–45.

26. Roy Reed, "Wallace Favors Review of Judges," *New York Times*, September 21, 1968, 17; Ben A. Franklin, "Politics: Wallace Finds Attack on Press and TV Is a Successful Campaign Tactic," *New York Times*, September 3, 1968, 34; "George C. Wallace: He's Not Just Whistling Dixie," *Science*, October 25, 1968, 456–59; Max Frankel, "Across the Land, Wallace Insists a Vote for Him Won't Be Wasted," *New York Times*, July 30, 1968, 27.

27. William F. Buckley, "George Wallace: Is He Really a Conservative?," *Los Angeles Times*, February 28, 1968, A3; Kazin, *Populist Persuasion*, 221–42; "Buckley Calls Wallace Votes Bad for Conservatism," *New York Times*, August 5, 1968, 27; William F. Buckley, "What George Wallace Means to Me," *Look*, October 29, 1968, 101–2; Penn

Kimball, "The Politics of Style," *Saturday Review,* June 8, 1968, 26–29, 62; "The 'Wallace Phenomenon' Gets a Big Hand," *New York Times,* September 8, 1968, E2; "Wallace Speaks His Mind," *Business Week,* October 19, 1968, 145–48.

28. "Honest George?," *New Republic,* November 2, 1968, 10; "The Clergy on George Wallace," *Christianity Today,* October 25, 1968, 36–37; Frady, *Wallace,* 21; Carter, *Politics of Rage,* 346–47; Michael A. Cohen, *American Maelstrom: The 1968 Election and the Politics of Division* (New York: Oxford University Press, 2016), 233.

29. George Gallup, "Nixon Leads HHH 43 to 31 Per Cent; Wallace Given 19," *Washington Post, Times Herald,* September 15, 1968, A2; Louis Harris, "Wallace Seen Gaining 'Respectability,'" *Washington Post, Times Herald,* September 30, 1968, A6; "Out of the Bottle," *Time,* September 13, 1968, 20; "Neither Tweedledum nor Tweedledee," *Time,* September 20, 1968, 25; "Wallace Sets Fire to the '68 Campaign," *U.S. News & World Report,* September 30, 1968, 32–33; Rowland Evans and Robert Novak, "Growing Wallace Strength Poses a Threat in Key States," *Washington Post, Times Herald,* September 20, 1968, A25; Roscoe Drummond, "Wallace, not Humphrey Bears Main Threat to Nixon Election," *Washington Post, Times Herald,* September 18, 1968, A25.

30. Roy Reed, "Wallace Race a Traveling Show: Songs, Spiels, Fun, and Prospect of Violence," *New York Times,* September 16, 1968, 43; Saravette Trotter, "Visiting Mr. Dildy, in Wallace Country," *Wall Street Journal,* October 31, 1968, 20; "Another Opinion: Wallace for President," *New York Times,* October 20, 1968, E15; Roy Reed, "Wallace's Rally Fills Vast Arena," *New York Times,* September 20, 1968, 32; Ben A. Franklin, "By Trial and Error, Wallace Shapes His Platform," *New York Times,* September 1, 1968, 32; George Lardner Jr., "Nation Wants Southerner as President, Wallace Says," *Washington Post, Times Herald,* October 18, 1968, A2; George Lardner Jr., "Wallace Denounces Nixon, GOP," *Washington Post, Times Herald,* September 12, 1968, A1; Walter Rugaber, "Wallace and Nixon Vie in South; Conservatives Shun Humphrey," *New York Times,* September 8, 1968, 78; Roy Reed, "Maddox Praises Wallace Courage," *New York Times,* September 15, 1968, 76; Roy Reed, "Texas Party Nominates Wallace at Last of the 'National' Conventions," *New York Times,* September 18, 1968, 1.

31. Roy Reed, "Revolt of States Seen by Wallace," *New York Times,* September 22, 1968, 1; George Lardner Jr., "Wallace," *Washington Post, Times Herald,* September 22, 1968, A1.

32. Martin Waldron, "Thinking of Presidency, Wallace Admits It's Frightening Thought," *New York Times,* October 11, 1968, 52; Carolyn Lewis and Walter Rugaber, "Wallace's Aides Disown 'Fiancee,'" *New York Times,* September 28, 1968, 20; "One Fan Too Many," *Newsweek,* October 7, 1968, 42–43.

33. "Wallace, in Chicago, Woos Northern Vote," *Washington Post, Times Herald,* October 1, 1968, A1; "Old Ironpants," *Newsweek,* October 14, 1968, 30–31; Walter Rugaber, "Hecklers Disrupt Talks by Wallace," *New York Times,* October 2, 1968, 28; Paul W. Valentine, "Protestors Drown Out Wallace Talks in Mich.," *Washington Post, Times Herald,* October 2, 1968, A2; Robert P. Hey, "Wallace," *Christian Science Monitor,* October 4, 1968, 1; Roy Reed, "Wallace Baits Hecklers to Rouse Backers," *New York Times,* October 4, 1968, 50; "Police Club Leftists after Wallace Rally," *Washington Post, Times Herald,* October 6, 1968, A6; Roy Reed, "Wallace Is Cheered by Thousands in Newark and Jersey City," *New York Times,* October 6, 1968, 75; "20,000 Hear Wallace Speak at Boston

Rally," October 9, 1968, *Washington Post, Times Herald*, A2; Wendell Berry, "American Pox," *Nation*, November 4, 1968, 457.

34. "Worrying about Wallace," *Nation*, September 2, 1968, 165; David Holmstrom, "East: Who Supports Wallace?," *Christian Science Monitor*, October 30, 1968, 9; Elliott Carlson, "The Cherished Myth of the Worker," *Wall Street Journal*, November 1, 1968, 16; "Worrying about the Wallace Impact," *Business Week*, August 17, 1968, 98; Ian D. Burman, "Wallace," *Christian Science Monitor*, September 25, 1968, 1; Rowland Evans and Robert Novak, "Auto Workers' Support for Wallace May Foretell a Political Revolution," *Washington Post, Times Herald*, September 30, 1968, A21; Jerry Flint, "Wallace Wins Over Humphrey in Auto Union Poll, 49% to 39%," *New York Times*, October 6, 1968, 75; B. J. Widick, "Why They Like Wallace," *Nation*, October 14, 1968, 358–59; "How Wallace Campaign Is Splitting the Labor Vote," *U.S. News & World Report*, September 23, 1968, 98–99.

35. Fred P. Graham, "Wallace Placed on Ballot in Ohio," *New York Times*, October 16, 1968, 1.

36. "Wallace and His Folks," *Newsweek*, September 6, 1968, 25–28; "Wallace's Army: The Coalition of Frustration," *Time*, October 18, 1968, 15–21; "The Wallace Factor," *Time*, September 27, 1968, 14–15; "Wallace: The Unspoken Issue," *Newsweek*, November 4, 1968, 35–36; Norman C. Miller, "Why Wallace?," *Wall Street Journal*, September 27, 1968, 14; Stewart Alsop, "The Wallace Man," *Newsweek*, October 21, 1968, 116; Edward Schneier, "The Scar of Wallace," *Nation*, November 4, 1968, 454–57; "Wallace Cashes In on the Dollar Issue," *Business Week*, October 26, 1968, 122–24; Crass, *Wallace Factor*, 133–43; Jody Carlson, *George C. Wallace and the Politics of Powerlessness: The Wallace Campaigns for the Presidency, 1964–1976* (New Brunswick, N.J.: Transaction Books, 1981), 6–18; Carter, *Politics of Rage*, 344–48.

37. Walter Rugaber, "Letters from 'The Folks' Tell Why They're Backing Wallace," *New York Times*, September 30, 1968, 40; Steven V. Roberts, "Wallace Backers Say Why They Are," *New York Times*, October 25, 1968, 32; "Microcosm of the Politics of Fear," *Life*, September 20, 1968, 38–40A.

38. "Dark Shadow of Mr. Wallace," *Washington Post, Times Herald*, January 7, 1968, B6; Stewart Alsop, "The Little Man in the Catbird Seat," *Saturday Evening Post*, March 23, 1968, 20; Kenneth Crawford, "Election Alarms," *Newsweek*, May 13, 1968, 36; "The Wallace Bogeyman," *Wall Street Journal*, July 30, 1968, 14; Merlo J. Pusey, "U.S. Could Be at the Mercy of Wallace," *Washington Post, Times Herald*, November 4, 1968, A25; "What If the House Decides?," *Time*, October 11, 1968, 26–27; Robert O'Brien, "What a Vote for George Wallace Could Mean," *Reader's Digest*, November 1968, 151–58; Gary Orfield, "A Proposal for Outfoxing Wallace," *Washington Post, Times Herald*, July 7, 1968, B2; Gary Orfield, "An Afterthought on Wallace Threat to the Election," *Washington Post, Times Herald*, August 25, 1968, B3; William C. Selover, "Election-Crisis Plan Pushed in House," *Christian Science Monitor*, July 26, 1968, 5; David S. Broder, "Compact of Major Parties Could Foil George Wallace's Bid to Decide Election," *Washington Post, Times Herald*, July 9, 1968, A15.

39. "Wallace Names Griffin a Possible Running Mate," *New York Times*, February 15, 1968, 24; Lesher, *George Wallace*, 424–25; Ben A. Franklin, "Chandler Is Held Wallace's Choice," *New York Times*, September 7, 1968, 21; Ben A. Franklin, "The New Wallace is a 'National Candidate' . . . ," *New York Times*, September 15, 1968, E2; Joseph A. Loftus,

"Chandler Suggests a 'Mr. Big' Decides for Wallace," *New York Times*, September 18, 1968, 28; "True to Himself," *Newsweek*, September 23, 1968, 28–29.

40. Walter Rugaber, "Wallace Still Has Not Decided Who Will Be His Running Mate," *New York Times*, September 23, 1968, 30; Thomas M. Coffey, *Iron Eagle: The Turbulent Life of General Curtis LeMay* (New York: Crown, 1986), 3–182, 247–440; Warren Kozak, *LeMay: The Life and Wars of General Curtis LeMay* (Washington D.C.: Regnery, 2009), ix–xiii, 69–364; "From LeMay to McConnell—a Change to the 'New Breed,'" *Newsweek*, January 4, 1965, 16–17; Gen. Curtis E. LeMay, "General LeMay Tells How to Win the War in Vietnam," *U.S. News & World Report*, October 10, 1966, 36–43; "General LeMay's God," *Christian Century*, February 22, 1967, 229–30; Walter Millis, "The Brutal Logic of Power," *Saturday Review*, January 29, 1966, 36; Arthur Prager, "Is the Arms Race in Reverse?," *Saturday Review*, June 8, 1968, 39–40.

41. Nick Proffitt, "LeMay Charges Nixon Plans Left-Wing Cabinet," *Washington Post, Times Herald*, October 9, 1968, A2; Carl Greenberg, "LeMay's Employer Denounces Wallace as a 'Demagogue,'" *Los Angeles Times*, October 6, 1968, AB; Lesher, *George Wallace*, 425; Randolph Pendleton, "Wallace Chooses LeMay for Ticket," *Los Angeles Times*, October 4, 1968, A1; Walter Rugaber, "Gen. LeMay Joins Wallace's Ticket as Running Mate," *New York Times*, October 4, 1968, 1; "Excerpts from Comments by Wallace and LeMay on the War and Segregation," *New York Times*, October 4, 1968, 50.

42. Rowland Evans and Robert Novak, "LeMay Casts Mushroom Cloud on Wallace Presidential Drive," *Washington Post, Times Herald*, October 7, 1968, A25; Max Lerner, "Wallace and Gen. LeMay Form an 'Overkill Team'" and "Let 'Em Eat Lead," *New Republic*, October 12, 1968, 9; "George's General," *Time*, October 11, 1968, 21; "Wallace's H-Bomb," *New York Times*, October 4, 1968, 46; "Wallace Keeps Silent on LeMay Racial View," *Los Angeles Times*, October 24, 1968, 25; Greenhaw, *Watch Out for George Wallace*, 38; "Magical Mystery Tour," *Newsweek*, October 28, 1968, 37.

43. Crass, *Wallace Factor*, 110–12; Archie Robinson, *George Meany and His Times: A Biography* (New York: Simon and Schuster, 1981), 277–79; "And the Pro-Humphrey Labor Chiefs Are Worried," *New York Times*, September 15, 1968, E2; Damon Stetson, "Politics: Meany Says Labor Will Fight Swing to Wallace among Union Members," *New York Times*, September 17, 1968, 38; Damon Stetson, "Labor Federation Supports Humphrey and Warns against Votes for Wallace," *New York Times*, September 19, 1968, 37; Anthony Ripley, "Reuther Asserts Wallace Is Peril," *New York Times*, September 23, 1968, 30; "Labor's Battle Cry Now: Stop Wallace," *U.S. News & World Report*, October 14, 1968, 108–9; James P. Gannon, "Silver Linings in George's Labors," *Wall Street Journal*, November 11, 1968, 18.

44. "Wallace—Invitation to Disaster," *New York Times*, November 3, 1968, 220; "The Election (I)—Why Not Wallace," *Washington Post, Times Herald*, October 31, 1968, A20; John Herbers, "Kennedy Asks Vote Rejecting Wallace," *New York Times*, October 25, 1968, 1; "Brooke Foresees a Revolt if Wallace Wins Election," *New York Times*, October 14, 1968, 41; "Ethics Group Labels Wallace Bid as 'Racial,'" *Washington Post, Times Herald*, October 2, 1968, A5; James Silver, "An Ex-Mississippian's Reflections on Wallace," *New Republic*, October 19, 1968, 17–19.

45. "SCLC Head Warns Philly Flock of Wallace Threat," *Chicago Daily Defender*,

October 31, 1968, 6; Dick Gregory, "What George Wallace Means to Me," *Look*, October 29, 1968, 98.

46. Robert L. Asher, "Muskie Hammers at Wallace for 'Philosophy of Violence,'" *Washington Post, Times Herald*, October 9, 1968, A2; Thomas A. Johnson, "Muskie, in Jersey, Calls Wallace 'The Man We've Got to Defeat,'" *New York Times*, October 24, 1968, 42; Robert B. Semple Jr., "Humphrey Links Wallace to Fear," *New York Times*, October 2, 1968, 1.

47. "Nixon, Wallace Alike on Law, Order—Thurmond," *Los Angeles Times*, September 15, 1968, E2; Robert B. Semple Jr., "Wallace Shadow Causes Nixon to Consider a 3d Party Appeal," *New York Times*, September 21, 1968, 17; Max Frankel, "Nixon Heads South in Attempt to Wrest South from Wallace," *New York Times*, September 27, 1968, 30; Max Frankel, "Nixon Says Rival Is Using Wallace," *New York Times*, September 28, 1968, 1; E. W. Kenworthy, "Nixon: A Tightrope in the South," *New York Times*, September 29, 1968, E1; Homer Bigart, "Politics: Nixon, Abandoning Silence on Wallace, Attacks Him and LeMay as Hawks," *New York Times*, October 4, 1968, 50; E. W. Kenworthy, "Nixon Strategy in South," *New York Times*, October 5, 1968, 20; E. W. Kenworthy, "Nixon Bids Protest Voter Think Twice on Wallace," *New York Times*, October 9, 1968, 1; James F. Clarity, "Rockefeller Sees Shift to Nixon by Many Now Backing Wallace," *New York Times*, October 10, 1968, 52; William F. Buckley Jr., "Nixon and Wallace," *National Review*, October 22, 1968, 1080–81; Henry Brandon, "The Wallace Effect," *Saturday Review*, October 19, 1968, 18; Barry Goldwater, "Don't Waste a Vote on Wallace," *National Review*, October 22,1968, 1060–61, 1079.

48. Jack Nelson, "L.A. Restrained in Welcome to Tired and Angry Wallace," *Los Angeles Times*, October 16, 1968, 3; Jack Nelson, "Ired Wallace Stomps Out on Hecklers," *Los Angeles Times*, October 17, 1968, 6; Ben A. Franklin, "Wallace Winds Up Drive in Georgia; Denounces G.O.P.," *New York Times*, November 5, 1968, 1; George Lardner Jr., "Wallace Blasts Pollster, Sees Nixon in Collusion," *Washington Post, Times Herald*, October 10. 1968, A1; Roy Reed, "Wallace Loses Some Momentum," *New York Times*, October 20, 1968, E2; Walter Pincus, "Wallace Says Bombing Halt Won't Rescue Humphrey," *Washington Post, Times Herald*, October 26, 1968, A2; Randolph Pendleton, "Wallace Calls Pollsters 'Liars,'" *Washington Post, Times Herald*, October 27, 1968, A30; James T. Wooten, "Wallace Assails 'Lying' Election Polls," *New York Times*, October 27, 1968, 71.

49. Carter, *Politics of Rage*, 12; Lesher, *George Wallace*, xi.

CHAPTER NINE

1. Robert Lewis Shayon, "The Show Biz-Politics Scene," *Saturday Review*, December 7, 1968, 61; Jules Witcover, *The Year the Dream Died: Revisiting 1968 in America* (New York: Warner Books, 1997), 430–35; Theodore H. White, *The Making of the President, 1968* (New York: Atheneum, 1969), 449–50; Edgar Berman, *Hubert: The Triumph and Tragedy of the Humphrey I Knew* (New York: G. P. Putnam's Sons, 1979), 226; Joe McGinniss, *The Selling of the President* (1969; reprint, New York: Penguin, 1988), 155–59; Lewis Chester, Geoffrey Hodgson, and Bruce Page, *An American Melodrama: The Presidential Campaign of 1968* (New York: Viking, 1969), 752–54; David

English and the Staff of the London *Daily Express, Divided They Stand* (Englewood Cliffs, N.J.: Prentice-Hall, 1969), 393–94.

2. Robert B. Semple Jr., "Nixon Works on His Strategy and Image," *New York Times*, August 18, 1968, E2; Robert B. Semple Jr., "Perils of Nixon's Strategy," *New York Times*, August 25, 1968, E4; "Republicans: Campaign from Mission Bay," *Time*, August 23, 1968, 14–15; Jules Witcover, *The Resurrection of Richard Nixon* (New York: G. P. Putnam's Sons, 1970), 364–66; "Law, Order, and Euphoria," *Newsweek*, August 26, 1968, 26–28; "All for One," *Newsweek*, September 2, 1968, 32–33; "Nixon Pins Hopes on the Middle," *Business Week*, August 17, 1968, 22–23; "As Nixon Campaign Takes Shape," *U.S. News & World Report*, August 26, 1968, 26; "Republicans: The Politics of Safety," *Time*, September 13, 1968, 19–20; "The Politics of Caution," *Newsweek*, September 16, 1968, 23–25.

3. Richard Reeves, "Nixon's Men Are Smart but No Swingers," *New York Times Magazine*, September 29, 1968, 28, 127–32; Chester, Hodgson, and Page, *American Melodrama*, 615–17; "The Nixon 'Talent Team,'" *U.S. News & World Report*, August 19, 1968, 28–29; Hugh Sidey, "Not a Candidate but a President-to-be," *Life*, October 4, 1968, 4; "Politics: Nixon Aides Say His Campaign May Be Costliest, Topping $20 Million," *New York Times*, October 8, 1968, 34; Tim Weiner, *One Man against the World: The Tragedy of Richard Nixon* (New York: Henry Holt, 2015), 19–21; Richard L. Strout, "Nixon's 'Victory Special' Rolls West—with Nostalgic Reporter," *Christian Science Monitor*, October 25, 1968, 12; Don Oberdorfer, "A Rally for Nixon Is a Thing of Art," *Washington Post, Times Herald*, October 3, 1968, 20; Chester, Hodgson, and Page, *American Melodrama*, 677–78.

4. "Scent of Victory," *Time*, September 27, 1968, 18–19; "Run, Dick, Run. Win, Dick, Win," *Newsweek*, September 23, 1968, 27–28; Chester, Hodgson, and Page, *American Melodrama*, 679–85; "A Confident Nixon Steps Up the Attack," *Business Week*, October 12, 1968, 32–34; John Osborne, "The Cool Confidence of a Winner," *New Republic*, September 28, 1968, 14–15; Saville R. Davis, "Nixon Campaign Confidence a Sharp Contrast to 1960," *Christian Science Monitor*, October 3, 1968, 3; Roscoe Drummond, "Nixon—Eight Years Later," *Christian Science Monitor*, October 12, 1968, 16; White, *Making of the President, 1968*, 378–84; George Gallup, "Nixon Tops His Rivals as Most Charismatic," *Washington Post, Times Herald*, September 25, 1968, A2; Louis Harris, "Public Prefers Nixon as a Leader," *Washington Post, Times Herald*, October 8, 1968, A17.

5. Michael J. Arlen, "The Air," *New Yorker*, September 21, 1968, 167–71; McGinniss, *Selling of the President*, 26–30, 49–96; "Verrry Interesting . . . but Wild," *Time*, October 11, 1968, 50–56; Jack Gould, "'Laugh-In' Team Back with a Nixon Line," *New York Times*, September 17, 1968, 95.

6. Gabriel Sherman, *The Loudest Voice in the Room: How the Brilliant, Bombastic Roger Ailes Built Fox News—and Divided a Country* (New York: Random House, 2014), xii–xiii, 30–59; Leonard Garment, *Crazy Rhythm: My Journey from Brooklyn, Jazz, and Wall Street to Nixon's White House, Watergate, and Beyond* (New York: Times Books, 1997), 128–37; McGinniss, *Selling of the President*, 97–111; "Nixon Makes TV Film," *New York Times*, July 21, 1968, 38; "'The Richard Nixon Show' on TV Lets Candidate Answer Panel's Questions," *New York Times*, September 22, 1968, 69;

Robert Lindeler, "Nixon's Television Aide Says Candidate 'Is Not a Child of TV,'" *New York Times*, October 9, 1968, 95.

7. English et al., *Divided They Stand*, 190–92; "How Nixon Does It," *Newsweek*, October 21, 1968, 32–33; Stewart Alsop, "The Quintessential Square," *Newsweek*, October 7, 1968, 118; Charlotte Curtis, "Pat Nixon: 'Creature Comforts Don't Matter,'" *New York Times*, July 3, 1968; Charlotte Curtis, "Nixon Family Keeps Working and Smiling," *New York Times*, August 8, 1968, 23; Marie Smith, "Mrs. Richard Nixon," *Washington Post, Times Herald*, August 4, 1968, G1–G5; "Five-Star Special for Republicans," *U.S. News & World Report*, August 19, 1968, 12–13; "Julie and David—Romance with a Political Punch," *U.S. News & World Report*, September 23, 1968, 14; "The New First Family—a Close-Up," *U.S. News & World Report*, November 18, 1968, 19.

8. Gloria Steinem, "In Your Heart You Know He's Nixon," *New York*, October 28, 1968, 20–35; Marquis Childs, "Nixon Still Finds Reporters Cool," *Washington Post, Times Herald*, October 25, 1968, A24; E. W. Kenworthy, "Nixon Is Found Hard to Fathom on Basis of Public Statements," *New York Times*, October 26, 1968, 21; Alan L. Otten, "Split-Level Nixon," *Wall Street Journal*, October 29, 1968, 20; Vermont Royster, "The 37th Man," *Wall Street Journal*, November 8, 1968, 16; Don Oberdorfer, "The 'Real Nixon' an Enigma," *Washington Post, Times Herald*, October 13, 1968, A1; Brock Brower, "A Vision of Victory at Last within Reach," *Life*, October 11, 1968, 34–43; "The Candidates Up Close," *Time*, October 18, 1968, 23–24; John Osborne, "The Summing Up of a Nixon-Watcher," *New Republic*, October 26, 1968, 15–17; "The Real Dick Nixon Stands Up," *Newsweek*, November 4, 1968, 28–29.

9. Ruth Rosen, *The World Split Open: How the Modern Women's Movement Changed America* (New York: Penguin, 2006), 159–61; Charlotte Curtis, "Miss America Pageant Is Picketed by 100 Women," *New York Times*, September 8, 1968, 81.

10. "Richard M. Nixon," *America*, November 2, 1968, 402–11; Pete Hamill, "Richard the Third-Rate," *Ramparts*, November 17, 1968, 34–35, 40; Arthur Schlesinger Jr., "A Skeptical Democrat Looks at President Nixon," *New York Times Magazine*, November 17, 1968, 45–47, 142–49; William Safire, *Before the Fall: An Inside View of the Pre-Watergate White House* (Garden City, N.Y.: Doubleday, 1975), 64, 74; Alan L. Otten, "In Defense of Images," *Wall Street Journal*, October 11, 1968, 16; "The Nixon Criterion," *Washington Post, Times Herald*, September 21, 1968, A12; Richard M. Nixon, "The Nature of the Presidency," *Vital Speeches of the Day*, October 15, 1968, 6–8.

11. Robert B. Semple Jr., "Nixon's Policy of Silence," *New York Times*, September 7, 1968, 20; "Nixon Approves Johnson's Speech on Vietnam," *New York Times*, August 21, 1968, 33; "Where the Candidates Stand on the U.S. Economy," *Time*, October 11, 1968, 93–94; "Nixon Denounces Humphrey Views," *New York Times*, September 7, 1968, 1; "Nixon Sharpens Attacks on Humphrey," *New York Times*, September 25, 1968, 28; E. W. Kenworthy, "Nixon Says Nation Could Not 'Afford' a Humphrey Rule," *New York Times*, September 24, 1968, 1; "Public Enemy No. 1?," *Newsweek*, October 28, 1968, 36–37; Michael W. Flamm, *Law and Order: Street Crime, Civil Unrest, and the Crisis of Liberalism in the 1960s* (New York: Columbia University Press, 2005), 173–76.

12. "Warren: Out of the Storm Center," *Time*, June 28, 1968, 11–13; "The Warren Court," *Newsweek*, July 1, 1968, 33; "Now a Changing Supreme Court," *U.S. News & World Report*, July 8, 1968, 31–32; "Courts Are 'Too Soft,' People Tell Pollsters," *U.S. News & World Report*, March 11, 1968, 19.

13. "Chief Confidant to Chief Justice," *Time*, July 5, 1968, 12–13; "Fortas at the Bar," *Time*, July 26, 1968, 17–18; "Judgment and the Justice," *Time*, August 2, 1968, 19; "The Fortas Film Festival," *Time*, September 20, 1968, 28–29; "What Went Wrong," *Newsweek*, September 23, 1968, 30–31; "The Fortas Defeat," *Time*, October 11, 1968, 24; "There Goes the Judge," *Newsweek*, October 14, 1968, 34; Kyle Longley, *LBJ's 1968: Power, Politics, and the Presidency in America's Year of Upheaval* (New York: Cambridge University Press, 2018), 160–84; Rick Perlstein, *Nixonland: The Rise of a President and the Fracturing of America* (New York: Scribner, 2008), 285–89; Joseph Crespino, *Strom Thurmond's America* (New York: Hill and Wang, 2012), 222–25.

14. "Billy's Political Pitch," *Newsweek*, June 10, 1968, 62–63; "The Politicians' Preacher," *Time*, October 4, 1968, 58; "The Election: Who Was for Whom," *Christianity Today*, November 22, 1968, 43–44; Kevin M. Kruse, *One Nation under God: How Corporate America Invented Christian America* (New York: Basic Books, 2015); Steven P. Miller, *Billy Graham and the Rise of the Republican South* (Philadelphia: University of Pennsylvania Press, 2009), 3–12, 131–38; Daniel K. Williams, *God's Own Party: The Making of the Christian Right* (New York: Oxford University Press, 2010), 88–94; "Billy Graham Says Nixon Is Not 'Tricky,'" *Washington Post, Times Herald*, October 1, 1968, A4.

15. "If Nixon Is President," *U.S. News & World Report*, October 7, 1968, 42–51; Robert Sherrill, "Nixon's Man in Dixie," *New York Times Magazine*, September 15, 1968, 32–33, 42–49; David S. Broder, "Nixon Sees Rival Camps in Dixie Deal," *Washington Post, Times Herald*, September 18, 1968, A1; John Osborne, "One Dollar for the First Black Face," *New Republic*, October 13, 1968, 15–16; Harry S. Dent, *The Prodigal South Returns to Power* (New York: John Wiley & Sons, 1978), 106–16.

16. Harrison E. Salisbury, "Nixon: Then and Now," *New York Times*, September 16, 1968, 1; Robert B. Semple Jr., "Nixon Visits Negro Slum and Warns White Suburbs," *New York Times*, September 22, 1968, 1; John Osborne, "Nixon and the Blacks," *New Republic*, December 14, 1968, 19–20; Robert B. Semple Jr., *New York Times*, September 13, 1968, 1; "Mr. Nixon on Integration," *New York Times*, September 16, 1968, 46; Chalmers M. Roberts, "O'Brien Lays 'Apartheid' to Nixon, Agnew," *Washington Post, Times Herald*, September 19, 1968, A8; Roland Black, "Nixon Capitalizing on Extremism," *Chicago Defender*, October 26, 1968, 32.

17. Jules Witcover, *White Knight: The Rise of Spiro Agnew* (New York: Random House, 1972), 240–63; Theo Lippman Jr., *Spiro Agnew's America* (New York: Norton, 1972), 167–73; "Everyone Knows Him Now," *Newsweek*, November 11, 1968, 38–39; "Mud at the Finish," *Time*, November 8, 1968, 30–32; "Last Blasts," *Newsweek*, November 11, 1968, 92–93; "Not Recommended for Adults," *New Republic*, October 5, 1968, 4; Vermont Royster, "Dum Spiro, Spero," *Wall Street Journal*, October 24, 1968, 18.

18. Lippman, *Spiro Agnew's America*, 154–67; Joseph Albright, *What Makes Spiro Run: The Life and Times of Spiro Agnew* (New York: Dodd, Mead, 1972), 220–45; William F. Buckley, "The Doubts about Agnew," *National Review*, November 5, 1968, 1132–33; "The Making of the Veep," *Newsweek*, October 7, 1968, 32–40; "The Counterpuncher," *Time*, September 20, 1968, 20–25.

19. Louis Harris, "Nixon Helped by Law-and-Order Issue," *Washington Post, Times Herald*, September 12, 1968, A2; "Poll Rates Nixon Best at Handling War," *New York Times*, August 25, 1968, 74; Robert Mason, *Richard Nixon and the Quest for a New*

Majority (Chapel Hill: University of North Carolina Press, 2004), 1–4, 14–36; John Bird, "Is Nixon Really the One?," *Saturday Evening Post*, November 2, 1968, 22–25; "The Silent Majority," *Christian Science Monitor*, September 9, 1968, 34; Robert L. Bartley, "Nixon and the 'Forgotten Americans,'" *Wall Street Journal*, September 5, 1968, 12.

20. Max Frankel, "Humphrey Seeks to Seize the Future," *New York Times*, September 1, 1968, E1; "The Professional," *Time*, September 13, 1968, 18; Rowland Evans and Robert Novak, "Mondale and Harris: Humphrey's Establishment Radicals," *Harper's*, October 1968, 88–95; "What's Wrong?," *Newsweek*, September 30, 1968, 27–28; Albert Eisele, *Almost to the Presidency: A Biography of Two American Politicians* (Blue Earth, Minn.: Piper Company, 1972), 366–69; Lawrence F. O'Brien, *No Final Victories: A Life in Politics—from John F. Kennedy to Watergate* (Garden City, N.Y.: Doubleday, 1974), 256–59.

21. Max Frankel, "Humphrey Shuns Plea He Disavow Johnson on War," *New York Times*, September 22, 1968, 1; Roy Reed, "Humphrey Likens Campaign to Underdog Truman's 1948 Race," *New York Times*, August 27, 1968, 24; Max Frankel, "Humphrey's View: There's Nowhere to Go but Up." *New York Times*, September 22, 1968, 181; "Faint Echoes of '48," *Time*, October 4, 1968, 16–18; R. W. Apple Jr., "Humphrey: Will Half-Measures Be Enough?," *New York Times*, September 29, 1968, E1; "Era of Democrats Ending?," *U.S. News & World Report*, September 16, 1968, 29–30; Robert C. Jensen, "The Mathematics Facing Humphrey," *Washington Post, Times Herald*, September 1, 1968, B6; Stewart Alsop, "The Case for Nixon," *Newsweek*, September 30, 1968, 116; "Liberals for Nixon and Other Realignments," *Time*, October 11, 1968, 20–21; Hugh Sidey, "A Party Dispirited with Itself," *Life*, September 20, 1968, 5; "What Should Humphrey Do?," *Time*, September 27, 1968, 15–17; "The Real Humphrey Must Now Stand Up," *Life*, September 6, 1968, 32B.

22. "Lurching Off to a Shaky Start," *Time*, September 20, 1968, 18–19; "Will 'The Real HHH' Stand Up?," *Newsweek*, September 23, 1968, 25–27; "LBJ vs. HHH on Vietnam: Where They Differ," *U.S. News & World* Report, September 23, 1968, 42–43; Robert B. Semple Jr., "In Pace, Mood, and Tone, Rivals Are Worlds Apart," *New York Times*, September 30, 1968, 1; Max Frankel, "Humphrey Finds Little to Cheer About," *New York Times*, September 15, 1968, E2; "The Campaign: Is Anybody Happy?," *Newsweek*, September 30, 1968, 23–24; "The Humphreys: Right Image for '68?," *U.S. News & World Report*, September 9, 1968, 17–18; "Hubert's Shadow," *New Republic*, October 12, 1968, 6; Robert H. Phelps, "Humphrey's Dilemma," *New York Times*, September 13, 1968, 52; Stewart Alsop, "Can Humphrey Win?," *Newsweek*, September 9, 1968, 104.

23. "The Biltmore," *New Yorker*, September 7, 1968, 26–27; Richard L. Strout, "'A Day in the Life of Humphrey': Fasten Seat Belts!," *Christian Science Monitor*, September 30, 1968, 5; "Covering the Candidates," *Newsweek*, October 7, 1968, 74; Tom Wicker, "In the Nation: Evil on Washington Street," *New York Times*, September 22, 1968, 190; Max Frankel, "Kennedy Hails Humphrey; Jeers Mar Rally in Boston," *New York Times*, September 20, 1968, 1; "Kennedy Measures Praise for HHH," *Washington Post, Times Herald*, September 20, 1968, A1.

24. "Dissidents' Dilemma," *Time*, September 20, 1968, 27; Max Frankel, "Politics: Humphrey Notes Opposition but Doubts His Critics Can Vote for Nixon," *New York*

Times, September 11, 1968, 28; Ken Reich, "McCarthy Declares He Won't Support Humphrey or Nixon," *Los Angeles Times*, August 30, 1968, 1; Marquis Childs, "Humphrey's Task Grows by the Hour," *Washington Post, Times Herald*, September 11, 1968, A11; Richard J. Levine, "Until November, Hostile Non-Cooperation," *Wall Street Journal*, October 10, 1968, 20; Gloria Emerson, "McCarthy Relaxes, Reflects, and Jests," *New York Times*, September 19, 1968, 1; "Then There Were Four," *Newsweek*, September 16, 1968, 29–30; Dominic Sandbrook, *Eugene McCarthy: The Rise and Fall of American Liberalism* (New York: Knopf, 2004), 214–15; Richard T. Stout, *People* (New York: Harper and Row, 1970), 376.

25. Martin Nolan, "Muskie of Maine," *Reporter*, July 13, 1967, 44–46; Douglas Kiker, "Washington," *Atlantic*, August 1967, 4–10; "The Making of a Running Mate," *Newsweek*, September 9, 1968, 37; "The Sleeper v. the Stumbler," *Time*, October 4, 1968, 19; Loudon Wainwright, "A Man at Peace with the Hard Facts," *Life*, October 4, 1968, 20B; Steven B. Roberts, "Edmund Sixtus Muskie Takes the Low-Key Road," *New York Times Magazine*, October 20, 1968, 32–33, 141–50; Rowland Evans and Robert Novak, "Phenomenon of the Campaign: Muskie's Rise from Obscurity," *Los Angeles Times*, November 7, 1968, B7; David Nevin, *Muskie of Maine* (New York: Random House, 1972), 3–6, 21–22, 26–27.

26. "Humphrey on What's Wrong," *Time*, October 25, 1968, 27; Theo Lippman Jr. and Donald C. Hansen, *Muskie* (New York: Norton, 1971), 16–18; Clayton Knowles, "Muskie Considers Nixon Misleading," *New York Times*, September 13, 1968, 50; Clayton Knowles, "Muskie Says Nixon Echoes Wallace," *New York Times*, October 15, 1968, 34; Eve Edstrom, "Muskie Raps Nixon's Silence on Wallace," *Washington Post, Times Herald*, October 31, 1968, A5.

27. Tom Wicker, "In the Nation: The Search for Hubert Humphrey," *New York Times*, September 26, 1968, 46; Douglas E. Kneeland, "Muskie Faced with Novel Role; He's Asked to Justify Humphrey," *New York Times*, September 29, 1968, 74; Robert C. Maynard, "Muskie Focuses on Defecting Liberals," *Washington Post, Times Herald*, September 30, 1968, A2.

28. Rowland Evans and Robert Novak, "Humphrey Drops Optimistic Mask and Bleakly Acknowledges His Woes," *Washington Post, Times Herald*, September 18, 1968, A25; Carl Solberg, *Hubert Humphrey: A Biography* (1984; reprint, Minneapolis: Borealis Books, 2003), 378–81; "Dick Nixon's Winning Ways," *Newsweek*, October 7, 1968, 30–31.

29. O'Brien, *No Final Victories*, 259–61; George W. Ball, *The Past Has Another Pattern: Memoirs* (New York: Norton, 1982), 444–47; Berman, *Hubert*, 215–18; Fred Harris, *Potomac Fever* (New York: Norton, 1977), 170–71; Eisele, *Almost to the Presidency*, 372–78; Ken Hughes, *Chasing Shadows: The Nixon Tapes, the Chennault Affair, and the Origins of Watergate* (Charlottesville: University of Virginia Press, 2014), 21–22.

30. R. W. Apple Jr., "Humphrey Vows Halt in Bombing if Hanoi Reacts," *New York Times*, October 1, 1968, 1; A. D. Horne, "Humphrey Loosens Ties to Johnson," *Washington Post, Times Herald*, October 2, 1968, A1; Richard H. Rovere, "Letter from Washington," *New Yorker*, October 12, 1968, 194–203; "Some Forward Motion for H.H.H.," *Time*, October 11, 1968, 19–20; Hughes, *Chasing Shadows*, 23–25.

31. "HHH's Bombing Halt," *Newsweek*, October 14, 1968, 31; R. W. Apple Jr., "Humphrey Shows Populists' Zest," *New York Times*, October 3, 1968, 1; Richard

Dougherty, "Humphrey's New Confidence: He May Have Found an Issue," *Los Angeles Times*, October 6, 1968, 1; Max Frankel, "New Humphrey Goal," *New York Times*, October 16, 1968, 31; Susan Brownmiller, "Backstage with Dick, Hubie, and George," *Vogue*, October 15, 1968, 96–97; Tom Wicker, "In the Nation: Once More, with Feeling," *New York Times*, October 17, 1968, 46; Allen J. Large, "'Law and Order'—into the Fuzzy Swirl," *Wall Street Journal*, October 22, 1968, 20; Max Frankel, "Humphrey Racial Stand," *New York Times*, October 19, 1968, 20; Kenneth Crawford, "President Shoppers," *Newsweek*, November 4, 1968, 40; "Fouls in the Final Rounds," *Time*, November 1, 1968, 15–16; "HHH's Catch-Up Campaign," *Newsweek*, November 4, 1968, 29–31.

32. "How Dr. Gallup Sees the Campaign Homestretch," *U.S. News & World Report*, November 4, 1968, 40–43; Max Frankel, "Humphrey Insists He Can Still Win," *New York Times*, October 15, 1968, 1; John W. Finney, "Humphrey Taunts Nixon as 'Chicken,'" *New York Times*, October 16, 1968, 1; Dorothy McCardle, "Muriel Humphrey Adds Special Campaign Spark," *Washington Post, Times Herald*, October 27, 1968, H1; "Humphrey Hammers against the Odds," *Business Week*, October 19, 1968, 34–36; "I Still Can Win," *U.S. News & World Report*, October 21, 1968, 54–60; "Mr. Vice President, Are You Going to Win This Election? Yes, I Really Believe I Am," *Saturday Evening Post*, October 19, 1968, 29–33, 78–81; "Can Hubert Give 'Em Harry's Hell?," *Newsweek*, October 7, 1968, 29–30.

33. "Tough Going," *Newsweek*, October 21, 1968, 34; Max Frankel, "Humphrey: From Issues to Invective," *New York Times*, October 23, 1968, 29; Rowland Evans and Robert Novak, "Humphrey's Surge in Strength Largely Anti-Nixon Sentiment," *Los Angeles Times*, November 1, 1968, B7; Jerry Landauer and Richard J. Levine, "Democrats Face Huge Campaign Deficit due to Higher Costs, Fund-Raising Woes," *Wall Street Journal*, October 24, 1968, 10; Alan L. Otten, "Typical Campaign Arena: New Jersey," *Wall Street Journal*, October 23, 1968, 18; "Problems of Dollars and Days," *Time*, October 25, 1968, 27–28; Flamm, *Law and Order*, 162–78.

34. Eugene McCarthy, "Confessions of a Fair Country Ballplayer," *Life*, October 18, 1968, 67–70; Eisele, *Almost to the Presidency*, 382–83; John Herbers, "McCarthy Still Won't Say Yes," *New York Times*, October 13, 1968, E2; William V. Shannon, "Where Will the McCarthy Vote Go?," *New York Times*, October 14, 1968, 46; Marquis Childs, "Picking Up Pieces after McCarthy," *Washington Post, Times Herald*, October 16, 1968, A16; "The Holdout," *Newsweek*, October 21, 1968, 37; Kenneth Crawford, "McCarthy: His Fashion," *Newsweek*, October 21, 1968, 46; "The Case for Making a Choice," *Commonweal*, October 25, 1968, 102–3; "McCarthy Half-Heartedly Backs Humphrey, Won't Run on Democratic Ticket in Future," *Wall Street Journal*, October 30, 1968, 2; Lawrence O'Donnell, *Playing with Fire: The 1968 Election and the Transformation of American Politics* (New York: Penguin, 2017), 395–97.

35. Hugh Sidey, "Prospects for a Postgraduate Historian," *Life*, May 24, 1968, 40; Jack Anderson, "LBJ in History," *Washington Post, Times Herald*, September 15, 1968, B7; Neil Sheehan, "President Appeals to Party to Back Humphrey," *New York Times*, September 18, 1968, 1; "He Meant What He Said," *Newsweek*, September 23, 1968, 29; George Christian, *The President Steps Down: A Personal Memoir of the Transfer of Power* (New York: Macmillan, 1970), 165–71; "Text of Johnson Talk Backing Humphrey," *New York Times*, October 11, 1968, 53; Max Frankel, "Johnson Seeks to Aid Humphrey,"

New York Times, October 6, 1968, 1; John Pierson, "LBJ and HHH: Less Reticence," *Wall Street Journal*, October 23, 1968, 18; Robert Dallek, *Flawed Giant: Lyndon Johnson and His Times, 1961–1973* (New York: Oxford University Press, 1998), 575–77.

36. Dallek, *Flawed Giant*, 577–79; Harry McPherson, *A Political Education* (Boston: Atlantic Monthly Press, 1972), 448–49; Hubert H. Humphrey, *Education of a Public Man: My Life and Politics* (Garden City, N.Y.: Doubleday, 1976), 404.

37. Eisele, *Almost to the Presidency*, 388–90; "Nixon Ahead, 42–40, in Final Gallup Poll," *New York Times*, November 4, 1968, 1.

38. Berman, *Hubert*, 226; "Down to the Wire," *Time*, November 8, 1968, 28–29; Tom Wicker, "Humphrey Surge Is Offering Aides a Hope for Upset," *New York Times*, October 27, 1968, 1; R. W. Apple Jr., "Humphrey Campaigns Like the Happy Warrior of Other Years," *New York Times*, October 30, 1968, 24; Max Frankel, "Humphrey Here, Bids Faithful Return," *New York Times*, November 3, 1968, 1; "Humphrey Claims 251 Electoral Votes," *Washington Post, Times Herald*, October 27, 1968, A1; Saville R. Davis, "Humphrey Tries to Ignite Democratic Coalition Fires," *Christian Science Monitor*, October 30, 1968, 3; Max Frankel, "Humphrey Drums on 'Trust' Theme," *New York Times*, November 1, 1968, 51; Bernard D. Nossiter, "Humphrey: Asks Voters for Miracle," *Washington Post, Times Herald*, November 1, 1968, A1.

39. Don Oberdorfer, "Nixon Is Preparing 'Three-Week Blitz,'" *Washington Post, Times Herald*, October 15, 1968, A1; Don Oberdorfer, "Nixon Hits HHH Tactics," *Washington Post, Times Herald*, October 16, 1968, A1; "Avoiding the Dewey Syndrome," *Time*, October 25, 1968, 25–26; "Nixon's the One," *Time*, October 18, 1968, 69–70; "Nixon Is Supported by 634 Newspapers," *New York Times*, November 2, 1968, 18; "A Preference for Nixon," *Life*, October 25, 1968, 42.

40. Marquis Childs, "Nixon Perfection May Be a Weakness," *Washington Post, Times Herald*, October 23, 1968, A24; John Osborne, "Something Eerie about the Nixon Crowds," *New Republic*, November 2, 1968, 13–14; Joseph Alsop, "Nixon's Campaign Panoply Masks Lack of Voter Ardor," *Washington Post, Times Herald*, October 14, 1968, A21; "Nixon's 2 ½ Problems," *Time*, October 18, 1968, 22; Rowland Evans and Robert Novak, "Nixon Now Facing Toughest Issue—a TV Debate Sought by Humphrey," *Washington Post, Times Herald*, October 11, 1968, A21; Rowland Evans and Robert Novak, "Possible Electoral College Deadlock Creates a Gnawing Doubt for Nixon," *Washington Post, Times Herald*, October 31, 1968, A21; Don Oberdorfer, "Nixon Bids HHH Take Popular Verdict," *Washington Post, Times Herald*, October 31, 1968, A1; Max Frankel, "Humphrey Backs House Election," *New York Times*, October 21, 1968, 1.

41. Garment, *Crazy Rhythm*, 143–44.

42. "In Deadly Embrace," *Newsweek*, September 9, 1968, 56; Hugh Sidey, "Vietnam and the Two Lonely Men," *Life*, October 11, 1968, 6; Thomas J. Foley, "Nixon Says Rival Has Confused Paris Peace Negotiators," *Los Angeles Times*, October 2, 1968, 1; E. W. Kenworthy, "Nixon Suggests He Could Achieve Peace in Vietnam," *New York Times*, October 8, 1968, 1; William V. Shannon, "A Confident Nixon Talks of Bipartisanship," *New York Times*, October 20, 1968, E2; Bernard D. Nossiter, "Nixon: He Attacks HHH for 'Loosest Tongue,'" *Washington Post, Times Herald*, October 24, 1968, A1.

43. Dallek, *Flawed Giant*, 582–83; "Watching for the Peace Signals," *Time*, October 25, 1968, 17–18; "Auguries of a Breakthrough," *Time*, November 1, 1968, 13–15; "The

Bombing Halt: Johnson's Gamble for Peace," *Time*, November 8, 1968, 24–27; "Inside Story: How the Decision Was Made to Halt the Bombing," *U.S. News & World Report*, November 11, 1968, 18–19; "The Bomb Halt Decision," *Life*, November 15, 1968, 84A–97.

44. Dallek, *Flawed Giant*, 582–83; Richard Nixon, *RN: The Memoirs of Richard Nixon* (New York: Grosset & Dunlap, 1978), 323–27.

45. Evan Thomas, *Being Nixon: A Man Divided* (New York: Random House, 2015), 178–79; "Vintage Nixon," *Washington Post, Times Herald*, October 27, 1968, B6.

46. Hughes, *Chasing Shadows*, 7–9; Clark Clifford with Richard Holbrooke, *Counsel to the President: A Memoir* (New York: Random House, 1991), 581–82; Anna Chennault, *The Education of Anna* (New York: Times Books, 1980), 173–77; Bui Diem with David Chanoff, *In the Jaws of History* (Boston: Houghton Mifflin, 1987), 236–37.

47. Hughes, *Chasing Shadows*, 9–10; Diem with Chanoff, *In the Jaws of History*, 238–45; "Saigon Balks," *Newsweek*, November 11, 1968, 46–51; "A Halting Step toward Peace," *Time*, November 15, 1968, 40–42; Walter LaFeber, *The Deadly Bet: LBJ, Vietnam, and the 1968 Election* (Lanham, Md.: Rowman & Littlefield, 2005), 153–60.

48. Dallek, *Flawed Giant*, 585–88; Hughes, *Chasing Shadows*, 37–44; Don Fulsom, *Treason: Nixon and the 1968 Election* (Gretna, La.: Pelican, 2015), 93–102.

49. "Why LBJ Stopped the Bombing," *U.S. News & World Report*, November 11, 1968, 39–40; Safire, *Before the Fall*, 84–88; John W. Finney, "Halt in Bombing Gave Nixon Scare," *New York Times*, November 9, 1968, 19; "Why Saigon Won't Talk," *Newsweek*, November 18, 1968, 54–55; "The Rocky Road to Paris," *Newsweek*, November 25, 1968, 38–44; White, *Making of the President, 1968*, 445–48.

50. Humphrey, *Education of a Public Man*, 8–9; Hughes, *Chasing Shadows*, 44–45.

51. Clifford with Holbrooke, *Counsel to the President*, 583–84; Hughes, *Chasing Shadows*, 45–52; Longley, *LBJ's 1968*, 243–50.

52. Chester, Hodgson, and Page, *American Melodrama*, 734; Thomas, *Being Nixon*, 180–81; John A. Farrell, *Richard Nixon: The Life* (New York: Doubleday, 2017), 342–48; John A. Farrell, "Tricky Dick's Vietnam Treachery," *New York Times*, January 1, 2017, SR9; Peter Baker, "Nixon Tried to Spoil Johnson's Vietnam Peace Talks in '68, Notes Show," *New York Times*, January 3, 2017, A11.

CHAPTER TEN

1. David English and the Staff of the London *Daily Express*, *Divided They Stand* (Englewood Cliffs, N.J.: Prentice-Hall, 1969), 400–401; "Nixon's Hard-Won Chance to Lead," *Time*, November 15, 1998, 22–26; "Finally, Nixon's the One," *Newsweek*, November 11, 1968, 31–34.

2. "The Loser: A Near Run Thing," *Time*, November 15, 1968, 33–34; Carl Solberg, *Hubert Humphrey: A Biography* (1984; reprint, Minneapolis: Borealis Books, 2003), 403–5; Richard Meryman, "A Man Abandoning Forever His Hopes of Being President," *Life*, November 15, 1968, 42–43.

3. George Lardner and Jules Loh, "The Wonderful World of George Wallace," *Esquire*, May 1969, 108–15, 125–28; "Wallace in Defeat," *Newsweek*, November 18, 1968, 51.

4. English et al., *Divided They Stand*, 405–10; Tom Wicker, "3 States Crucial," *New York Times*, November 6, 1968, 1; Tom Wicker, *One of Us: Richard Nixon and the American Dream* (New York: Random House, 1991), 382–83.

5. "Who Will Vote in November," *U.S. News & World Report*, August 12, 1968, 28–29; "At Grass Roots—What People Say," *U.S. News & World Report*, October 14, 1968, 51–53; Walter Lippmann, "The Hard Choice," *Newsweek*, October 7, 1968, 27; Walter Lippmann, "The American Predicament," *Newsweek*, October 21, 1968, 27; "Promises, Promises," *Newsweek*, October 21, 1968, 30–32; "Thoughts on an Election," *Wall Street Journal*, October 31, 1968, 20; Stewart Alsop, "Are We Still on God's List?," *Newsweek*, November 11, 1968, 124; Kenneth Crawford, "Middle-Class Revolt," *Newsweek*, November 18, 1968, 52; Lewis Chester, Geoffrey Hodgson, and Bruce Page, *An American Melodrama: The Presidential Campaign of 1968* (New York: Viking, 1969), 607–9.

6. "Gallup: Humphrey 'Probably' Would Have Won—if the Election Had Come a Few Days Later," *U.S. News & World Report*, November 18, 1968, 132–33; Louis Harris, "Polls: An Insight," *Newsweek*, November 11, 1968, 34–35.

7. "The Anatomy of the Vote," *Newsweek*, November 11, 1968, 35; "Closing Out Campaign '68," *Newsweek*, November 18, 1968, 49; "The Way the Voting Went—and Why," *U.S. News & World Report*, November 18, 1968, 40–43.

8. Raymond Moley, "Nixon Has Re-established the Two-Party System in the U.S.," *Los Angeles Times*, November 11, 1968, B7; William V. Shannon, "Some Early Thoughts on President Nixon," *New York Times*, November 11, 1968, 46; Thomas Griffith, "What the Election Wasn't About," *Life*, November 15, 1968, 36–40; "The Shape of the Vote," *Time*, November 15, 1968, 21; John H. Averill, "New Foundation Held Vital Need of Democratic Party," *Los Angeles Times*, November 8, 1968, 1; Alan L. Otten, "Changing Lineups," *Wall Street Journal*, October 25, 1968, 16; George Lardner Jr., "Wallace Emphasizes His Impact," *Washington Post, Times Herald*, November 6, 1968, A9; George Lardner Jr., "Wallace on Political Future: 'We'll Have to Play It by Ear,'" *Washington Post, Times Herald*, November 7, 1968, A8; Ben A. Franklin, "Was It the Last Hurrah of George Corley Wallace?," *New York Times*, November 10, 1968, E2; Ben A. Franklin, "Wallace Tempers Defeat of Party by Claiming Credit for Republicans' Victory," *New York Times*, November 7, 1968, 23.

9. "LBJ's Place in History: A Professional View," *U.S. News & World Report*, December 2, 1968, 52–54; Eric F. Goldman, "The Wrong Man from the Wrong Place at the Wrong Time," *New York Times Magazine*, January 5, 1969, 23, 82–88; Tom Wicker, "Requiem for the Great Society," *Saturday Evening Post*, January 25, 1969, 30, 62–70; Robert G. Sherrill, "Looking Back at Johnson," *Nation*, January 13, 1969, 42–45; "The Johnson Years," *Newsweek*, January 20, 1969, 18–23.

10. Wicker, *One of Us*, 390; "HHH: Very Much at Peace," *Newsweek*, November 18, 1968, 50; "The Exodus Begins," *Time*, November 22, 1968, 15; Robert B. Semple Jr., "Humphrey Meets Nixon in Florida; Pledges Support," *New York Times*, November 9, 1968, 1.

11. Winthrop Griffith, "He Is Not What He Was, and He Is Not Yet What He Will Be," *New York Times Magazine*, March 30, 1969, 32–33, 132–40; Hubert H. Humphrey, *Education of a Public Man: My Life and Politics* (Garden City, N.Y.: Doubleday, 1976), 430–38; Solberg, *Hubert Humphrey*, 411–70.

12. Ben Stavis, *We Were the Campaign: New Hampshire to Chicago for McCarthy* (Boston: Beacon Press, 1969), 199–201; Susan Brownmiller, "Gene McCarthy Is Waiting for a Sign," *New York Times Magazine*, July 20, 1969, 10–22; Dominic Sandbrook, *Eugene McCarthy: The Rise and Fall of American Liberalism* (New York: Knopf, 2004), 215–99.

13. Adam Clymer, *Edward M. Kennedy: A Biography* (New York: Perennial, 1999), 143–54; Theodore H. White, *The Making of the President, 1972* (New York: Atheneum, 1973), 74–84.

14. Jules Witcover, *Party of the People: A History of the Democrats* (New York: Random House, 2003), 571–76; Rick Perlstein, *Nixonland: The Rise of a President and the Fracturing of America* (New York: Scribner, 2008), 694–99; Jefferson Cowie, *Stayin' Alive: The 1970s and the Last Days of the Working Class* (New York: New Press, 2010), 84–124; Richard M. Scammon and Ben J. Wattenberg, *The Real Majority* (New York: Coward-McCann, 1970).

15. Julian E. Zelizer, *Governing America: The Revival of Political History* (Princeton, N.J.: Princeton University Press, 2012), 81–87; Michael A. Cohen, *American Maelstrom: The 1968 Election and the Politics of Division* (New York: Oxford University Press, 2016), 349–52; Penn Kemble, "The Democrats after 1968," *Commentary*, January 1969, 35–41; George Will, "What Happened to the Democratic Coalition?," *National Review*, April 8, 1969, 325–27, 349; Joshua Muravchik, "Why the Democrats Lost," *Commentary*, January 1985, 15–26; Allen J. Matusow, *The Unraveling of America: A History of Liberalism in the 1960s* (New York: Harper and Row, 1984), 395.

16. Walter Rugaber, "Wallace Is Left with Nostalgia," *New York Times*, December 8, 1968, 48; Dick Barnes, "Wallace Backers Work to Keep Party Alive," *Washington Post, Times Herald*, December 8, 1968, E3; Dan T. Carter, *The Politics of Rage: George Wallace, the Origins of the New Conservatism, and the Transformation of American Politics* (Baton Rouge: Louisiana State University Press, 1995), 369–70, 386–95; Stephan Lesher, *George Wallace: American Populist* (Reading, Mass.: Addison-Wesley, 1994), 428–52; George C. Wallace, "Failure to Resist Evil Is Evil in Itself," *George C. Wallace Newsletter*, May 1969, 1; George C. Wallace, "Warren, Fortas Gone—Chance for Change," *George C. Wallace Newsletter*, July 1969, 1; George C. Wallace, "Our Greatest Victory So Far," *George C. Wallace Newsletter*, June 1970, 1; "The Wallace Victory—Meaning for 1972," *U.S. News & World Report*, June 15, 1970, 22–25.

17. Carter, *Politics of Rage*, 371–450.

18. Carter, *Politics of Rage*, 433–68; Lesher, *George Wallace*, 470–506; Michael Riley, "Confessions of a Former Segregationist," *Time*, March 2, 1992, 10; Michael Beschloss, "The Art of Losing: How Wallace Blazed the Way for Buchanan," *Newsweek*, March 11, 1996, 43.

19. Chester, Hodgson, and Page, *American Melodrama*, 746.

20. "Mr. Nixon's Challenge," *Wall Street Journal*, November 12, 1968, 20; "To the President-Elect," *Life*, November 15, 1968, 48B; "Nixon's Next Challenge," *Business Week*, November 9, 1968, 27–32; "Exclusive Interview with President-Elect Nixon," *U.S. News & World Report*, November 18, 1968, 38–39; "President Nixon: What Will He Be Like?," *Newsweek*, November 11, 1968, 36–37; "An Interregnum without Rancor," *Time*, November 22, 1968, 12–13; "Hands across the Interregnum," *Newsweek*, November 23, 1968, 31–36; "Toward the Nixon Inauguration," *Time*, January 17, 1969, 13–14; Max Lerner, "The Liberals' Odd Silence on Nixon: Could It Be Guilt?," *Los Angeles Times*, November 22, 1968, B7; Stewart Alsop, "The Demonsterization of Nixon," *Newsweek*, February 24, 1969, 104.

21. Garry Wills, "The Enigma of President Nixon," *Saturday Evening Post*, January 25, 1969, 25–27, 54–58; Chester, Hodgson, and Page, *American Melodrama*, 777.

22. John A. Farrell, *Richard Nixon: The Life* (New York: Doubleday, 2017), 371–96; Heather Cox Richardson, *To Make Men Free: A History of the Republican Party* (New York: Basic Books, 2014), 280–81; Jules Witcover, *White Knight: The Rise of Spiro Agnew* (New York: Random House, 1972), 298–371; Robert Mason, *Richard Nixon and the Quest for a New Majority* (Chapel Hill: University of North Carolina Press, 2004), 37–160.

23. Farrell, *Richard Nixon*, 416–533; Ken Hughes, *Chasing Shadows: The Nixon Tapes, the Chennault Affair, and the Origins of Watergate* (Charlottesville: University of Virginia Press, 2014).

24. Kevin P. Phillips, *The Emerging Republican Majority* (New York: Arlington House, 1969); Michael A. Cohen, *American Maelstrom: The 1968 Election and the Politics of Division* (New York: Oxford University Press, 2016), 336–39; Robert O. Self, *All in the Family: The Realignment of American Democracy since the 1960s* (New York: Hill and Wang, 2012), 276–398; Michael Kazin, *The Populist Persuasion: An American History* (New York: BasicBooks, 1995), 245–60; Cowie, *Stayin' Alive*, 1–209.

25. Geoffrey Kabaservice, *Rule and Ruin: The Downfall of Moderation and the Destruction of the Republican Party* (New York: Oxford University Press, 2012), 252–362; Richard Norton Smith, *On His Own Terms: A Life of Nelson Rockefeller* (New York: Random House, 2014), 543–677.

26. H. W. Brands, *Reagan: The Life* (New York: Anchor Books, 2015), 185–238; Rick Perlstein, *The Invisible Bridge: The Fall of Nixon and the Rise of Reagan* (New York: Simon and Schuster, 2014); Natasha Zaretsky, *No Direction Home: The American Family and the Fear of National Decline, 1968–1980* (Chapel Hill: University of North Carolina Press, 2007), 223–45.

INDEX